MODERN TEACHING OF PHYSICAL EDUCATION

MODERN TEACHING OF PHYSICAL EDUCATION

[Strictly According to the UGC Syllabus for B.Ed. Course]

By

M.U. QURESHI

ANMOL PUBLICATIONS PVT. LTD.

NEW DELHI - 110 002 (INDIA)

ANMOL PUBLICATIONS PVT. LTD.
4374/4B, Ansari Road, Daryaganj
New Delhi - 110 002
Ph.: 23261597, 23278000
Visit us at: www.anmolpublications.com

Modern Teaching of Physical Education

First Published, 2004

ISBN 81-261-1985-3

PRINTED IN INDIA

Published by J.L. Kumar for Anmol Publications Pvt. Ltd., New Delhi - 110 002 and Printed at Mehra Offset Press, Delhi.

Contents

Preface

Education is a vast discipline and Teachers' Training is a vital part of it. The responsibilities of the educationists and educators are focused on the task of providing better training to the future teachers for their better learning and proper development. Needless to say that this responsibility can only be exercised, if the trainers are equipped with the required knowledge of the subject concerned. That's why it becomes essential for making adequate provisions for each course to the student-teachers or teacher trainees. The present series is designed for providing a solid workable base for all course-papers. It has been prepared strictly according to the syllabus of the B.Ed class, prescribed by the UGC for different universities.

No doubt, there are so many other books on the subject, available in the market, written by worthy authors. However, every writer has his or her own style and way of presentation. The present work also has its own features and characteristics.

In preparation of this series of texts, the editor had to refer to the works of other authors and information sources. The editor feels a deep sense of gratitude for incorporating their ideas in the text. Hopefully, this series would serve as a 'ready to refer' tool for all teachers, teacher-students and others.

—Editor

1

Introduction

The body of a child develops every day. Terman says that the differences in the bodies of a child and a grown-up exists in every nerve and vein. Difference is there even in the proportion of different limbs and also in the bones. A child has softer bones than the grown up persons and the heart-beat is also quicker in his case. The child like a soft and undeveloped object is easily affected by external factors. This difference is not found only in the development of bodies of adults and children but is also found in the children of the same age-group. It is not necessary that physical development should be uniform in all children. There are certain factors that causes different changes in the same child at different ages. The physical exercise which is useful at a certain age, may not be so at another age. So is the case with the diet, which doing good at one stage may prove unwholesome at the other. These things necessitate that the child should be given greater care than adults. Those who are responsible for promoting the development of children should be especially careful about all these things.

There are two factors that affect the development of a child. They are (1) heredity and (2) environment.

Heredity is the sum total of all such things that a child inherits from his forefathers. It has its root not only in the mother and father of a child, but in the remote ancestors as well. The child who is born after completing nine months in mother's womb, has fairly an old history of his existence. There are certain such forces acting in him as existed in his early forefathers also. These things which are quite new in the child appear to be so because of the reason that the primitive man is no more amongst us for giving us an opportunity to see for ourselves those very things present in him.

What are the things which a child gets from heredity? It is a difficult question. No definite answer has been given to it as yet. The only thing which can be said with certainty is that a child gets certain physical and racial qualities from his forefathers. If it were not so, the entire creation would have come to an end and there would not have been the possibility of Factors Influencing Child Growth and human beings giving birth to human beings, horses to horses and elephants to elephants. A living creature inherits its form and feature from its parents. Eyes, hairs, body complexion, fingers in hand and foot, physical stature, childhood etc. are certainly such things that are inherited. Sex organs, muscles, skeletons, blood-vessels are hereditary. In the physique and nature af a child, certain qualities of their forefathers are existant proving thereby that the forefathers have a great hand in shaping the child in its present form. Healthy and well-formed body and numerous ambitions are inherited properties of an individual and so are the diseased body and several other defects. Evidently, one cannot afford to neglect the influence of heredity in the development of a child.

We have stated above that a child inherits from its forefathers a number of qualities. After birth, these qualities of a child are influenced by the environment as well. The environment determines to a great extent the direction of development and also plays a significant role in slowing down or speeding up the process of development. In two different environments, children from the same parents develop distinctly two different personalities. A child getting good training and upbringing from parents and respect in the society ultimately, becomes a responsible and respectable citizen and attains a stature in which the entire nation may feel a pride. Just reverse is the case of the child denied all love in the family, and uneducated and hated by the society. He is seized of antisocial feelings. It can, therefore, be concluded that favourable or unfavourable environments affect accordingly the development of a child.

Environment includes all those things that influence the child both prior to and even after birth. These may be divided in three groups, namely :
(1) pre-natal, (2) intra-natal and (3) post-natal.

If during pregnancy, the mother does not get nourishing food and fresh air and has to live in unhealthy environment, the child's health will also be affected. In the sameway, alcoholic drinks taken by the expectant mother, affect the health of a baby in the womb because these get mixed in the mother's blood and consequently tell upon the health of the baby. In the absence of nourishing food the baby in making in the womb gets the required material from the bones and particularly from the teeth of the mother. Thus, in the absence of proper nutritious diet, the mother will naturally become weak and the baby, too, will turn weak. His bones will not be strong. Injury to a pregnant woman can result into the death of her unborn child; can cause abortion or some kind of deformity in the child. This in turn will retard his mental development. Thus, it should be seen that while the child remains in the mother's womb, the blood of the mother, food, air and her way of living create an environment which has a healthy influence on the development of the baby.

Hereditary Diseases—Hereditary diseases, too, have their ill effects on the development of a child. Diseased and unhealthy parents beget diseased and unhealthy children. Children of parents suffering from veneral diseases, like gonorrhea and syphlis, are constitutionally weak and easily fall victims to eye defects, skin troubles and various diseases.

Effect of Drugs– Drugs like quinine and iodine have detrimental effects on the born baby in the womb. There is always a possibility of abortion, deformity or even death of the baby in the womb, if the mother uses these medicines during her pregnancy.

Mother's Age– Mother's age is another factor that counts in the development of the baby. A very young mother's child is generally weak and complications too arises during delivery. On the other hand, the babies of very aged women, too, are likely to be unhealthy.

But a healthy woman of mature age gives birth to a healthy and strong baby.

There are chances that the baby might get injured or contract infectious diseases at the time of birth. Sometimes, head injury causes deformity of brain causing bleeding of brain nerves. This results in derangement of mind and deformity of body. Infection, too, has its bad effects. It is, therefore, very important that due attention is paid to the child during birth and every possible precaution is taken to ensure that no injury is caused to the new-born child.

As in the case'of pre-natal period when nutritious diet taken by the mother affects the development of the baby, in the same way during post-natal period, nutritious food is necessary for the mother to ensure healthy growth of the child. In the absence of good and balanced diet the mental and physical development of the child is retarded. Proper nutrition helps the physical development. When the child gets balanced diet all-round physical development takes place and the child gains power, height, weight and proportion. The body has power to resist diseases. Because of this power of resistance that proper .mental development takes place. Lovely complexion, smooth, and glossy hair, bright eyes, shining teeth, sound sleep, good appetite and upright body indicate the health of a child who has been brought upon nutritious diet. Contrary to this, those who do not get balanced diet can neither enjoy sound health nor possess good appetite. Their body is also not properly developed and the mental growth, too, is retarded.

Sunshine and fresh air play as important part in the healthy development of a child as nutritious food. Children born in slums and other unhealthy surroundings do not attain proper physical and mental standards. They fall victims to various diseases and neither get a sound sleep nor good appetite. Fresh air, sunshine and clean surroundings are essential for the Factors Influencing the Child Growth and proper development of a child. Those houses where sunshine does not reach become damp and children living in them suffer from diseases of throat, cough and respiratory organs. It these places, germs of malaria and yellow fever easily breed. Children living in such places may easily fall victims to diseases.

The body-builds of an adult and those of a child differ. Even there is a difference between the builds of two boys of the same age-group.

Development is conditioned by heredity and environment. Physical and other qualities are the gifts of heredity. Environment may be divided in three categories: (1) Pre-natal, (2) Intra-natal and (3) Post-natal.

During pre-natal period, the baby is influenced by the diet of the mother, her care, hereditary diseases, the effect of drugs like quinine and iodine and the mother's age. During intra-natal period, the effect of injury or infection; and in the post-natal period nutritious diet, fresh air and healthy surroundings count.

Women have to undergo great trouble and difficulty during pregnancy. Hence their special care is necessary during this period, otherwise not only their health will be impaired in all respects but also of the growing would-be in the womb. Many women in India are not fully aware of the nature of the particular care that they should take. So some of them breath their last in the process of child-birth.

Necessary Food for the Expectant Lady—The expectant lady in addition to her own nutrition has to supply nutrition to her baby in the womb. The essence of a substantial portion of the food that she takes goes to the nourishment of the baby that she is carrying in her womb. During this period she is in particular need of adequate quantity of calcium, phosphorus and vitamin D. So her food should consist of such articles; which may naturally provide these essentials to her. After the child birth the nursing mother has to breast-feed her baby for a few months. Therefore, the food for her during pregnancy should be such as to enable her to breast feed her baby after delivery adequately. We list below some items of food necessary for an expectant lady:

1. Milk about a litre. It must not be over-boiled.
2. Sweet and fresh seasonal fruits and fresh vegetables. It should be seen that the vegetables are not overcooked.
3. Non-vegetarian diet must not be taken for more than once a week if necessary at all. One egg per day may be given.

4. Pulse and bread prepared from fresh flour will be quite helpful.
5. Butter may be given daily.
6. Only a little ghee may be given if considered necessary.
7. Salt with iodine property should be taken. Some fruits and vegetables rich in iodine may also be taken.

Other Precautions—It should be seen that the expectant lady does not suffer from constipation. In-take of adequate quantity of fruits and vegetables will remove constipation, if some time it is there. Pelvic measurement should be taken during advanced pregnancy. Such a measurement will forewarn about some surgery, if it is necessary in the process of delivery. Expectant lady should be protected from infectious diseases and should be kept separately, if there is a fear of some epidemic.

Provision for Maternal Care—It will be better if in every locality there is a maternal unit within a radius of about 2 km. This unit will take care of the lady after delivery for the first few days. This unit should be manned by experienced medical doctors, surgeons, midwives and nurses. At this there should be some provision for pathological examination of blood, urine and stool. The heart and lungs of the expectant lady should be examined and her pelvic measurement should also be taken. The expectant ladies and nursing mothers should be given necessary information regarding normal pregnancy. They should also be acquainted with symptoms of abnormal cases. Here they should also be taught about taking proper care of young children. Some nurses or midwives should be deputed for going door to door for educating such expectant ladies who observe veil-custom.

The nursing mother and her baby should be kept at the maternal unit at least for 5 or 6 days, unless a longer stay is warranted becasue of certain complications. Six or seven weeks after the delivery the nursing mother should be re-examined by some lady doctor of the unit either at her home or at the unit itself. This re-examination will be better done at the unit itself because the necessary appliances and instruments will be ready at hand there. The nursing mother while leaving the maternal unit after delivery should be encouraged to come for re-examination after 6 or 7 weeks. People should be advised for utilizing the services of the unit whenever necessary.

The following should be done at the time and after the delivery of child birth:

1. As soon as the baby is born one per cent of silver nitrate solution should be dropped in his eyes. This measure will protect the eyes from any disease during me first few months.
2. The new-born baby should be allowed adequate rest.
3. It is better if the baby is kept on the mother's milk for a few months or for as long as possible for the baby's health. If the mother's milk is not adequate for him, some fruit juice containing vitamin 'C' may be given to him in addition to cow's milk. Cow's milk will serve as a good substitute, if the mother's milk is not sufficient for the baby. After six or seven months a little well cooked ordinary food may also be given once or twice a day in addition to cow's milk. These days several baby foods are sold in the market. The same may also be utilized after consulting a physician.
4. The baby should be given bath daily, but in this process any cold-exposure must be avoided.
5. Children should be always kept away from persons suffering from any serious disease.
6. These days physicians prescribe a number of injections on one month's interval. Accordingly children should be given these injections.
7. Periodical examination of children should be made for detecting any possible developing ailments.
8. Various habits pertaining to feeding, sleeping, rest, and bath etc., should be regularized at fixed hours as far as possible.
9. Particular care should be taken for their balanced diet.

2

Health Education

The school is responsible in many ways for the mental, physical, moral and spiritual development of future citizens of the State, although the responsibility of the family. State and other concerned persons in this regard can in no way be ignored. Therefore, it is a sacred duty of a school to give a prominent place to health education in its several schemes directed in the interest of the growth of children. So far, our schools have miserably failed in this respect, and the educational authorities as well, are no better in this matter. The sooner this state of affairs ends, the better.

It is true that our country is so poor that most of our children do not get balanced and nutritive diet. Therefore, some people remark that it is a farce to talk of health education of children, if they do not get nutritive diet. Some grain of truth cannot be denied in this remark, but it is also true that we are deprived of the maximum advantages of even poor resources due to our ignorance of the basic knowledge of health rules. Therefore, it is necessary to remove this ignorance of ours. The State, school, family and others should extend due co-operation in planning an active health eduction programme for children. Only then, we can contribute our mite to the building of a bright future for our children.

The Objectives

The main aim of school health education programme is to acquaint the teachers and students with health rules so that they may be healthy and inspire others to be so.

By a health education programme, we want to bring to the notice of the students the evil consequences of various intoxicants and other bad habits so that a healthy environment may be built up within and outside the school.

In the health education programme we want to pay due attention to the rules of mental health as well. At the same time, we also want to endeavour to inculcate various social virtues in children. For this we shall include various types of plays, games and sports in the health education programme.

Various Programmes

Cleanliness—The cleanliness of the school environment is the first thing to be attended to. The rooms, play-ground, lavatories, urinals and other places should be kept entirely clean. It should not be difficult for any school to attend to these basic things, howsoever, poor it might be financially. But many schools ignore this vital necessity and their rooms and the total environments are full of all kinds of unhygienic conditions. It hardly needs mention that this situation adversely affects the health of children.

Arrangement for Adequate Light and Fresh Air—In the foregoing pages we have emphasised at several places the importance of sufficient light and fresh air in the school. This should be considered as one of the most important constituents of health education programme.

Health Examination—Every student in the school should be medically examined at least thrice a year according to a prefixed programme. The result of this examination should be communicated to the concerned teachers and guardians in order that the necessary may be done for the child. The progress of health of each student should be carefully watched on the basis of the medical examination result. For this, each teacher should be required to perform his share of the responsibility, and due allowance should be given for this in assigning teaching load to him so that he may not feel overworked.

Education in Physiology and Hygiene—Every student should be made conversant with the basic elements of physiology and hygiene. For this, at least one period a week should be devoted. Some suitable lecture by some physician or specialist at least once a month should also be arranged.

Good Refreshment and Pure Water—Pure water must be available in the school. If there are wells, they must be kept in perfect hygienic conditions. Sellers of fruits and other edibles should be carefully inspected and they must not be allowed to play with the health of students by selling rotten and stale things. The school should also arrange for some refreshment in the mid-day. This refreshment should consist of nutritive elements.

Physical Exercise—The students get mental exercise in learning the various subjects, but most of them do not get the necessary physical exercise. For this, facilities of various types of games, sports and plays should exist in the school in order to cater to students with various abilities, inclinations and aptitudes. All the students should be encouraged to participate in these according to their individual interest. Both the Indian and Western styles of games, sports and plays should be organised.

Fundamental Issues

The students should be told in detail about the health rules that they must observe. Their attention should be specially drawn to the following basic elements:

1. The benefits of early to bed and early to rise. The ratio to be observed between the time to be given to study, play and rest.
2. The basic elements of balanced diet, how the diet may be made adequately nutritive.
3. How to save one from infectious diseases.

4. What to do for the health of teeth, eyes and other organs of the body.
5. The structure of the various organs of the body.
6. Importance of health in life.
7. The meaning of purity of water, air and food.

Different Methods

We are mentioning below some of the most important methods of health education which a school should adopt:

1. The teacher should observe all the health rules. He should not present any bad example before his students.
2. The students should be given to read books and magazines dealing with health rules and principles.
3. The cleanliness of students should be examined every day with great sympathy.
4. The entire environment of the school should be kept healthy. The room, play-ground, urinals etc. should not be dirty.
5. The specialists should be invited to deliver lectures on health rules from time to time.

Health of Mind

We have dealt above with physical health of students But physical health cannot be separated from mental health, as the mind and body are interdependent. Therefore, it is in the interest of physical health itself that due care is also taken of the mental health of the students. In fact, both the physical and mental aspects are necessarily included in the term health. The teachers should keep in mind the following for promoting mental health of students:

1. The teacher should be impartial in his behaviour. He should give due affection and care to all the students. No student should feel ignored.

2. The mental development of the student should be studied from a psychological point of view.
3. The students should be given free environment for the development of various personality traits. They should have opportunity for cultivating various social virtues.
4. Parental co-operation should be sought in removing the bad habits found in students. Under no circumstances the student should suffer from any inferiority complex.
5. Great ideals should be presented before the students from the lives of great personalities of the world.

QUESTIONS

1. Describe the factors to be kept in view in organising a health education programme in a school.
2. Draw an outline of an ideal health education programme for your school.

3

Fundamental Principles

For understanding the principles of health education for school life, it is very important to study the science of health because one cannot grasp the health rules without its help. In this chapter we shall study the scope and uses of health education pertaining to school life.

The study of the science of health is necessary for a man both in his capacity as an individual, and also as a member of the society. The first aspect of the study covers the physical and mental development. It includes the study of the entire physical activity, motion, respiration, eating and the functions of brain, such as thinking, feeling and activities directed towards the achievement of a certain objective. The study is carried on in close association with environment. The study of science of health is important socially as well. An individual's health and development is intimately related to his social surroundings. The society influences the development of an individual considerably. Environmental study in its thoroughness is, therefore, the pre-requisite for the full knowledge of an individual's health.

Hygiene is an integral part of physiology which imparts knowledge to us about the functions of various limbs of the body in a healthy condition. Hygiene tells us the methods and rules for leading a healthy and disease free life. To have a complete grasp of these rules and methods it is necessary to acquire a knowledge of physiology as well.

Scope and Sphere

Hygiene has a wide scope. It embraces all those sciences which contribute to the long and healthy life of human beings. Ignorant people generally fall prey to superstitions, and attribute the causes of various diseases to divine displeasure, evil spirits and witchcraft etc. Obviously, these are false notions and can be removed only by proper study of the science of health.

School health education is a vital part of general hygiene. It includes all such instructions that enlighten a student about activities and functions contributing to preservation and promotion of health. By means of school-hygiene, the spread of disease in the school-going children can be checked and their eradication can also be attempted. Thus, an attempt is made to increase the life-span of students. A thorough knowledge of health rules underlines the need of the study of anatomy and also the symptoms of common diseases of children. In this connection, practical knowledge of causes and diagnosis is equally necessary. School hygiene includes the knowledge about the environment, equipments and routine of the school as well.

A question may be asked as to why is it necessary for the would-be teachers to know about school-hygiene ? The answer is quite obvious. A teacher's primary duty is to look after and bring about the mental development of students which is possible only when there is a sound body guaranteeing a sound mind. Hence, a knowledge of school-hygiene for a teacher is very necessary. Only from a healthy seed comes out a healthy plant. So only a healthy child can ensure the growth of a healthy man. It shows how necessary it is to give proper attention to health from the early childhood. School-life during which period, the teachers prepare a child for the future is thus quite important in the life of a man. Hence, it is necessary for the teacher to know about the science pertaining to health. It is now an important part of a school's programme. It is the teacher's duty to be aware of various health problems of the child and make constant efforts to draw the attention of students and guardians to these problems and also help them in effecting improvements wherever necessary. A teacher failing to perform this duty exposes his students to various hazards affecting health.

Value of Nutrition

A large number of students in the school lack nutritive diet and also healthy living environment. Such students develop many physical defects. They generally have flat and contracted chests, thin and curved legs, flat foot, round shoulders and bent trunks. Sometimes, there is no symmetry in the formation of shoulders. They are uneven. The unhealthy living surroundings also contribute to these physical deformities and unhealthy appearances. They are susceptible to contagious diseases, which in their turn cause a lot of disturbance in their studies. Teachers, besides paying attention to the living environment and nutrition, should also take into consideration the schools's arrangements for light and air in the class-rooms and proper seating-arrangement. All these have a cumulative effect upon the health of children. Instances are not lacking of schools situated in dark lanes with small and damp rooms with no proper seating arrangements and ventilation. There is no gain-saying that students shut up in such a school can never maintain good health. The environment affects a child not only physically but psychologically and morally as well. It demands unceasing effort on the part of teachers to provide them with a congenial atmosphere for study. If the teachers pay due attention to the diet, environment, sanitation, dresses, health and mode of living of the students, they will certainly make positive contributions in giving the country citizens with sound health and character.

Significance of Physiology

The area of science of health is widespread and for mastering this subject it is necessary to have a knowledge of physiology, body movements and anatomy. School-hygiene should be studied with a personal and social angle.

The knowledge of school hygiene is very necessary for the teacher, because he is concerned with the mental development of the child and the relation between a healthy mind and a healthy body is too well-known to be emphasised. Home atmosphere, circumstances, food, condition of the educational institution, the design of its rooms etc., influence the health of the children. Teachers should also pay attention to the ways of living, dresses and food habits of students.

QUESTIONS

1. What is meant by science of health ? What other sciences have to be studied for getting a sound knowledge of this science ?
2. What ends should be in view while studying the science of health, and what should be its aim ?
3. Why is the knowledge of science of hygiene necessary for a teacher?

4

The Infrastructure

The Management

According to the Indian Constitution 'Health' is a state subject. But at the national level as well our Central Government has established a Health and Family Welfare Ministry. This ministry is directly responsible for health problems in the centrally administered areas. The State governments are completely independent regarding public health and medical relief problems. The Central Ministry of Health and Family Welfare advises the state governments on certain problems and gives adequate financial aids for the control of certain diseases, like malaria and small-pox. Besides, it run many research centres and institutes for finding out suitable measures for controlling certain diseases. The Ministry also works as a co-ordinating agency for various national health progammes and it collects informations from various international organisations in other countries and passes on the same to the Health Ministries of the various states in the country. The Central Health Ministry also prescribes and determines standards for various medicines and certain food materials.

The Central Health and Family Welfare Ministry is under a cabinet minister. There are a number of secretaries and deputy secretaries to assist him. A directorate is also attached to it. The Director General of Health services is the chief of this directorate. A number of deputy-directors and assistant-directors are appointed to help the Director General in the performance of his duties. In 1956, the Government of India established the Central Health Education Bureau. The Directorate of Health services was also divided into various units such as—1. Medical Care and Hospitals, 2. Public Health and 3. General Administration.

The Public Health Department runs the All India Institute of Hygiene and Public Health. Besides, the Institute of Communicable Diseases and Central Research Institute are also run by this department.

State Setup

There is a Health Ministry in each state under a cabinet minister. There is usually a deputy-health minister as well, if the nature of the work so requires. There are a number of secretaries, deputy-secretaries, and assistant-secretaries for his help. In many states there are Director of Health Services. He is the chief medical officer and head of medical education. There are a number of deputy and assistant directors under him.

District Setup

There is a Chief Medical Officer (CMO) in each district. He is usually the head of the district hospital. Two medical officers have been placed under him. One of them is concerned with the health of the public and the other with medical treatment.

Health Services in the District—Each district has a number of dispensaries, health centres and clinics. The state government is directly responsible for running these services. A number of workers are trained for looking after epidemics, maternity homes and child clinics under the direct care of medical doctors and surgeons officially appointed for the purpose.

Below we shall understand some other aspects of health services programme generally in each state of the country.

Services in Hospitals

The following services are generally given under this category—

(1) To provide financial aid to medical students.

(2) To educate the public about the specialized services rendered by the hospitals and clinics running at various places in the state.

(3) To nurse the patient admitted in hospitals or outside registered for the same.

Child Care

There have been scattered attempts in this field prior to independence. But since 1948 the Government of India took the full responsibility for running these services. Although health has been a state subject, still the Central government gives adequate financial aid to all the states for these services. A number of advisors have been appointed to advise the India Government, for this purpose. The Central government sees that the various state governments run their health services satisfactorily. The Government at the centre has the following aims in relation to health services run by various states:

1. To establish ideal health services through out the country.
2. To establish maternity and child welfare bureaus in the country under the supervision of the State Government.
3. To improve the training of workers employed for running health services.

The state governments are running the following health services under the guidance of the Central Government:

1. Over seventy thousand maternity beds have been arranged in the country.
2. Over ten thousand lady health visitors have been appointed in addition to over eighty thousand Dais.
3. Over 20 thousand maternity and Child Welfare units have been opened by the various state governments.

4. About 20 thousand Primary Health centres have been started in the country.
5. Training of midwives has been organised and hundreds of them are trained every year.

Nurse in Public Service

Nursing service is a development of the twentieth century and it is in its infancy in our country. The following are some of the main functions of the public health nurse:

1. To give suggestions to mothers for the right keep-up of their babies.
2. To help the medical doctors in examining patients.
3. To render first-aid, whenever necessary.
4. To encourage the public for utilizing the public health services available in the locality.
5. To educate the public regarding protection from epidemics.
6. To help families when there are some patients there.
7. To inspect how the patients are being looked after by their relatives and family members.
8. To look after patients.
9. To help people to obtain medical assistance for their patients.

Welfare Projects

Community Development Projects are primarily to encourage agricultural productions. But sanitation, public health, women and children welfare and cottage industries have also been their jurisdiction in certain respects under each community project. In the state there are a number of Community Development Blocks. Each block is put under a Block Development Officer (B. D. O.). In each state there is a State Development Commissioner, a Deputy Development Commissioner and a number of District Development Officers and District Development Committees. Under the B. D. O. a number of services are run. One of these services is health. In each Development Block there are primary and secondary health centres. The following are the services rendered under these two heads:

Primary Health Centre—Each development block has this primary centre which consists of a dispensary and a medical ward of six beds. The Maternity and Child Welfare Centre is related with this primary centre. For each primary health centre there are two doctors, two compounders, two sanitary inspectors, four vaccinators, two health visitors, four midwives, six trained Dais, one sweeper and a cook.

Secondary Health Centres—Under each block there is a secondary health centre which runs a hospital of 40 beds. For this centre there are an Administrative Medical Officer, an Assistant Public Health Engineer, Malaria Inspector, Senior Health Visitor, a male Medical Officer, a lady doctor, a laboratory technician, a clerk, a steno-typist, a pharmacist, some cooks, at least one nurse, antimalaria staff and a sweeper.

Colombo Plan

About twenty countries organised a conference at Colombo and founded a Colombo Plan Fund for encouraging health services in each participating county. Under this plan our country obtained 12 lakh pounds as an aid for health services. As a result The All India Institute of Medical Sciences, was established at New Delhi. Our government obtained aid from Canada for treatment of malaria and tuberculosis and other allied medical services.

The UNICEF

The short form of this unit of U. N. O. is UNICEF. This unit does not get any aid from U. N. O. but the member-nations have organised a separate fund for it. Our government contributes about sixty lakh rupees every year to this fund and it has also obtained crores of rupees as aid for running its primary health centres. UNICEF gives aid to about 4000 primary health centres, 9,000 secondary health centres, 250 hospitals and 200 laboratory equipments. It is with the help of UNICEF that one B..C. G. programme a penicillin factory at Pimpari, D. D. T. factory at Delhi and other health projects have been started.

The WHO

India is a member of this organisation since its inception in 1948. Its main office is at Geneva. Its main purpose is to protect and promote health. This organisation tries to obtain informations regarding health and medical treatment problems and disseminates the same to the member-nations which are over 131 today. The member-nations contribute to the maintenance of this organisation and in turn obtains financial aids for their own health services. India contributed to it over twelve lakh dollars in 1980 and obtained from it over 15 lakh as a help. This organisation has given financial assistance to over 220 health programmes. W. H. 0. has sent visiting Professors to more than twenty Medical Colleges in our country. The foundation day of this organisation is celebrated as the World Health Day (7 April) through out the whole world. For administrative purposes this organisation has six divisions—each for countries within the following groups.

1. Africa—main office at Brazaville.
2. South-East Asian Countires—head office at Delhi.
3. Europe—main office at Copehegan.
4. America—head office at Washington.
5. Western Pacific Countries—head office at Manila.
6. Eastern Meditarianean Muslim Countries—head office at Alexandrea.

Education in Medicine

Medical Education—There are about 150 medical colleges in our country today. Besides, there are about 20 Dental Colleges as well. There is a provision for training of nurses at Bombay, Banglore, Ahmedabad, Hyderabad, Chandigarh, Indore, Poona, New Delhi, Madras, Vellore and Trivendram. Many big hospitals also are running courses for training of nurses. Some institutions like Ram Krishna Mission, Red Cross Society, and Andhra Mahila Sabha are running nurses training centres. The Central government gives aid to these institutions. There are about 600 nursing colleges and health schools for training of midwives and health inspectors.

Today greater emphasis is laid in our country on Post-graduate medical education and Research. A number of centres are doing this work in our country. The central governments gives grants to these centres.

A Central Health Bureau was founded in 1956 with a view to encourage health education in the country. This bureau has seven technical departments. The main purpose of this bureau is to make the curriculum of health education popular in children, teacher-trainees and teachers working in schools. This bureau gives technical help for health education in various states and centrally administrated territories. So far about twenty such bureaus have been started in various states and centrally administered territories. They have been opened in about forty districts as well.

Indian System of Medicine—Our government has encouraged the Ayurvedic and Unani system of medical treatment as well, but at many places integrated courses have not been a success. So the graduates of these courses suffer from an inferiority complex before the allopathic doctors. However, today there are over 15 under-graduate colleges are giving medical education according to the Indian system. Some voluntary organizations also are giving this education. The Central government tries to see that a minimum standard of education is maintained in these colleges. Provision for post-graduate education has also been made in these colleges.

About 100 colleges all over the country are giving medical education according to the homeopathic system. Out of these, six are government institutions.

There are separate central boards for Ayurvedic, Unani and Homeopathic systems of medicines. The members of each of these boards are usually nominated by the government. The purpose of these boards is to prescribe a minimum standard for medical education for these respective systems.

Health Education—Under this are included all those educative informations that are helpful in maintaining the health of the individual, community and the race. Evidently, its scope is very wide. However, primarily, it starts with the health of children who form the units of the society in general. Pertaining to child's health investigations are made for finding out causes of diseases and methods of their cure. In short, the aims of health education may be stated as below :

1. To teach children health laws and to guide them for observing the same.
2. To acquaint children with causes and cure of their diseases.
3. To help the teachers and other workers in the school in learning the methods of improving health.
4. To guide the guardians and parents as to how they can maintain their own health and that of their children.
5. To help the community in understanding health problems and their solutions.

QUESTIONS

1. Describe the nature of health services in our country at the national and state levels.
2. Write short notes on:
   (a) Maternity and child welfare services in India.
   (b) Public Health Nurse.
   (c) Primary and Secondary Health centres under the Community Development Projects.
   (d) World Health Organization.
3. Give a short account of medical and health education in country.

5

Basic Difficulties

Factors at Work

Poverty is one of the main causes of bad health of our Indian people. No doubt, we have ample resources, but the same have not yet been fully explored and exploited, with the result that we have remained poverty-striken since centuries. Per capita income in our country is very low. At the same time, some people are so rich that they do not know how to spend their money, on the other hand, there are innumerable ones who cannot manage their two square meals a day. Evidently, the distribution of wealth in our country is very uneven.

Balanced diet for most of the people in our country is a dream. Lack of education is also another reason of bad health of our people, because they are ignorant of the laws and principles of good health. Lack of cleanliness is another cause of our bad health, because unhygienic condition breeds germs of various types of diseases. There is an urgent need of education in hygiene and health principles in our country for educating the general people in this area. Huge population in the country is another cause of the bad health of the people. Every year there is a great increase in the size of population. This result into lowering of standard of living, because production is not increased at the same rate.

Move for Reforms

After independence our government has been trying to improve the health of the people. Before 1947 the average age of an Indian had been 27 years. But due to government and our own efforts now the average age of an Indian has been raised to fifty years. The standard of living has also improved.

It may be noted that improving of public health is mainly the responsibility of the state government. But the Central government is equally interested in the matter. Hence there is a Ministry of Health and Family Welfare under a Minsiter of the cabinet rank in the Central government. This ministry gives grants to state governments for improving the health of the people. Under its health programmes may be included prevention and eradication of seasonal epidemics, establishment of a primary health centre in each community block for providing preliminary medical aids to the neighbouring people. The Central government helps the state government in running district and sub-divisional hospitals by providing medicines, appliances and residential facilities to the hospital staff. It also helps in building up new hospitals in various parts of the country.

Nutrition Programme—Most of our people either suffer from malnutrition or undernutrition. Children, expectant and nursing mothers are generally victims to this. For improving their health the Ministry of Health and Family Welfare and the Education and Social Welfare Ministry have started certain nutrition programmes in many states. The following are some of the main aspects of this programme:

1. To provide food to children of some primary schools.
2. To give some nutrition to children of some kindergarten schools.
3. To distribute some necessary medicines to expectant mothers and young children.
4. To provide Vitamin A pills to some children for preventing blindness.
5. To distribute milk without butter and double bread combined with Vitamin A to children in the tribal areas.

6. To give food to children of pre-school age in densely populated dirty localities.
7. To encourage the people to produce nutritious food commodities and to consume the same in a healthy manner. For spreading information about nutrition, so far about 20 films have been produced in various regional languages. Demonstrations and exhibitions are also organised for making people conscious about the rudiments of balanced nutrition. The Central government is encouraging research in the area of nutrition.

The Precautions

Several programmes at the national level have been organised for prevention of many diseases. We are hinting at some of them below:

B.C.G. Vaccination Programme—In 1949 the B.C.G. vaccination programme was started for cure of T. B. patients and for prevention of this disease in others. By 1987 about 45 crores persons were clinically examined for detection of T. B. and above 27 crore were vaccinated against T. B. One crore T. B. patients were detected and 350 hospitals in the country were made for T. B. patients. The National T. B. Institute Banglore runs a reorientation course for medical practitioners. The Vallabh Bhai Chest Institute and Chest Institute Delhi runs a T. B. and Chest disease post graduate diploma course. There are more than 250 T. B. centres for looking after T. B. patients in the country.

National Filaria Control Programme—The Central government is running this programme since 1955. Under this programme underground drainages are constructed in cities and town affected by filaria in order that mosquitoes and larvas may not breed in the open. Opening of filaria hospitals and destroying mosquitoes and larvas responsible for filaria are the other main aspects of this national programme. A survery has revealed that about 20 crore persons reside in areas prone to filaria. Aboutly crore of these are those who have definite symptoms of filaria. Several units have been established in urban areas for destroying larvas. These units cover about 30 crore persons.

National Malaria Control Programme—This programme was started in 1953. In 1958 this programme was changed into National Malaria Eradication Programme. The whole country has been included in this programme, except the sea coast areas above the 5000 feet level because malaria has no influence at such a high level. The Central government started this programme, but the state governments have also been given responsibility for carrying out this programme. The World Health Organization also gives financial aid for this programme. About 50,000 units are active today for eradication of malaria. Each unit covers about 15 lakh persons. This programme has been very successful till 1970-71 when the percentage of patients fell to 0-15 from 10-0 in 1955-56. But since 1979 it is reported that the percentage is going again up, because the mosquitoes are getting immune to disinfectants. The area organisations in Lucknow, Shillong, Hyderabad, Baroda, Bhuvaneshwar and Delhi train workers for this programme. At the state level under the State Health Department there are a number of officers and workers appointed for eradication of malaria, such as Director of Health Services, Dy. Director of Malariology, District Medical Officer of Health, Malaria Officer Incharge of a unit and a number of executives and administrative officers, mechanics, accountants, store keepers, clerks and a host of malaria inspectors.

National Trachoma Control Programme—Since 1963 this programme is in operation. This programme is run in U. P., Bihar, Rajasthan, Assam, Haryana, Jammu and Kashmir, Gujrat, H. P., Meghalaya, Manipur, Karnataka, Kerala, M. P., Punjab and some other states under the guidance of the Central government. By 1987 about 20 crore persons were covered under this programme which mainly pertains to health education.

National Small-pox Eradication Programme—Under this programme certain selected persons are again vaccinated for prevention of small-pox. This work was started in 1962. In the beginning about 21 crore vaccinations were done and 22 crore persons were revaccinated. This disease has been partially controlled. In 1972 there were about 28,000 small-pox patients and 5,500 out of these died and in 1987 there were about 1 lakh small-pox patients and about 30,000 died out of them.

Unhealthy State

Poverty, ignorance and huge population causes bad health. Some efforts for improving health of the people the Central and State governments are rendering positive services for this. This following programme are noteworthy in this context.

1. Nutrition Programme.
2 Programmes of prevention of diseases—B.C.G. Vaccination, Filaria, Malaria, Trachoma and Small-pox control programme.

QUESTIONS

1. Discuss some of the main causes of poor health of people in India.
2. Describe any three programme for control of certain diseases.

6

Body Structure

There are a number of bones in the human body. If skin and flesh are removed from the body, bones will remain. This skeleton is an awe-inspiring object to look at. But this skeleton is the rock foundation of the human body. This bony structure is also called the skeletal system. This bone structure is commonly known as skeleton.

Specialities of Skeleton—The skeleton is no rigid or immobile like a house. The most important feature of the skeleton is that it can bend or take turn at many places according to a man's desire. Muscles in the body help its movement. Its flexibility helps the acrobats in a circus to perform various body tricks and people witnessing their performance become inclined to think that the body is boneless.

Setup of Bones

The total number of bones in a human body is 206 which are as follows:

(1) Eight bones in the upper part of skull and 14 on the face totalling in all 22.

(2) Twenty-five bones in the chest.

(3) Sixty-four bones in the upper part. Each hand has 32 bones.

(4) In the lower portion, there are 62 bones. Each leg has 31 such bones.

(5) Twenty-six bones are found in the rear.

Besides, there is a bone between the larynx and the chin and six bones in both the ears. In this way, the bones total 206. 'What is the utility of so many bones' is a question that naturally arises. The answer to this question is evident. These bones also help in the movement of the body. Every part of the human body is made of a number of bones and not by a single bone. This two has its utility. Had there been only one bone in a particular part of the body it would have become entirely useless, had that single bone been broken in on account of injury. But because of the presence of a number of bones in a particular part of the body an injury caused to some bone does not invalidate that part entirely. Of course, there is a considerable pain when a bone is broken but in course of time, with proper treatment, it becomes allright. Moreover, the presence of so many bones make the skeleton considerably strong as compared to a single bone skeleton.

Bones are tubular and therefore light and strong. The cavity in them is filled with a substance known as marrow. According to the shape and size, these could be divided in the following categories :

(1) Flat bones : Bones of the skull are flat.

(2) Short bones: Bones of the fingers and toes are short.

(3) Long bones : Bones of the hands and legs are long.

(4) Cubical bones: Bones of the knee and wrists are cubical.

(5) Irregular bones : Bones of the spinal chord are irregular, and

(6) Cuneiform bones: These bones are pointed at one end and gradually turn thick, as in the ankle.

The unique thing about the bones is their hardness. The body remains hard and strong as a result of this quality of the bones. Calcium and some salts cause this hardness in the bones. Calcium phosphate, carbonate flouride and magnesium phosphate are important in this respect. Calcium phosphate is found in abundance in the bones.

Different Parts

Skeletal system may be divided into three categories:

1. Skull, 2. Trunk and 3. Upper and lower extremities.

The skull is further subdivided into two parts : 1. Cranium and 2. Face. The first part consists of eight bones. It is like a strong box. Brain remains safe in it. The eight bones that constiture this cranium are as follows:

1. Frontal bone which forms the forehead.
2. Skull-roof and the two side partial bones.
3. There is a bone in the back of the skull. This is known as occipital
4. Two bones in both the temples are known as temporal bone. Besides the above six bones, there are two more bones. One is known as spheroid bone and the other known as ethmoid bone.

The Skeleton

These eight bones of the skull are joined with each other by a fixed and well-organised joint. There are a number of holes in the skull tube. The biggest hole in the tube is in the rear portion towards the back where spinal chord joins the brain. Some veins of the nerves come out from other holes and blood vessels come and go.

In the case of children, the above-mentiond eight bones are not joined with each other. There are two fontinalis in their skull. One 's known as anterior and the other as posterior fontinalis. These remove the danger of the skull cracking during birth and provide it with strength to stand the impact. These fontinalis join each other at the age of two. One should be very careful to protect the child against head injury during the first two years.

The face consists of 14 bones which are listed as below:

(a) Superior maxillary or upper jaw bone, (b) Inferior maxillary, (c) Two molar or cheek bones, (d) Two palate bones, (e) Two nasal bones, (f) Two spongy bones, (g) Two rachrymal bones, (h) One vomer bone.

Out of these bones, the inferior maxillary is movable. This can move upwards, downwards, sideways, inside and outside. Chewing the food is possible only with the help of this bone. On the face open up the cavities that protect our sense of hearing (ear), of smelling and breathing (nose) and of seeing (eyes). These cavities protect these important organs from outside injuries. The middle portion of inferior maxillary is known as chin. On its upper portion are 16 cavities for teeth.

The trunk consists of vertebral column, ribs, sternum, shoulder girdle and the hip bones.

Spinal chord is the base of the human body. This is known as vertebral column. This begins from the neck and goes down nearly two or three inches above the anus. This column consists of 26 different parts which are interconnected. Each of these parts is called the vertebrae of the spinal chord. These structures are unique. These bulge out and feel rough when touched.

In the spinal chord of children there are 33 irregular bones. Five of the last nine bones out of these 33 join and turn into a single bone. Likewise, the remaining four combine to form another bone. It is because of this phenomenon that there are only 26 bones in the spinal chord which have been grouped as under :

(a) Seven cervical vertebral form .the neck.

(b) Twelve dorsal thoracic vertebral form the back.

(c) Five lumbar vertebral form the waist region.

(d) Out of nine pelvic vertebral which form the pelvic region, the first five are called sacrum, while the remaining four are separate and can turn this way or that. The two vertebrae of the lower part are interconnected and are fixed.

Except the first two and the last nine vertebrae, others are almost similar in shpae. The beginning part of vertebrae is like a stone-studded ring. Just like in a stone-studded ring the stone in fixed part is thick and broad and the remaining portion is thin. The front part is known as the disc, while the circular one is called the neural arch. Many portions of the two parts are projecting. On both the sides of neural arch are projecting parts known as transverse process.

In the back portion of the neural arch there is a projection. This projection is pointed. These pointed projections are interjoined with the result that vertebrae are strongly interilinked. Muscles also stick to these projections and with their help the back can easily bend.

The discs of the vertebrae are placed on each other, and thus they sit tightly on one another forming a tube. This is called the vertabral canal. Through this canal passes the spinal chord which resembles in shape to a thick rope. The veins coming out of medulla oblongata-throughout vertebrae spread throughout the body. These nerves help us to know and feel different objects and they also control the function of the various parts of the body. Between the two vertebrae is the pad of cartilage. The pad of cartilage saves the bones from friction and there .is no fear of a bone striking against the other during a fall or a jump.

The vertebrae of the various parts vary according to need. The lower vertebrae are comparatively larger and heavier than the upper ones. The neck vertebrae are the lightest, while waist region ones are the heaviest. It is but natural because the body weight is heavier at the waist as compared with that at the neck.

Besides the above, there are other differences between the vertebrae. The projections near the vertebrae of neck bear holes. The pointed projection in the back portion of the vertebrae behind the chest are very long. All the projections in the waist region vertebrae are thick and strong.

The first and the second vertebrae of neck have some peculiarities in them. In the first vertebrae, there is an arch whose back pointed projection is very small, its upper portion are two smooth projections. On them rest the back-bones of the skull. In the upper parts of neck's second vertebrae is teeth-like projection which fits in with the first vertebrae neural arch. The head moves in various directions with the help of these teeth-like marks.

The structure of the spinal chord is not like a straight rod. It has several curves. Some of its portion appears to bulge outside while others seem to bend inwards. The neck portions seem to be bending outwards. In the back side of the chest there is a long arch like pit and waist region seems to bulge outwards.

These curves have their own advantages. The important ones are given below:

(a) These curves add strength to the backbone while man carries head-loads.

(b) Provide strength to the backbone when it expands or relaxes.

(c) Help the extremities of the stomach and chest bones.

(d) Provide room for the interrelation of back's powerful muscles.

Wrong sitting positions during student life sometimes result in certain deformities. The number of curves are either get reduced or increased owing to wrong sitting positions. The back, too, turns ugly and deformed and there remains a possibility of hunch appearing in the back.

The chest, too, is a box like the skull. The heart and the lungs lie safe in this box. The chest bones are six to seven inches in length. The upper portion of the chest is broad and narrows downwards.

The chest is divided into three parts:

(a) In the upper-portion collar bones join each other.

(b) In the centre seven ribs on each side join.

(c) The lower portion is made up of cartilages.

There are twelve ribs on each side of the chest. In the front, a bone in the middle of the rib joins them. This broad bone is called the sternum, in this way, there are 25 bones in the chest. Seven pairs of bones are joined in the chest while three pairs join the seventh pair, but these three pairs of bones have no relation with the chest. The last two pairs of the ribs are small and do not reach the sternum. These are, therefore, called the floating ribs. Every two ribs are joined in the middle by muscles. These muscles are outercoastal muscles. During respiration, the bony structure of the chest lifts itself upward and goes downwards due to expansion and relaxation of the muscles.

The respiratory and the food tubes come down through the upper part of the bony chest structure. At this very place, a number of blood vessels and nerves come down from the neck to the chest and vice versa. In the lower portion of this body structure lies an arch-like cover of muscles known as diaphragm. This separates the chest from the stomach. Through this passes the food tube from the chest to the stomach.

The structure of the upper extremities is joined to trunk through a circle of bones. This circle is called shoulder girdle. The shoulder girdle is formed by the collar-bones in the front and the shoulder blade in the rear. Like ribs, the collar-bone is joined to the sternum through cartilage. The shoulder-blade rests on the rib bones in loose and plain way. The bones of the shoulder girdle are thin and can easily turn in one or the other direction.

Each arm has the following parts:

(a) Collar-bone, (b) Scapula, (c) Upper arm, (d) Forearm, (e) Wrist and Palm. (f) finger

The division of bones in them is as under :

Collar-bone is on the uppermost portion of the chest. It has only one bone. Scapula is a single bone; one bone in the upper arm; two bones in the forearm; eight bones in the wrist; five in the palm; 14 in the fingers. This brings the total of bones to 32 in the an arm and 64 in both the arms

Ordinarily, the structure of the lower extremities resembles that of upper extremities. Pelvic, thigh, leg and calf are included in the lower extremities. The division of bones under this category are as follows : the hip bone, the thigh bone, the calf bone, two leg bones, seven knee bones, five foot bones and fourteen bones of the toes. The total in this way comes to 31. Due to difference of one bone in wrist and knees, the structures of upper and lower extremities vary. The wrist has eight bones, while the knee has only seven.

The structure of lower extremities is joined with the trunk by the hip girdle. The hip has a broad and special type of bone. Hips are two in number. The two bones of the hip are joined with the back in the waist region by a triangular bone called sacrum. Below the two bones are the genital organs of the male and female. Despite the two bones being connected through sacrum, the back-bone below the sacrum is not joined by the tail bone. In the pelvic girdle are the genital, reproductory and excretory organs of males and femals.

In comparison to male's pelvic girdle the female's is less deep but broader. The shape of the pelvic girdle is like a bottomless pot.

The three parts of the hip girdle which are as follows are worth mentioning:

(1) The broad upper part known as ilium.

(2) The narrow lower part called ischium.

(3) The broad front part named pelvis.

During childhood, the above three parts are visible separately but in course of time they gradually join each other on the outer part of the hip girdle. The junction creates a round cavity which is called tibia. In both the hips, there is a round cavity in which fit in both the thigh bones properly.

Like the upper arm there is a bone in the thigh called fibula. This is the longest and the strongest bone in the body. Its upper end is round like ball and fits properly in the hip bone. The lower portion of this bone is somewhat broad and is joined to the leg bone at the knee. It is a very strong joint. There is also a traingular bone on this place called tarsal bone. This bone can be shaken or moved.

Below the knee there are two bones in the leg like the arm. These are called metatarsal bone and joints. The metatarsal bone is narrow and comparatively weak. The upper part of the tarsal bone is comparatively thick and broad. It joins the fibula at the knee. The lower portion of the tarsal bone which is narrow in conjunction with acetabulum makes its inner projection.

There are seven acetabulum. These form the knee. One of these thick bones is joined with the tarsal bone. Another bone with a curve downwards forms the heel.

Like the palm, there are five bones in the feet. The toe bones are joined with them. The total number of the bones is 14. Two in the first toe and three each in the rest total 14.

Joints in Body

It is evident from the last chapter that the skeletal or bone structure has many joints at places. Those places where two bones or cartilages join each other are called joints. These joints are divided in two categories :

(1) movable, and (2) immovable. The joints of the skull are the specimens of immovable joints.

Movable joints are of four categories:

Bell and Socket Joints—In this kind of joint the round end of a long bone fits in the socket of another bone. The bones in these joints are so placed that the interlinked bones can be moved freely. The shoulder and hip joints are the unique examples of this category of joints.

Hinge Joint—In this variety of joint the joining bones can cause action forward and backward. The action of these joints is similar to the action of the upper lid and lower pan of a box joined by a hinge. The elbow, knee and finger joints fall in this category. The unique thing about these joints is that the joining parts can move forward and backward but not sidewards. There is a large number of such joints in our body.

Pivot Joint—In this kind of joint one bone forms a peg and the other moves over it. This joint is found between the atlas and the axis vertebrae. The head can easily be moved forward, backward or sidewards position on the basis of this joint.

Gliding Joint—Under this category of the joint, one bone is joined by the other through a cartilage. This joint possesses the quality of gliding to some extent. The wrist bones and the vertebrae of the spinal chord are interconnected on this principle.

The bones on each joint are tied by white ligament fibrous bonds. The action of these ligament fibrous bonds are rope-like. They keep the bones in their proper places. There are muscles on the joints which are joined with bones through the white ligament fibrous bonds.

There exists an efficient arrangement of keeping the joints intact. At this spot (joint) the ends of the two joining bones have a fibrous membrane which is very strong and tape-like in shape. There is one more thin membrane which makes a peculiar type of sack at the ends of the bones. This sack is called the capsule of the joint. There is a layer of cartilages on the ends of the bones in this sack. This cartilage, too, is covered by a smooth and very thin membrane. A smooth oil-like lubricant continuously comes out of this membrane which protects the bones from striking against each other. This liquid acts like a lubricant in a machine, and ensures functioning of these joints.

Joints are very necessary for the skeleton. In the absence of the joints, the man can neither move his hand or feet nor move from one position to another. Had there been no joints, all the bodily movements would have an impossibility and there would have been no movement in the man. Then, he would have been just like a wooden statue. The uniqueness in the human body lies in the fact that the joints are according to the needs of a particular portion. The utility of each organ of the body depends on these joints.

When defects appear in joints the functioning of the various organs, too, become defective. The knee joints generally fall victims to defects. Defective knee-joints are very common among many players. Under defective joints they feel pain during movement of the body from one position to another. Walking, sitting or standing becomes a painful process for players with defects in their joints. Similarly, other joints, when in a state of unhealthiness, cause pain in the movement of organs concerned. Chronic pain in joints often results in tuberculosis or rheumatism. The hip and the knee-joints commonly suffer from rheumatism.

Sometimes the bones of joints are dislocated. Such a dislocation makes the affected parts motionless and useless.

The children who suffer from such a dislocation of bones should be given leave from the school and advised to take rest. They should further be advised to take nutritious food and inhale fresh air.

The Diseases

Many diseases often appear in the bones of children. The cause generally lies in the inadequate and unhealthy diet, lack of mother's milk, use of tinned milk and lack of fresh milk. Unhealthy home atmosphere, lack of fresh and open air and sunlight are factors which, too, contribute to bone diseases. Malformation occurs in the bones in individuals living in unhealthy conditions and the following changes appear in their bones:

(a) Square Head—Due to defects caused in the bones of the skull, the head often becomes square and forehead bulges unusually forward.

(b) Beaded Ribs—The chest, becomes somewhat thick at the spots where cartilages join the ribs.

(c) Pigeon Chest—This deformity is caused by the defects in the chest bones. Consequently, sternum bulges forward causing cavity on one side.

(d) Carved Spine—The vertebral column bends on one side when there are defects in its bones and kyphosis appears. Sometimes it turns on one side resulting in scoliosis.

(e) Softened Bones—Children's bones are soft and are likely to become deformed due to unusual pressure. Sometimes, when the child starts walking, some defects develop in his leg bones and they become deformed. As a result of this deformation, knees turn thick, leg muscles become slanting and feet turn flat. Besides, other deformities, too, are caused. The ends of the long arm and leg bones become particularly thick.

(f) General Debility and Yellow Complexion of the Body—General debility and yellowness in children retard the full development of muscles. They turn weak and diseased. Ligaments, too, become loose and weak. Delay is caused in cutting of milk teeth and if somehow they come out decay sets in early. The teeth-roots become weak and turn blackish. Teeth worms appear which cause hollowness in the teeth.

(g) Bulging Out Stomach—Sometimes, it is observed that the stomach of the child unusually bulges outwards giving it more prominence than to other parts of the body. This deformity is caused by soft and weak muscles.

(h) Lack of lime salt affects the pelvic girdle which becomes narrow causing considerable difficulty in easy delivery.

(i) Related Development of Nervous System—As a result of this factor, the child starts speaking, walking and running at a delayed stage.

(j) Often defect in bones are the root cause of cold, cough, bronchitis, pneumonia, etc. Resistance to these diseases is also lowered.

The Defects

1. Particular attention should be paid to physically weak children in schools. Neither hard physical labour nor mental should be forced upon them. Generally, teachers make the child stand in the class for a long time. This practice should be avoided and the physically weak child should, in no circumstances, be subjected to this punishment.
2. Nutritious food is very necessary for weak children. Their food should consist of such edibles that are bound in calcium and vitamin D. The mother's food, too, should be rich in calcium and vitamin D. Children of mother having enough calcium and vitamin D do not fall prey to any disease during teething period.
3. Young children generally fall victims to the dreadful disease of rickets. Fresh air is absolutely necessary guarding the children a ganist this disease. They should also get enough sunshine. Their house should be open and ventilated. There should be no dampness in houses. Children should be asked to play in open Parks is is very useful in this respect.
4. Children suffering from tuberculosis should be isolated. They should not be allowed to come to school. Sterilised milk should be provided to them. Heliotherapy, too', proves very useful for such children. Focussing of sun's ultra-violet rays on the affected bones is also a very effective treatment of bone tuberculosis.
5. Particular attention should be paid to the sitting positions of the children in order to protect them against deformities like kyphosis. They should be trained to sit and rise properly and stand erect.

6. For removing the ugliness of a flat foot, sufficient rest should be given to the feet. Such feet should be guarded against excessive fatigue. Standing on the toes proves highly beneficial in this deformity. Such children should not wear heavy boots.

Skeletal structure of the human body is dynamic. It is not a motionless or rigid structure, but flexible and full of motion. This structure consists of 206 bones: 22 in skull, 25 in chest, 64 in arms, 62 in legs and 26 in the back part. Bones are tube-like, and are divided into six categories—(1) Flat, (2) Shoot, (3) Long, (4) Cubical, (5) Irregular and (6) Cuneiform.

The skeleton is divided into three parts—skull, trunk and upper and lower extremities. The skull is further'sub-divided into two parts—

(1) Cranium and Face. Cranium has eight, while face has 14 bones.

The trunk includes vertebral column, ribs, sternum, shoulder girdle and hip girdle.

Vertebrae are like a stone-studded ring. They vary according to need and circumstances. Some are small, some are big and many others bear holes in them.

Sternum is like a box in which lie the lungs and heart well-protected.

Upper extremities are divided into six parts—(1) Glenoid cavity, (2) Scapula, (3) Upper arm, (4) Forearm, (5) Wrist and (6) Palm. The lower extremities constists of—(l) Hip, (2) Thigh, (3) Leg, (4) Knee and (5) Foot.

The structure of movable joints is unique in as much as they are tied with ligament fibrous bonds. There is a membrane through which seeps out an oil-like lubricant. This helps the smooth functioning of the joints. The joints control and help the movement of the various parts of the body. Defects in the joints cause many diseases. Bone diseases cause a number of deformities in the body causing square head, beaded ribs, pigeon chest, curved spine, flat foot and unusual outward bulging of the stomach.

Following is the teatment for the above mentioned deformities:

Avoiding excessive physical labour and taking of rest, nutritious food, open and fresh air, sun-light and useful exercises and practising of the proper way of sitting, standing and rising.

The human body is made up of very small cells. These cells can be seen through a microscope. The cells play an important part in the making up of a human body. A small particle of the semiliquid substance called protoplasm is known as cell. Protoplasm is formed when oxygen, hydrogen, nitrogen, carbon and sulphur combine. The inner portion of the cell is called the core or kernel. This thing is like a globe or an egg in shape and controls the-working of the cell. Different kinds of cells do different kinds of work. Their shape differs according to their work. Many of the same variety of cells are known as tissues. There are many varieties of tissues like fat tissues, bone tissues and muscular tissues. The fat tissues are made up of fat cells, bone tissues of bone cells and muscular tissus are made from muscular cells. In a nut-shell, the different kinds of tissues are made of different cells. The tissues build up the various parts of the body. Every part of the body has a different function to perform.

The human body is like a well-organised, well-administered and well-planned city where nature has kept in view everything and has made the best possible arrangements. The circulation'of blood feeds the body, the discharge from bowels and sweat keep the body clean. The respiratiory system is meant to fill in fresh air and expel the foul one. Arrangement for keeping contact with the outside world has been made possible through the nervous system. Bones and skeletons are to keep the body straight and muscular system for joining the bones and making them move according to need. For execution of different work there are various groups known as systems. The systems are of nine kinds as mentioned below:

Muscular System—This system provides power of movement to various parts of the human body. Muscles are connected with bones or strong tissued nets. The tissued nets are known as joints or nerves.

Skeletal or Bony System—The skeleton keeps the body straightened and upright, but not stiff or unbending like the wall of a house. The skeleton has been so devised that it can take turn or bend at many places. Bones are joined with each other. The joining substance is known as connective tissue. The skeletal or bony system is the main base of the body.

Respiratory System—The main function of this system is to provide oxygen to the cells, expel out carbon di-oxide and bad water from the body. Lungs and respiratory tubes form a part of this system.

Circulatory System—The various organs in this system take the food inside. Food is the most essential thing for sustaining life. These organs digest the food. Stomach, intestines, liver etc., are the main organs under this system. These organs carry the useless and waste products to the other organs that throw them out. Throwing the waste out is the main function of the larger intestine.

Excretory System—Under this system come the lungs, the larger intestine, kidney and the skin. The function of these organs is to throw out stool, sweat and urine etc., from the body. Much foul matter reach the blood. When the blood reaches kidney all this foul matter is discharged out through urinary passage. In the same way, sweat and stool are discharged out of body.

Digestive System—The main organs which come under this system are saliva-producing glands, the mouth, alimentary canal, stomach, intestines, liver and spleen. With the help of these organs we carry the food in the stomach and digest it.

Nervous System—The nervous system of the body controls and directs all the other systems. The brain, spinal chord and the entire network of nerves constitute the nervous system. Their function is to control the activities of the entire human body.

Reproductive System—This system" of the human body relates to the activities concerning the genital organs and the birth of children. In this are included the visible and hidden genital organs of male and female. When discharged ovum and sperm of these organs of male and female unite another human being is produced. The race thus continues to exist.

Lymphatic System—Under this system come the lymphatic capillaries and glands through which the tissues receive their diet and the foul matter is thrown out.

Muscular System

The entire human body is covered with skin. If skin is peeled off red flesh will become visible. If we make a picture of human body without skin, it will be revealed that flesh is not in a uniform position on the body. At some places it is in larger quantities, while at other it is in smaller quantity. Besides, it is peculiar in make. Its both ends are thin and contracted; while the middle portion is broad and swelled. These pieces of flesh are called muscles. They exist both on the outer and the inner parts of the body. By outer part is meant the head, hands, legs and chest. In these parts muscles embarace the bones. Besides, there are some muscles which being in the inner part of the body do not remain joined with bones. Such muscles are found in the blood vessels, heart, stomach, intestines, etc. There are about 500 muscles in a human body.

Categories of Muscles—Muscles are divided into two categories: (1) voluntary and (2) involuntary. Voluntary muscles are those which function according to a man's wish and are under his control. But there are certain muscles which do not function according to our dictates. These are known as involuntary muscles. Heart, stomach, muscles of the urinary tract and inestines come under the category of involuntary muscles. These continuously contract and expand. The action of heart cannot be controlled according to human desire. Similarly, function of the intestines are also beyond man's control. The food continuously goes down from the intestines. The retina of the eye contracts to light and expands in darkness. This, too, cannot be controlled by man's desire.

Construction of Muscles—The size and shape of the muscles varies from one another. Some are big, other are small, some are long and some are round. Leg muscles are big, while those of the eyes are very small. Their shape and size are governed by their functions. Voluntary muscles, too, are of different sizes. Leg and hand muscles are thicker in the middle as compared to ends. There are tendons on their ends through which they are joined with bones. Some muscles are joined with the upper membrane of the bone. Muscle's one end is joined with one bone and the other end with another bone and it remains in the upper position. The upper end is known as source or origin while the lower end is known as the entrance. The main part of the muscle is known as stomach has contractible cells in it.

Functional System of Muscles—The main function of these muscles is expansion and relaxation. When the muscle contracts, bone on both ends come nearer. The length of the muscle at this time is reduced but its breadth increases. This action becomes quite clear when the action of the bleep muscle is examined in the upper arm. This muscles is joined near the joint of shoulder with the shoulder blade.

Its belly is just in front of the hand bone, but it is not Joined with it. When it contracts it turns small, thick and round and the fore arm bones near the upper arm. One can understand this action by feeling the upper arm. When the tricep behind the hand contracts, the forearm straightens up. In the same manner, the expansion and relaxation of the muscles take place in various parts of the body. The movement of the different-parts of the body rests on the contraction and relaxation of these muscles. The expansion and relaxation of muscles is made possible through the help of bones. In order to bring the forearm nearer to the upper arm, its outer bone is joined with elbow and only then the bicep contracts and raises the forearm. In the same way, for extending the forearm, the tricep behind the hand takes help. This muscle joins the elbow resulting in the extending of the forearm.

A number of muscles combine and make efforts to cause an action. An action is not caused by a single muscle. For example, in keeping the body erect, both the muscles in the front and on the rear act. The front muscles try to force the body-forward while the muscles on the back try to keep the body in a backward position. As a result of this action and reaction the body remains in an upright position. The same action by many muscles causes movement of body in various manners.

It will be worth while noting here that muscles expand and relax on receiving orders from the nervous system. That is why in serious head injury or shock to nervous system turns the man senseless. It is so because during an injury or a shock, the instructions from the mind are not passed on to muscles by the nervous system and the muscles remain loose.

Ingredients for the Formation of Muscles—Muscles are formed with the help of many things. Threefourth part of muscles comprises of water and the rest of protein and natural salts. Milk, almond, gram, meat, eggs are the main protein which provide food and strengthen the muscles. These things provide energy to the muscles as a result of which they function properly. Heat is generated in the body by taking these things. When the muscles do not work, a starchy substance is deposited in a large quantity. During action this substance is used by muscles. When muscles have to work more the quantity of this substance is reduced. Muscles remain healthy only when they work and get reasonable rest.

Development of Muscles—Strength and development of muscles depend upon nourishing diet and physical exercise. In the absence of these two, the muscles do not get sufficient diet and consequently turn weak. Lack of fresh air tells adversely on the muscles. For keeping them strong and healthy, proper rest should be given to them. Rest gives opportunity to throw out foul matter from within and new energy is generated in the muscles. Useless and foul matter creates fatigue and laziness in the body.

Utility of Muscles—Body is stimulated to action due to muscles. Had there been no muscles in the body, it would not have been possible to eat, drink, see, speak, laugh, sing, walk and write etc. The muscles keep the body in the desired position and help those parts where there is absence or shortage of bones.

General Structure—Small cells are the main constituents of the human body. These protoplasms are made up of oxygen, hydrogen, nitrogen, sulphur and carbon. Groups of cells are known as tissues. They are of different kinds and form the various parts of the body.

The human body is like a well-planned, well-administered and well-organised town. There are nine systems which perform all the functions of the body. These are as under:

1. Muscular system, 2. Bony system, 3. Respiratory system, 4. Blood circulatory system, 5. Excretory system, 6. Digestive system, 7. Nervous system, 8. Reproductive system and 9. Lymphatic system.

Musculatory Stystem—Muscles are of two kinds : (1) Voluntary and (2) Involutary. Their shape and size differ. They are long, short, round and broad. They are further divided in three parts : (1) Source or origin, (2) Stomach and (3) Entrance place. Contraction and relaxation are their main functions. Movement in the body 'is caused by their contraction or relaxation. They keep the body in different positions. Water, protein and natural salts are necessary for them. Their health and strength depend on fresh air, protein, rich food, exercise and adequate rest. During rest they throw out foul matter out of the body. The discharge of foul matter gives new strength to the muscles.

QUESTIONS

1. What are the special features of the skeleton ? Give a description of bones in various parts of body.
2. Describe the various parts of the skull. What are their functions ?
3. Describe the structure of the vertebral column. What is its relation with the various parts of the body ?
4. Write a short note on the upper and lower extremities of the human body.
5. What categories of bone-joints are found in the body ? Describe them with illustrations.
6. Write a brief note on the structure of movable joints in the body.
7. Throw light on the importance of joints in the body
8. Which deformities are caused by which defect in the bones? Give a brief account.
9. What measures should be taken to protect the bones from becoming deformed ?
10. "The human body is like a well-planned and well-organised town." Comment.

7

Controlling System

Nervous system is also known as cerebro-spinal system or marrow fibre system. This is a complicated but well-organised system as compared to other systems, in the body. All other body systems are controlled by this particular system. The nervous system rules over all other systems. The main organ of nervous system is the brain, the king of the body. The brain which lies surrounded by eight bones in a safe place rules the body, controls the functions of all the body organs and goes on receiving information from every nook and corner of the body. Body will remain inactive without brain. In its absence there would neither be blood circulation, nor respiration nor would other parts of the body function.

This system is made up of a particular type of cells. These differ from other common cells. There is a nervous cord called axon. Besides, there are many small fibres which have many brands called dendrites. Jointly, these fibres are called neurous. The colour of nerve cells is light grey. Therefore, these cells are known as grey matter. Their vessels being white are called white matter.

The axons are covered by medullary sheath. The dendrites though joined to the nearest branches of nerve cells are not attached to each other. These places are known as sinaptic junctions. Each activity of the body is felt through the action of this system. Nervous feelings are transmitted by dendrites like the electric current from one nervous cell to another. Their feeling power is so sensitive that we have no idea of the time although activities continuously take place. A network of such axons and dendrites are spread all over the body which carry the feeling instantly to the spinal cord. The feelings of repeated actions are each time conveyed by the sinaptic junctions to spinal cord or brain. Repetition of action reduces the power of sinaptic junctions as the result of which each time the action is repeated, transmission of feeling becomes easier and faster. It is due to this reason that repeated practice of work makes it easier. Lesson repeated many times become simple and easier to remember because of this action. Sometimes, the feeling transmission power becomes dull. This is due to tiredness of sinaptic junction on account of overwork. Alcoholic drinks and other narcotic drugs also occasionaly make it dull.

Nervous System

Nervous system is made of two different but interrelated systems:

(a) Central or Cerebro-Spinal System.

(b) Peripheral Nervous System.

Central or Cerebro-spinal System is divided into two parts, (1) The safely placed upper part in the skull (brain), (2) The safe smooth, long and circular part in the vertebral column (Medulla oblongata).

Significant Parts

The brain is not only an important part of this system but is also the most important part of the body. It is oval in shape and its front portion is comparatively narrow but thick. The weight of a young man's brain is 1/50 of the total body weight. The weight of a man's brain in the age group of 15 to 49 years is about 1300 grams and that of a woman in the same age group is approximately 1100 grams.

The nature has kept the brain inside the membranes to keep it particularly safe. The membranes are (1) Duramater, (2) Arachnoid, and (3) Piamater.

Duramater is thick and strong. It is placed below the skull bones. It protects the brain like a soldier. After this comes the archnoid which is thin and soft. The membrane placed still below is called piamater. It is very thin and attached to the brain. A network of blood vessels is spread in it. Besides, there are a number of projections and cavities in the brain. Projections are called convolutions and cavities are named fissures. Piamater also penetrates fissures, as it is attached with the brain.

The brain is divided into four pans : (i) Cerebrum, (ii) Cerebellum, (iii) Pons Variole and (iv) Medulla Oblongata.

This is the biggest part of the brain. The fissure divides it into two parts. These parts are called hemispheres. One is called the right and the other the left hemisphere. These two are separated by a longitudinal cerebral, but in the lower part they remain joined by marrow tissues. This joining bond is called corpus collosum.

There are a number of fissures and convolutions. These are like furrows in a field. Fissures divide the brain into many parts. Each part is called centre. These have definite functions assigned to them. They are named after the nature of their functions, e.g., taste centre, hearing centre, smelling centre, seeing centre etc. The depth of fissures is related to human intelligence. Intelligent man's fissures are deeper but they are shallower in the case of mediocres.

Cerebrum is full of grey and white matter. Grey matter covers the white matter. Grey matter is called cortex. It is made up of nervous cells and nervous fibres. The nervous fibres enter the cortex. The cortex of an intelligent man is comparatively thicker than that of a mediocre's.

The grey matter is made up of various kinds of marrow nerves. There are about 300 crores of cells in the brain. Some of these cells are needle-shaped. Their middle portion is make up of lifejuice. The core is in their centre. Arms come out on all sides of this core. In addition, a long wire comes out of each cell. The white matter is generally made of them. These wires go from one part of the cerebrum to another, from one hemisphere to another and to cerebellum, medulla oblongata and vertebral column. Each marrow fibre is independent. Their arms, too, are independent. Although their branches are intermingled, yet these are not related to each other. The marrow cell with all its arms is known as neuron.

The needle-shaped cells are of many varieties. Some are small, some of middle size and many are huge-sized. There is one more variety of cell which lies in the nerve cell and helps it.

The white matter is a group of marrow tissues. It comes out of the marrow cell of grey matter from medulla oblongata and other parts of the brain.

Its functions are varied and complicated. These functions are related to thinking, remembering, desire, will-power, feeling, execution of works etc. This is the centre of intelligence and knowledge. On its strength we think, take decisions, learn, understand and remember. In this part of the brain emotions like love, hate, fear, joy, sorrow and anger are generated and felt. Ace of these functions are entrusted to different parts.

It has been proved by experiments that if a person's brain is damaged, he will have no initiative to execute a work on his own. He will get the stimulus for external activities through medulla oblongata. He will move his limbs but will not feel inspired to do anything voluntarily. Such actions are called relaxations.

Injury to the cerebrum causes unconsciousness but the man regains consciousness after treatment. Emotions are born again. This shows clearly that every action of the body is controlled by cereburm. Defects in cerebrum destroy the intellectual power of the man. Narcotic drugs affect this vital part and men using alcoholic drinks and other narcotic drugs lose their intelligence and sometimes the addicts turn insane.

Those children whose cerebrum is comparatively smaller in size are mentally weak. Intelligent children have larger cerebrums.

A small nerve centre in the rear and lower part of cerebrum is called cerebellum. It is like a flat ball in shape and is about four to five ounces in weight. The cerebellum is divided into two parts. Like the cerebrum, this too, is grey in the upper part and white in the lower part, and has convolutions and fissures. The fissures in cerebellum are less wider but deeper in comparison to cerebmm. Brain's piamatter goes to a large extent in the cerebellum.

If the cerebellum is cut into two parts, the parts would look like a tree. There are cells in large numbers in the grey matter. The white matter is made up of wries that come out from the cells of grey matter. Nerve fibres go from cerebellum to cerebmm and medulla oblongata. Similarly, the nerve fibres also come from these parts to cerebellum.

Cerebellum controls the actions of muscles. Movements of limbs like, walking and running are controlled by it. Defects in cerebellum put an end to these activities of the human body. The man can neither run, nor walk, nor can perform such functions which need the combined efforts of many muscles.

Cerebellum orders some muscles to relax and others not to do so. When these two orders of the cerebellum are carried out properly by the muscles, the smooth movements of limbs take place. The movement of body limbs is the responsibility of cerebellum. The right part of cerebellum assists the left part of cerebrum while the left part of cerebellum in the same way assists the right part of cerebrum. Thus, the functions of cerebellum is to maintain uniform movement of the body parts.

It is a dam, like the nerves fibres bridge which originates from above the medulla oblongata and joins both the parts of cerebellum. It also joins the medulla oblongata with cerebrum. All the nerves' fibres originating from cerebrum pass through it. These nerve fibres pass over each other in such a way that those originating from right hemisphere of cerebrum pass through fibre bridge on the left side and reach the muscles in the left portion of the body. In the same way, those fibres originating from the left hemisphere go to the body. Because of this set up an injury caused to the cerebrum's right hemisphere stops the functioning of the left part of the body and injury to left hemisphere results in die stoppage of the functions of right body part. In front of the Pons Variole there is a disc-like gland which is called pituitary gland. It plays an important role in the mental and physical development.

Medulla oblongata is that part of the brain which is situated behind the pons variole and the lower part of cerebrum. It is a cylinder-like gland made up of marrow tissues and is connected in the upper part with cerebrum and through the lower part to cerebellum. Spinal cord starts from its lower part. Contrary to other brain parts, the white matters remain above the grey matter in the medulla oblongata. Medulla oblongata is very thick and broad near the pons variole but is narrow near the foramen magnum. It is about a quarter of an inch in length. All the tissues going from spinal cord to brain pass through it. In its middle are situated the blood circulatory, respiratory, digestive and other centres. The medulla oblongata is. therefore, an important part of the brain. The life depends on it. Injury to it causes instant death. Of the twelve pairs of tube originating from the brain six come out in front of the medulla oblongata and the rest come out from the rear.

Spinal cord is like a rope made of nervous tissues. It starts from the foramen magnum. It is about 18 inches long in males and about 17.5 inches in the females. It is also covered with a layer of three membranes. There is a crevice in the front portion and another in the rear portion. These crevices are so deep that they join each other. Between them is a very narrow passage through which passes the central canal. Like the brain it, too, is made up of grey one. There are cells in the grey matter and fibres in the white matter.

If the spinal cord is cut vertically and examined we will find the grey matter in the shape of the English letter 'H'. Its both arms are slightly curved. One arm is in the front and one in the rear of spinal cord. The front arm is called the anterior and the rear one the posterior nerve root.

The formation of spinal cord grey matter is like that of the brain. This is also made up of narrow cells and fibres coming out of them. Spinal cord white matter is made up of matter that is covered by fibres. These fibres come and go to each part of the brain. In this way, these carry instructions to ail the parts of the body. The fibres of the right part of the body reach the left part of the brain while those of the left part go to the right part of the brain. These control the movement of muscles. Therefore, if the root of any of these fibres get out, the movement of the muscles connected with that fibre, stops. These can experience feeling and touch. These conductor nerves start from the anterior nerve root and later are connected with the posterior nerve root. Their fibres bring sensations experienced by touch from the skin that covers the various parts of the body. That is why these are called feeling roots.

A person does not feel any sensation or pain or other things in the part where these fibres become defective but the connected muscle continue to operate and move. Thus, it is evident that each nerve of spinal cord is related to the feeling and speed.

The nerve fibres that constitute the white matter of spinal cord and the nerve centres situated in the grey matter has important functions to perform. The white matter has that transmission and receiving power that enables the brain to transmit and receive information from each part of the body. The actions and feeling of the right body part are communicated to the left portion of the brain and those of the left body part are received in the right portion of the brain. The same arrangement exists in the brain for giving instructions to the left and right part of the body. Illness or injury to the spinal cord puts a stop to the transmission and reception of instructions. We can neither move our body part nor feel the pleasure or sorrows, if the spinal cord is affected by illness or injury. If the spinal cord near the neck is affected by injury or disease paralysis will be caused, although the person may not die, but if the inner part of the spinal cord in the neck is affected, it will result in instantaneous death, because from this spot starts nerve fibre and go to the diaphragm muscle. These control and guide the movement of body parts. Since the diaphragm is related to the respiratory function of the body, it will not be possible to breathe in the case of the above described injury to the spinal cord resulting in the death of a person.

The grey matter of the spinal cord is also not less important. The neuron which makes the grey matter is related to the movement of those muscles in which reach the transmission fibres of the front roots of the spinal cord nerves. Voluntary movements are not caused in the grey matter of the spinal cord like the grey matter of brain. If the spinal cord is injured or diseased at a particular spot, the actions of the muscles of the body part below it which are controlled and directed by the front roots of the nerves will not be possible according to desire. The movement of these parts below the injured spot will not react to desires. And how can it be possible when their connection with the brain is cut off ? If these parts are goaded some movement will take place, but the brain will not play any role in it. In such conditions, the sensory wires get instructions from the spinal cord and then some movement is caused without the help of the brain. These movements are called reflex actions. These take place due to external factors without our knowing them. The brain plays no part in these movements. Such movements are conducted by the small centres situated in the grey matter. The contraction of the retina when we enter into light from darkness or its expansion when we go from light into darkness is an important example of reflex action. These take place automatically. One does not .feel them. During this relfex action the spinal cord acts like a subordinate officer who issues order in the absence of the higher officer and communicates it to him. This order remains in force if the higher officer approves of it, but if he disapproves of it, he cancells it and issues a fresh order in its place. The main aim of the reflex actions is to protect the body.

Peripheral System

A periphery is made up of very thin nerve fibres coming out of neuron. Nerve fibres are attached and properly tied up with each other by the ligaments. According to functions, these are divided into two categories :

(1) Afferent, (2) Efferent.

The afferent nerve fibres carry information to the brain or spinal cord and the efferent nerve fibres bring instructions from the brain and give them to muscles, glands or blood vessels. We experience through afferent nerve fibres the feelings and impulses generated by the touch, smell or other actions. It is because of this nature of their function that these are also called sensory nerves. The efferent nerve fibres inspire movements of the muscles. These are, therefore, called motor nerves. If due to the inspiration of certain motor nerve, a gland secretes, that particular type of nerve is then named secretory nerve. The serve which broadens or narrows a blood vessel is known as vaso motor.

Twelve pairs of peripheries originate from the lower part of the brain. These are called skull peripheries. These are articularly related to sense organs such as, olfactory nerve, auditory nerve, lasting nerve, optic nerve and neck etc. Some of these peripheries are sensory and. some are motor.

Olfactory nerve—This nerve is related to smell. The olfactory nerve starts from the mucous membrane of the nose and it enters the brain and joins the olfactory centre.

Optic nerve—this nerve is spread over the opitc lobes. These are attached with each other near the pituitary gland in the lower part of the brain.

Oculomotor nerve—It is purely a motor nerve. It is related to the muscles which turns the optic lobes in various directions.

Oculomotor—This is also an optic motor nerve but this is related with the movement of the eye.

There is one more nerve related to the movement of the eyes.

Trigerminal nerve—Trigerminal nerve is the biggest nerve of the brain. This is divided in three branches and is, therefore, called trigeminal nerve. One of its branches which spreads over optic lobe, nostrils, mouth, teeth, cheek and tongue is called sensory nerve. All actions and messages reach the brain through it. Out of the remaining two branches, one goes to the upper jaw muscle while the other to the lower jaw muscle as the result of which the jaws move while we take food.

Facial nerve—This nerve controls the movements of facial muscles.

Auditory nerve—It is related to hearing. It goes to the ear drum.

Glosso pharyngeal nerve— This nerve is divided into two parts, one of which spreads in the hind part of the tongue. We feel the taste of the food through it. The other branch goes upto throat and helps in swallowing the food. This is also called the tongue and throat nerve.

Vagus of pnemo-gas nerve—This nerve is related to lungs, liver and stomach. Its area of action is widespread. It is, therefore, called distributory nerve as well.

Spinal nerve—This is a motor nerve going to particular muscles of chin.

Lower tongue nerve—It is called the lower tongue nerve because it lies in the lower part of the tongue. It controls the actions of the tongue muscles.

Role of Spinal Cord

Thirty-one pairs of nerves start from the spinal cord with spacing. Eight in the neck, twelve in the sternum, five in waist, five in liver and the rest in other regions. Each nerve is joined with the spinal cord by two parts. The front part is called ventral root and the back part the dorsal root. Both die roots join each other near the spinal cord. These joined roots make the nerve.

All the spinal cord nerves are mixed nerves. Each nerve has two fibres out of which one is sensory fibre and the other one is motor. The sensory fibres come from the different parts of the body, join the spinal cord and convey messages. Through them the spinal cord feels the impulses and senses of the different parts of the body. These fibres are. therefore, called sensory fibres. The other fibres come from the inner part of the spinal cord, go to different body parts and create movement in them. These are, therefore, called motors.

Sympathetic Setup

Every nerve of the spinal cord is related to sympathetic nervous system. On both the sides of dorsal are two strings. There are projection like ganglias on both of these strings at some interval. These ganglias are yellow in colour. This is why this nervous system is also called yellow nervous system. The nerves coming out of this system are called yellow nerves. A number of branches come out of these ganglias. Some of these join the branches of the nerves coming out of the spinal cord and some join the blood vessels of the inner body part. The movement of inner parts are caused by this system. This system controls and directs the body actions during emotional activities like fear, grief, impulses, hate, love, comfort. For example, when the man is terrified, his face turns yellow. During the fear emotion the feeling of this nervous system are affected causing less flow of blood. Consequently, the face turns yellow in the absence of blood. Similarly, during joy, the face turns red, and one does not feel hunger during grief.

Nerve Centres

The centres relating to blood circulation and perspiration etc., are fully developed in the child at birth. These are independent centres. Brain has no control over them. Other centres develop gradually. They by and by gain strength and control. As the time passes, the external factors change and there come changes in reactions as well. The control centres develop first. Then develop the afferent centres which provide strength to see bright objects and listen to loud tones. Gradually, the child begins to recognise the difference between various lights and sounds. These centres do not develop separately. These are interrelated. With the development of each centre also develop the fibres which keep contact with other centres. In this way is established a relation between the sound-producing object and its sound and colour, shape and size. It is due to this that the child as soon as it hears a sound, the picture of the sound-producing object is drawn in his brain with the result that the child soon learns to establish relations of words with the objects and feelings.

This development takes place properly in a healthy child. The following factors which influence the blood circulation also affect the development of brain:

1. Weakness and indisposition.
2. Alcoholic drinks and other narcotic drugs.
3. Lack of fresh air, sufficient light, reasonably nourishing food, exercise, sleep etc.
4. Defective functioning of ductless glands. Besides the above, heredity also affects the mental development to a large extent.

The following special nerve centres are worth mentioning:

1. The auditory word centre. 2. The visual word centre. 3. The writing speech centre. 4. The writing centre.

The auditory word centre lies in the left part of the brain. The development of this centre takes place when the child starts to recognise and understand the words.

The visual word centre is a special part of optic centre and is related to the movement concerning the recognition by the child of the shadow of words. This centre develops when the child starts learning the letter.

The centre which controls the movement of lips and tongue is called the motor speech centre. It develops when the child starts speaking.

With the development of the visual word centre, the writing centre also develops. This centre is a special part of the centre that controls the muscles of the right hand. The last two centres' development takes place later as compared to the earlier ones. These centres are also interrelated like the other centres. Because of this interrelationship the man can write the heard or seen letters and can read them also. All the above four centres are realted to the brain.

Word Deafness—It is necessary for the teacher to have a proper knowledge regarding the development of the above centres. The auditory centres of some children are not fully developed. They, therefore, fail to distinguish between the sounds of some letters. This state of affairs called the word deafness. It is because of this factor that a child turns a mediocre.

Word Blindness—Word blindness is caused when the visual word centre does not develop properly. The child as the result of blindness fails to recognise the sound of the written letter.

The Mentally Retarded

The following are the categories of children having defects : (i) Backward child, (ii) Dull child, (iii) Feebleminded child, (iv) Imbecile child, (v) Idiot child, (vi) Morally defective child.

Caring for the Handicapped

Generally, people fail to distinguish between a backward and a dull child and think that there is no difference between the two kinds, but a difference does exist. Backward children are those who have a normal brain but for certain reasons do not progress like other children of the school and remain backward.

In a backward child, although the number of nerve cells and fibres remain normal, yet they do not develop to the extent they ought to. Lack of full development causes indisposition and educational backwardness. Sometimes, the child remains backward in the class due to defects in hearing and seeing. Dumbness is also the cause of this educational backwardness. Lack of nourishing and balanced diet also fells adversely on the full development of brain. Rickets and tonsils also give rise to mental defects. Adenoids cause deafness in a child. The respiration, too, becomes defective. As a result of these, the child becomes indisposed and backward. Lack of sound sleep is another factor contributing to backwardness. Other reasons that create backwardness are continuously changing the institution, late admission in the school and absence for a considerable period from school either due to illness or other reasons.

The backwardness cuased by the above factors may be removed if the contributory factors are removed. The eyes. ears, nose and throat of the child should be got examined by doctors. Even slight defects should be carefully treated. Nourishing and balanced food should be given to the child. The children suffering from eye or ear defects should be sent to institutions of the blind, deaf and dumb.

Backward Children

The dull children are those who are inferior in intelligence to children with normal brain but are better than the feeblemined children.

The cause for dull intelligence is the shortage of nerve cells relating to higher intellectual activities in the body. As the result of this shortage, the mental development is slow and the child lacks in efficiency and chartacter. The child is not capable of learning any subject. Generally, this defect is born with the child and it is diffcult to get rid of it. The intelligence quotient of such children is between 70 and 85 as compared to a normal child, i.e., their I. Q. is 15 to 30 less than that of a normal child.

Such children start speaking and walking late. Their teeth also cut late. Their faces give a lethargic and dull expression. They walk lazily. They lack concentration and reasoning power. Their habits are dirty and every action is slow.

Particular attention should be paid towards the studies of such dull children. The moment suspicion arises about the dullness of a child, he should immediately be shown to a doctor. Children with extremely dull mind are not suitable for ordinary schools. Their education should be arranged separately. They should be imparted some practical, and vocational training with a definite purpose. Their education should be so patterned that more physical work is involved in it. For example, they should do gardening, carpentry, leather work, book-binding, tailoring, weaving of blankets and durries etc. For the girls of this category; arrangement should be made for learning tailoring, weaving, cooking, washing etc. They should be given more opportunity for physical exercises, sports and dance etc. Scouting and girl guide training is also useful. They should be asked to clean the house, wash clothes, polish shoes aad other household work in order to create in them the feeling of responsibility.

Special educational institutions should be opened for such students where fresh air and sunshine are in abundance. There should also be big fields where they may play freely. Classes should be small and there should not be more than 20 students in a class. Personal attention of the teacher is necessary in the case of children with dull mind. The lesser the number of children in a class the more attention the teacher will be able to pay. Arrangements for mid-day meals should also exist for such children.

8

Wealth of Sight

The eyes are the most important organ of the human body. It is through them that we see every object in the world. Information regarding the objects that we see immediately reaches the mind. Sometimes, we feel headache, fatigue, lack of interest, backwardness, disinclination and mental disturbances etc., when defects appear in our vision, this shows how vital eyes are for us and how important, it is to protect them against defects and diseases, it is necessary to have a knowledge about their functions and structure in order to save them from falling victims to defects and diseases.

Wealth of Eye

Eyes are made of optic lobes. These lobes are hollow from inside and are slightly flat. Their front part is a little projecting. The diameter of the optic lobes is approximately an inch. The optic lobes are situated in the middle of cheek bone's cavities. The outer part of these cavities is filled with fat that protects the optic lobes from injuries. It may thus be seen that eyes are safely placed in a string and well-guarded bone fort. The front of the eyes is protected by eyelids with eye-lashes on them. The eye-lashes protect the eyes while the eyelids remain open. The inner part of the eyelids that comes in contact with the eyes is covered with a smooth and soft membrane. This membrane is transparent and is called conjunctiva. This is also an eye's protector in as much as it guards the eyes against the attack of germs of various diseases. The membrane remains wet due to its own secretion as well as on account of tears coming out of lachrymal (tear) glands.

Lachrymal glands lie in the upper and outer corners of each eye cavity. Tears are produced by these glands. The function of tears is to protect eyes from dust, germs and other objects and remove them out of eyes. Another function of the tears is to keep the eye surface clean. The secretion from tears glands accumulates in the lower layer of conjunctiva. It then passes through a small duct in the bone to nose. When tears are produced in large quantity it flows direct from the eye over the cheeks. The nose, too, at this time becomes wet due to excessive secretion from lachrymal glands.

There are a number of sebaceous glands at the root of eye-brows. These glands are useful in two respects. Firstly, they keep the ends of the lashes wet and smooth as the result of which the upper and lower eyelids do not rub against each other to an irritating extent causing friction. It also helps eyelids to rise and fall effortlessly and smoothly. Secondly, these glands create a stricky border which allows only .the unwanted and excessive quantity of tears to fall down direct over the cheek. Sty (boils) appears on the eyelids when openings of any of these glands are blocked.

The eye wall consists of the following three layers. Each layer has two cells which are full of transparent matter:

(1) The outer wall which consists of sclerotic (white of the eye) and cornea.

(2) The middle layer which consists of choroid and iris.

(3) The inner layer which consists of retina.

The Formation

The sclerotic has a hard fibrous membrane and surrounds 5/6 part of the eyelid. It is transparent in the front so-'that light may enter through, it. This much portion is known as cornea. It covers the coloured pan of the eye. Light enters the eye through cornea.

The functions of the sclerotic are to protect the inner part of the eyes, to keep the eyes circular and to save them from deformit. The shape of the eyes turns ugly when sclerotic extends or gets' damaged. In the second part, it is attached with the thick cord-like optic nerve. There are a number of muscles attached with the outer part of the sclerotic. These muscles help the optic lobe to turn in different directions.

A blackish brown membrane inside the surface of sclerotic and attached to it is called choroid. The matter which darkens the inner part of optic lobes and protects it from dazzling lights remains in the cells of this surface. Those animals and birds which are deficient in that black matter cannot see clearly objects in the daylight. Those persons who are sunblind are also deficient in this black matter. Such persons turn blind during daylight. Like the sclerotic, choroid, too, is joined with the optic nerve from behind.

A disc-like black cover situated behind the comers at some distance is called iris. On the inner surface of choroid are visible a number of lurry spread, while on the outer surface is disc-like collection of a number of furry muscles. The iris visible in the cornea is made up of fibres of contracting muscles. The matter that gives different colours like blue, brown, black etc. remains deposited in the iris in different quantities. A small hole in the centre of iris is known as pupil. There are two kinds of disc-like and horizontal-involuntary muscle fibres in the iris. The main function of these fibres is to control the size of the pupil and also the light that enters the eyes. The disc-like muscular fibres contract in the light which narrows down the pupil's opening.

Just behind the iris is situated a pair of bi-convex lenses about half an inch in diameter. It is like a circular, flexible, crystalline and translucent. It divides the optical lobe in two parts. It is a solid gland made of soft, gelationus live tissues. It remains in contract with furry muscles. When the muscles contract the lens gets pressed and the hanging bonds relax. The lens as the result of the above action becomes more bi-convex. The lens power of contraction and expansion is called the accommodation power. Due to the accommodation power the eye fixes itself at particular position while reading or concentrating on minute details. The eyes are not tired much when seeing distant objects because the ciliary muscles do not contract and remain in natural position. The eyes should be rested and practised to see distant objects after concentrating on some object. The function of the eye lens is to throw the light rays on the screen like the camera lenses.

It has already been stated earlier that the lens divides the optic lobe into two parts. In the front part there is a colourless fluid which is called acqueous humour. In the rear portion, there is another liquid which is transparent like jelly. This liquid is called vitreous humour. These two fluids project the light rays entering the eyes so that these rays fall properly and at the right place on the retina and help the proper functioning of the eyes. The vitreous humour provides strength and size to the optic lobe.

After the choroid layer comes the retina. The retina is made up of optic nerves. The retina has a number of layers. The most important of them are called rods and cones. The functions and shape of rods and cones vary. The rods help us to see in dark while the cones help us seeing in day-light. The rods and cones transmit the effect of light on the brain for analysis through the help of optic nerves. The images seen in the retina are produced because of the above action of the rods and cones. The place at which the effect of light is analysed is known as yellow spot. The images become distinct, when the light rays are centred on this spot. This spot helps us in executing minute works. It is like the sensitive lens of the camera. This spot is the centre of clear vision. Only cones are firmly fixed here. Outside, both rods and cones are fixed together. The number of cones is less outside the retina.

The other important part of the retina is called the dark spot. The optic nerves enter the optic lobe at this spot. This part of the retina does not help in seeing because rods and cones do not exist there.

The Functioning

Four straight and two oblique muscles are attached to the optic lobe. The optic lobe turns in different directions with the help of these muscles. Four straight muscles coming from behind the optic lobe enter on both the sides in the upper part. The optic lobe moves upwards, downwards and sideways with the help of these muscles. The oblique muscles enter slantingly in the upper and lower part of the optic lobe. Their contraction makes the eye move on its axis.

With the help of the above two varieties of muscles, the optic lobe can move in different directions. Generally, both the eyes move in a direction simultaneously. This keeps the axis of optic lobes at equi-distance.

The Vision

The sight depends on the action of the light rays coming from an object and falling on the lens. It is necessary for clear vision that the light rays coming from an object should be centred on the retina. This creates an image of the object seen on the retina. The light rays coming from an object within a distance of 20 feet are generally widespread while those from a more distance object are parallel or equi-distant. The eyes see both the objects and have the power to deal with both kinds of light Rays. The widespread as well as the parallel light rays need bending before centring on the retina. It is possible only with the help of a double bi-convex lens. It has the power to bend and turn the rays oblique. With this action of this lens, images of objects coming from near as well as from distance are formed on the retina.

The accommodation power of the lens by increasing its curve and bend, focusses the light rays on the retina forming the images of the objects from which the light enters the eyes, whether these objects be at hand or at a distance. The parallel light rays coining from a distance object focus on the retina without its exerting any pressure, but the light rays coining from the nearer objects exert pressure on the retina, because they need curving and blending before focussing on the retina. Here the accommodation power is needed most. The nearer the object the greater pressure it exerts, because the light rays need curving and blending before focussing on the retina. In so doing when the ciliary muscles force the choroid and ciliary outwards their hold on the suspending bonds of the lens loosen and the lens projects outwards. The nearer the object the greater will be the contraction of muscles as the result of which the lens will project forward. The eye muscles are more strained when a man writes from a short distance. This makes the muscles weak as the result of which the sight becomes defective.

The Shortcomings

There may be many kinds of defects in the vision. We are mentioning some of these below :

The Diseases

The sclerotic expands in the direction of its weakest part behind when excessive strain is exerted on it and it finds itself unable to bear it. As a result, the optic lobe becomes larger than the normal size in the rear portion in comparison to the front portion. This creates greater distance between the lens and the yellow spot. Under such conditions, the parallel light rays coming from a distant object focus before reaching the retina. The result is that the image formed on the retina becomes blurred.

The use of a concave lens makes the light rays spread before these enter the eye with the result that the eyes focusses them on the retina. In this way, short-sightedness may be overcome.

The cause of short-sightedness may be classified into two categories :

(1) determining factors and (2) pre-disposing factors.

Factors at Work

Strain is not exerted on any muscle for seeing an object at a distance of about 20 feet or so, but strain has to be applied for seeing a nearer object. The position of the eye undergoes certain changes like bending or getting curved while viewing nearer objects, reading small letters or sewing or doing needle work. Both the eyes are drawn towards each other. This pulling work is done by the connected inner muscles. Ihe nearer the object the more the eyes are drawn towards each other. This naturally results in greater strain on the eye muscles. Due to bends and curves, images are formed on the yellow spot of the retina. This causes enlargement of the sclerotic which is the main reason responsible for short-sightedness.

These factors may be divided into the following categories:

Poor and Unbalanced diet—Lack of nourishing and balanced diet also causes mypoia. The sclerotic and other eye tissues of children who do not get nutritious and balanced diet get weak as a result of which they become incapable of bearing more strain.

Diseases—Body diseases also cause myopia. The sclerotic too becomes weak along with other body parts due to ailments. Consequently, its power for bearing strain diminishes along with other body limps and the eyesight becomes weak and defective.

Heredity—Heredity is also a factor that is responsible for this eye disorder. The child inherits a weak sclerotic from his parents which in course of time causes myopia.

(1) The child brings the book nearer to his eyes and bends over it while reading. He cannot read a book from a reasonable distance. He cannot also read what is written on the black-board and if he somehow reads, it is full of mistakes. (2) The child feels headache. (3) His eyelids and eyes get swollen. (4) Water trickles down from his eyes. (5) He feels itching in the eyes. (6) Stye appear on eyelids. (7) The eyes appear dull and sluggish.

The Cure

(1) If the above stated symptoms appear in a child the teacher should get him examined by the school physician and proper treatment be arranged.

(2) The children should be taught the right way of sitting while reading, writing or doing needle work.

(3) The habit of reading books in a correct manner should be developed in the child.

(4) Such children should sit in the front row in the class.

(5) They should be advised to use contact lenses.

(6) The children with these defects should be sent to such schools where their treatment may be possible and the advance of the disease may be checked.

Other Problems

This defect arises when the optic lobes becomes very small or flat. This defect comes by birth. With the appearance of mis defect, the light rays do not focus properly on the retina. The light rays coming from a distant object focus behind the retina. Consequently, a clear image is not formed on the retina. This defect may be removed to some extent through accommodation. This causes curves in the light rays and they concentrate on the retina.

The eyes of the children become small and go deeper in the socket when the defect of long-sight or hypermetropia occurs. The pupils contract. The children experience headache, blinking and redness appear in the eyes. Water also trickles down from their eyes. Children should be advised to use convex lenses for overcoming this defect.

This defect is caused when unequal curves of cornea are produced on retina. This causes obstruction in the proper focussing of the image as the result of which the image becomes indistinct. With the appearance of this defect, sometimes one part of an eye suffers from short-sight while another part of the same eye suffers from long-sight. In this state of the eye when a man sees across he can only see one line clearly. This condition arises because some part of the image is formed on the retina while some part is formed in the front of as well as behind the retina also.

The two eyes cannot see in the same direction at the same time when this disorder sets in. This disorder is of two kinds according to the position of the eyes. In one case, the eye sees in the direction of the other eye. The squint eye appears to be dropping in this kind of disorder. In the second category of the disorder, the eye sees in the opposite direction of the nose either upwards or downwards.

As soon as symptoms of this defect appear in an eye, a specialist should be,consulted. Use of correct glasses is beneficial in this disorder. The defective eye should be put to more use. This will give it more power and the defect will thus disappear gradually. Operation of the eye is also useful and the enlarged muscles or the contracted ones are set right.

Loss of Sight

Blindness is caused when swelling appears in the eyes of children. Gonorrhoeal contagion at the time of the birth causes this disease and as a result the power of transparency of the cornea is lost. Short-sigtendness may also cause blindness. Congenital syphlis or cataract may also causes blindness. Injury to the eye or some other contagions, too, produce blind-ness.

The school doctor should be informed about such children and proper treatment should be provided with the consultation of an eye specialist. Every child's eyes should be examined at least once a year. This will reveal to the doctor the presence of the disease or disorder, if any, and due treatment should be given in the early stages.

Children Care

Generally, eye defects are overcome by the use of proper glasses, but there are some defects that continue to develop. Children suffering with such defects should be given particular care and arrangements should be made for special type of education for them. The children with defective vision may be divided into the following categories :

(1) Short-sighted or myopic children. (2) Semi-blind children. (3) Blind Children.

Teching Myopic Children

Such boys should be admitted in special institutions and should be left in the care of teacher there. Personal alternations is needed for their education. Not more than sixteen or at the most 20 students should be kept in a class. These children cannot strain their eyes too much in reading or writing. They should therefore, be given more oral education. In educating them, books with bold prints and charts should be used more; The black-board should be used for writing. Such education should be imparted to them which does not overstrain their eyes and which may also help them in future in earning their livelihood. They should be encouraged and taught drill, dance and other sports. They should also be told to work in sufficient light. Their eyes should be examined at reasonable intervals in order to know the progress or deterioration of the sight and a chart should be maintained about this report for guidance.

Teaching Semi-blind Children

This category comes between the total blindness and short-sightedness. It, in the opinion of the eye specialist, the children's semi-blindness is ordinary, arrangements should be made for their education along with the myopic children but if semi-blindness of these children is in an advanced stage, special arrangements for their education should be made or they may be admitted in the institutions run for blind children.

Teaching the Blind

In this category, besides totally blind children, such other children are also included which are unable to read books due to defective vision. Such children should be admitted in a school meant for blind children with specially trained teachers. In these classes, the number of students should not exceed more than ten in a class.

They should be educated through Braille system. In this system, education is imparted through raised words, dots which stand for different letters.

Vocational training in weaving of cane chairs, baskets, mat and polishing and carpentary should be given to these children.

Other Diseases

The following are some important eye diseases worth mentioning :

(a) Stye, (b) Swelling of eyelids or Blepharitis, (c) Conjunctivitis, (d) Keratitis, (e) Cataract.

When the merbomian glands on the eyelids swell, small boils or stye appear on the eyelids. These are caused by over-straining the eyes, rubbing them with dirty hands or uncleaned towels and also due to the indisposition of the body.

These should be treated by mango leaves or plum leaves. They are cured easily by this treatment. Applying lead oxide mixed with oil, too, produces beneficial effect.

In this disease, the eyelids swell and become thick. They turn red. Sometimes, a thin coating is formed on their ends and eyelashes fall down.

Germs enter the eyes when these are rubbed by dirty hands or towels causing this disease. The disease is also caused in the absence of nourishing and balanced diet. Sight defects also appear due to swelling eyelids.

The eyes should be washed with a solution of soda bi-carbonate. After washing them, germicidal ointment should be applied on the eyelids. Fomentation of the eyes also proves useful.

This disease causes redness in the eyes and tears begin to trickle down. The dirty discharge from the eye dries up over the eyelashes in the night as the result of which the two eyelids stick to each other. It is a contagious disease. It causes pain in the eyes. During the day-light trouble increases, as eyes cannot bear the sun-light.

For curing this disease it is necessary that eyes should be washed with lukewarm water and germicidal ointment applied on them. It is not advisable to put any bandage over eyes during this period, because it will create dampness, darkness and heat which is an ideal condition for the multiplication of germs. The bandage will also not allow the dirty thick white discharge from the eye to come out. The child suffering from this eye trouble should not be allowed to attend the class so that other children may not catch the infection. The child should be sent to an eye specialist for treatment.

In this disease white blisters appear round the cornea which cause considerable pain to the eye. Sometimes, due to the growth of these blisters, the sight is completely lost. This disease generally appears when the child is five year old. Defects in the teeth, poor diet, adenoids and the habit of inhaling air through mouth are some of main causes of this disease. This disease should be treated by sun-rays or artificial light rays (ultra-violet rays or infra-red rays). Such children should go to special school.

The transparent power of the eye lens is lost in this disease. Consequently, the lenses become full of darkness. Injury to the eye or ordinary eye troubles lead to this disease. The eye suffering from cataract should be operated. Special type of glasses should be used during the disease so that light rays may focus correctly on the retina. Cataract generally appears in old age.

The main parts of the eyes are—sclerotic cornea, choroid, iris and retina.

The sclerotic protects the inner parts of the eye and saves them from deformity. In it there lies a number of muscles that help the eye to move in various directions.

Choroid has an element in it that protects the eye against the dazzle of light.

This is a disc-like black screen. The pupil lies in it and behind it, there is the eye lens. Eyes are capable of seeing minute objects because of the accommodation power of the lens.

The important layers in the retina are called rods and cones. Rods help the eye to see in darkness while cones helps to see in light.

The movement of optic lobes depends on the six connected muscles.

Vision defects are of the following kinds :

Short-sightedness or myopia, long-sightedness or hypermetropia, astigmatism, squint and blindness etc.

The common eye disease are stye, blepharitis, conjunctivitis, keratitis, cataract, etc.

QUESTIONS

1. Describe in detail the structure of the human eyes and explain it with the help of illustrations.
2. What do you understand by defective vision ? What are its symptoms and how can these defects be removed.
3. Give an account of the common eye diseases.

9

Wealth of Ear

Ears have a very important place in the education of children, because they hear and grasp through ears whatever the teacher teaches in the school. The sound waves reach the brain through the ears. The ear can be divided into the following parts:

(1) External ear, (2) Middle ear, (3) Internal ear.

The Structure

The external ear is made up of catilages. It has two main parts. The first part is known as pinnae (or shell-like structure) which has a number of projections. These are known by different names. The other main part is made up of fibrous tissues.

In the middle of pinnae is a pit wherein sound waves concentrate. The auditory canal lies in the surface of this pit. The auditory canal is a cave-like zigzag one inch long canal that enters the skull. The entire canal is covered with a thin flesh lining with tiny hairs. There are a number of small glands in it which secretes a poisonous, sticky and bitter kind of wax. This secretion is commonly known as ear wax. Foreign matter does not find its way in the ear because of the zigzag constructing of the auditory canal and the presence of hairs and ear wax. The presence of these objects creates obstruction in the easy passage of foreign matter into the ear. Small insects which somehow enter the ear stick to the wax and get destroyed.

The inner mouth of the auditory canal is covered with a disc-like thin membrane. This is known as eardrum or tympanum. The eardrum separates the external ear from the middle ear. When excessive wax is produced in the ear, it is deposited in the auditory canal causing obstruction to the passage of sound waves to the eardrum. At this time, the man slightly becomes hard of hearing. When such a state of affairs is reached it is advisable to get the wax removed and ear cleaned. Sometimes, people use wooden pricks or pins to remove this wax. This is not desirable because there is every likelihood of the eardrum being injured. Holes in the eardrum cause deafness.

The middle ear is the inner cavity which is quarter of an inch thick. This lies between the eardrum and the internal ear. The middle ear is full of air. The eardrum separates it from the external ear. Inside there is a narrow duct called throat-ear duct. This duct goes up to the throat. Equal pressure of air is maintained on both the sides of the eardrum on account of this duct. This duct saves the eardrums from bursting during violent explosion or loud noise which all of a sudden puts pressure on the eardrum. At such times, the air inside passes over to the throat and the eardrum is saved from bursting. Throat swelling can inflict the middle ear by travelling through this duct. Children commonly suffer from this trouble. Severe cold, catarrah and adenoids create obstruction in this passage causing tension in the eardrum. The result is that hearing becomes hard because there is less vibration in the eardrums.

There are three bones which are bound with each other through ligaments. We hear clearly because of the free movement of these bones. These bones carry the vibrations caused by sound waves to the inner ear. The hearing power is affected when ligaments of these get defective.

These bones are named after their shape and size and are called hammer, anvil and stirrup.

Hammer Bone—The hammer bone lies near the eardrum. It is hammer-like in shape. The upper thick and broad pan is called its head while the lower narrow part is called neck. When we hear attentively, this muscle contracts and stretches the eardrum. This makes the man hear every word clearly. It is joined with the anvil behind the eardrum.

Anvil Bone—The shape of this bone is like the anvil of a goldsmith. It is joined in the front with the hammer bone and in the rear with the stirrup bone. Both these joints are movable.

Stirrup Bone—Its shape is like an iron stirrup. It is because of this shape that this bone is called stirrup bone.

The above three bones are joined with each other and it is because of this that whenever eardrum is shaken, the three bones are also shaken.

The internal ear is a complex mechanism which lies below the temple bone. Because if its peculiar and complicated shape it is also named snail ear. Inside it there is a close membrane sack which is filled with a clean fluid. This fluid is called endolymph. The membrane sack is called membranous labyrinth. It is a necessary pan of the hearing organ. The auditory canal ends here. Membranous labyrinth has three parts:

(a) Vestibule, (b) Cochlia, (c) Semi-circular canals.

Vestibule—This forms a central cavity in the internal ear. It is situated between the pouch-shaped cochlia and the semi-ciruclar-canals. It grasps the sound from the cochlia in the front and from the semi-circular canals in the rear. In its outer wall there is an egg-like hole which is called vestibule orifice. In this orifice there is situated the broader part of stirrup. A membrane covers this orifice.

Cochlia—It is snail-like in shape and lies in the lower part of the vestibule. It is attached with the middle ear through a circular hole. This hole remains covered by a membrane. There are a number of holes in the surface of cochlia through which nerves enter.

Semi-circular Canals—These canals spring from the rear and upper part of the vestibule. These canals are three in number. These canals are situated in different planes and after making right angles against each other they join the openings of vestibules. One end of each nerve is swollen. Inside, there spread the fibres of auditory nerve. These have no direct relation with hearing but they maintain the balance of the body.

There are two small membranous sacks in the vestibule. One of these sacks lies in the upper rear part, while the other one remains in the lower front part. The sack in the rear part of vestibule is larger compared to the front one. Three membranous canals join it. Another thin canal emanating from the front part is joined with the cochlia.

The Mechanism

The vibrations of every sound-producing object create vibrations in the, air as a result of which sound waves are produced. These sound waves travel .at a velocity of 1100 feet per second and collect in the external air from where they enter the auditory canal. The sound waves spread in all directions around the object in the manner of those water waves that are produced round the stone which is hurled in water. The water waves start in all directions from the place where stone falls and it appears that water reaches the shores along with the point where the stone falls and some movement is produced but this water does not go along with the waves to the shore. It moves only to a little distance from where the stone had fallen. A similar condition exists in the vibrations of air also. The vibration is most near the sound-producing object but the intensity of vibration decreases as the distance increases. It is on account of this reason that the sound is loud nearer the sound-producing object and gradually the sound becomes less audible as the distance increases.

This has already been stated earlier that sound waves enter the external ear with air. From there they enter the auditory canal and strike against the eardurms. The eardrums shake due to sound waves striking against them. With eardrum the three bones also get into motion. Being outside the eardrum the movement of these bones are in another direction. This movement in turn sets the fluid inside the vestibule and cochlia in motion. The information regarding the vibration in the fluid are carried to the auditory centre of the brain through auditory nerve and thus we sense sound.

There are different categories of deafness:

Deaf and Dumb—Persons being deaf by birth also turn dumb.

Semi-dumb—Some persons turn deaf during childhood. They having some experience of hearing and-being not totally deaf can be educated by speech method.

Deaf—Some persons turn deaf after learning speaking. They can be successfully taught through speech method.

Partially Deaf—This means hard of hearing.

The Deafness

Defects either in the external, middle or internal ear cause deafness. Deafness is either by birth or occurs at any time during life. The causes of deafness may be divided into the following categories:

(a) Obstruction caused in the auditory canal either by the accumulation of too much of wax or by enlarged tonsils or adenoids. The auditory canal's end gets blocked by the enlarged tonsils and adenoids with the result that air does not reach the middle ear. Consequently, the child turns deaf.

(b) Injury caused to the eardrum by some external object turns the child deaf.

(c) The child begins to hear hard if the middle or the external ear is diseased. Whooping cough, pneumonia, influenza, scarlet fever, measles and enlargement of tonsils create throat trouble and the germs of the disease reach the middle ear through eustachian tube. This causes swelling of the middle ear and pus is also formed. This pus falls on the hole of eardrum and the infection reaches the sound carrier bones. This causes defects in the mechanism of hearing.

(d) Defective auditory nerve or faulty development of hearing centre turns the child semi-deaf and dumb. Injury is another contributory factor.

(e) Meningitis is also responsible for turning a child deaf.

The Symptoms

(1) Continous strickling of pus from the ear, (2) Child appearing tired and lethargic, (3) Buzzing sound in the ear, (4) Pain in a ear, (5) Headache, (6) Inhailing air through mouth, (7) Lack in concentration, (8) Bending of head in a direction while reading, and (9) Unable to hear everything that the teacher tells, because of not seeing the face of the teacher.

Ear Care

It is necessary to pay attention to the following for the safety and health of the ears:

(1) Teeth, nose and throat should be kept clean. The infection of throat reaches the middle ear through eustachian tube and adversely affects the hearing.

(2) Ears should not be cleaned through hard things like wooden picks or pins, because thereby eardrums are likely to be damaged.

(3) Ears should be got cleaned at regular intervals so that dust may not stick in the auditory canal.

Test for Hearing

Audiometer is the best medium of testing a man's hearing. A number of head phones are attached with the gramophone of audiometer which are used for examining specially made gramophone records. Sound that gradually become weaker are produced by these records. The child hears and notes down on a notebook. In this way, his hearing is tested. This test, although satisfactory is costly.

For testing the hearing power whispering test is also applied. Generally, this method is used in schools. In this test sound is gradually weakened from a distance of 20 feet to the extent when it is no audible. Sometimes, it becomes difficult to perform this test in the noisy atmosphere of the school.

Hearing power is also tested through watch sound. In this method the hearing power of the student is compared with that of the normal hearing power of the examiner. The result of this test is expressed as a fraction for each ear. The result of this test is expressed as a fraction for each ear. The result of this test may be affected by the noise of the room. Difference in the sound of watch, too, may affect the result. This test is, therefore, not very reliable.

Role of Education

Many things told and explained in the class-room prove futile for the children with defective hearing, because they do not hear all of it. So special arrangements should be made for the education of such children. Children hard of hearing should be sent to special schools. They may also be sent in ordinary schools but they need the care of an expert teacher. Their classes should not contain more than ten students because it is only then that the teacher will be able to give his personal attention to each student. In such cases such children are influenced by others also and in this way they are not at any disadvantage.

Separate arrangements should be made for semi-deaf children and they should particularly be given vocational education. Vocational education is absolutely necessary for children who are totally deaf. Such children may be educated in tailoring and embroidery, weaving, dyeing, cooking, carpentry, leather work, book-binding etc. Particular attention should be paid towards their physical development because deaf and dumb children are generally found to be indifferent towards their health. They should he encouraged for taking regular physical exercises. Arrangements should also be made for games and sports so that their proper physical development may take place.

Some Diseases

A slight pain in the ear should he taken as an indication of some disorder in the ear and immediate attention should be paid to it. Swelling in the middle ear generally causes pain. Sometimes, ear discharge begins to flow out. Scralet fever, measles, cough and adenoids, too, cause mistrouble.

Early treatment should be started in such condition because not only it affects the middle ear causing deafness but the infection may also reach the temple bone and in that case, the consequences may be very serious. It may also affect the brain or its membrane. Fatal diseases may appear. It is because of these that the ear discharge or ottorrhoea should not be neglected.

The ear is divided into three parts: (1) External ear, (2) Middle ear and (3) Internal ear. There is an inch long cave like-canal in the pinnae called auditory canal. The inner orifice of the auditory canal is covered by eardrum. Foreign matter cannot enter in the ear because of the zigzag formation and the presence of hair and wax inside it.

The middle ear lies between the eardrum and internal ear. Eustachian tube lies in the middle ear. It balances the pressure in the air. There are three bones in the middle ear called hammer, anvil and stirrup.

Internal ear situated in the temple is a very complex mechanism. Inside it there is the membranous labyrinth which has three canals called vestibule, cochlia and semi-circular canals. Semi-circular canals are three in number.

Hearing Mechanism—The vibrations of the sound-making object produce vibrations in the external ear, auditory canal, eardrum, three bones, setting in motion of the fluids in vestibule and cochlia-hearing centre in the brain affected through auditory nerve and thus man hears and understands the sound.

Deafness is of four categories : (1) Deaf and dumb, (2) Semi-dumb, (3) Deaf, (4) Hard of hearing. They should be given vocational and practical education. Hearing testing : (a) Audiometer, (b) Whisper test and (c) Watch test.

QUESTIONS

1. Describe briefly the various parts of the ear.
2. Explain through an illustration how the brain grasps the sound waves and understands them.

10

Wealth in Mouth

The food is chewed with teeth. Hence the teeths are important part of our digestive system. The fact is that the teeth play a very important role in keeping the body healthy. Their main function is to chew the food. They make the food easily digestible. The incisor teeth cut the food in small pieces and the grinding teeth chew and turn the food in pulp. Teeth also help in sounds. Our pronunciation becomes faulty in their absence.

Wealth of Teeth

According to kind and shape teeth are of various kinds. They may be divided into four categories:

Incisor teeth—These teeth cut the food into small parts. They are flat and their edges are sharp. With the help of these sharp edges the food is cut into pieces.

Canine teeth—These are long and pointed as compared to incisor teeth. This variety of teeth make hole in the food and tear it asunder. They are, therefore, called canine teeth.

Premolars or Bicuspid teeth—These teeths chew or crush the food. They crush the food with their edges.

Molars or Grinding teeth—The rectangular edged teeth are called molars or grinding teeth. Their edges are sharp. Their function is to grind the food property. These are very strong. The third or the last tooth of this category is called the wisdom tooth.

The teeth may be divided into the following three parts in view of their structure:

(i) Fang or root, (ii) Neck, (iii) Crown.

Fang or root—The pan of the tooth in the cavity of jaw-bones is called the fang or the root of tooth. Incisor and canine teeth have one root, the crushers have two and the grinding teeth have three roots.

Neck—The neck is that part of the tooth which remains in gums.

Crown—The upper and the visible part of teeth is called the crown of the teeth. It is covered with a particular type of cover. This cover is known as tooth enamel. This enamel is the protector of teeth. It saves the teeth from injuries from hard objects. It differs in formation with the common bone. This particular element of the tooth named enamel protects the tooth from decaying. Sometimes, cavities appear in it which result in the loss of dentine.

Enamel is hidden on the neck. In the root a cement-like object takes its place. It is yellow in colour and properly fixes the roots of the teeth inside the gums. The inner part of the tooth is made up of a substance called dentine. There is a cavity in the middle of the tooth. This is known as the central cavity of the tooth. It has got a particular type of kernel called the tooth marrow. This is, in fact, the strongest part of the tooth. It possesses blood capillaries, fibrous tissues, cells and minute nerves. This is the live part of the teeth. In it there are nerves which make us feel the comforts and pains in the tooth. The blood capillaries that lie in it provide food to the tooth and carry out the harmful matter. There is pain in this part of the tooth when defects arise in it.

Gums—Gums are made up of thick fibrous tissues. On one side these are attached with the teeth neck and on the other with the aw-bone. Above the fibrous tissues is a lining of mucous membrane containing blood.

Structure of Teeth

The foundation of teeth is laid during the pre-natal period. When the body is six month old its first teeth begin to show. The process of teeth cutting goes on for a period of two years and twenty teeth come out during this time. The teeth of healthy children are out in this fashion. The cutting of teeth in the weak and unhealthy child is delayed. All the teeth appear in children by the time they attain the age of three years. The first teeth which cut the lower incisors, then the upper incisors, later on the front premolar is cut. Last to cut are the rear premolars. These teeths are known as the milk teeth and their number is 20 in all. These teeths start falling out from the age of six and in their place are cut the real and permanent teeth. When the permanent teeth are ready for cutting they push the milk teeth ar.d take their place. This process of cutting permanent teeth continues till the boy is of 12 years in age. These permanent teeth are cut early in the case of healthy children. The last four premolars make their appearance in the last. These are called the wisdom teeth. When the mouth is fully developed, the number of teeth too increases and they total in all 32.

The development of teeth thus may be divided into two parts:

(1) Temporary or Milk Teeth.

(2) Permanent or Food Teeth.

The number of temporary teeth in each jaw is as under :

(1) Incisor — 4
(2) Canine — 2
(3) Molars — 4
Total — 10 x 2 = 20 teeth.

The number of permanent teeth in each jaw is as follows:

(1) Incisors — 4

(2) Canine — 2

(3) Premolars — 4

(4) Molars — 4

Total — 16 x 2 = 32 teeth.

The Diseases

Two teeth diseases are outstanding and need mentioning : (1) Carries or worms in the teeth and (2) Pyorrhoea.

Like other diseases this, too, is caused by past and present circumstances. The following come under the former:

(1) Lack of good and nourishing food, (2) Heredity, (3) Lack of hard foods, and (4) General debility.

Diet Problem

Calcium, Vitamin 'A' and 'D' and phosphorous are necessary to keep the teeth healthy. Their absence affects the teeth. These are equally needed by children, old men and women, mothers and pregnant women. Everyone should get these nourishing things in sufficient quantity.

Teeth will remain in healthy condition if the enamel is healthy. Calcium is needed in an ample quantity in order to make teeth healthy and strong but to digest calcium, properly vitamin 'D' should be present in food in abundance. In its absence the teeth do not get calcium in sufficient quantity. So in order to keep the body supplied with calcium one should take milk, curd, butter, green vegetables, fish, eggs and salads.

The mother's health affects the baby's health too. During prenatal stage and infancy, the child gets this entire nourishment from the mother's body. The mother should, therefore, get adequate nourishing diet. Her diet should consist of enough milk, eggs, so that her body may get the needed amount of calcium, phosphorous, vitamins 'A' and 'D'. Cod liver and other fish oils remove the deficiency of vitamins 'A' and 'D' to a large extent. Oranges and dried grapes should be taken for procuring vitamin 'C'. These things are necessary to build strong teeth.

For the healthy growth of teeth, mother's milk is very beneficial. During infancy, the animal milk affects adversely the teeth of children. The teeth of those babies who are not fed by their mothers are generally unhealthy and ugly. The mother should at least feed her child with her own milk for a period of six months. It is during this period that teeth are cut and they require nourishing food. The child should, therefore, be given milk, cod liver oil, orange juice and the yolk of the egg. He should be given turnips, carrots, cabbage and cauliflowers when he grows. By taking these things he gets the needed substance for the proper growth of his teeth.

Generational Factor

Besides the nourishing diet, another factor that affects the teeth is heredity. As other characteristics of a child are affected by heredity, so are the teeth as well.

Lack of hard food also affects the strength and growth of teeth. Its lack does not give enough exercise to the gums and jaws, as the result of which the teeth do not get enough nourishing matter. Tiie proper circulation of blood, too, does not take place. For the proper development of teeth, the use of jaws and gums is necessary. Hard food should therefore, be given to children. They should be provided with carrots, turnips, beet-roots radishes, apples, guavas, papayas, melons and mangoes. Their use not only will give exercise to gums and jaws but clean the teeth as well. The children should develop a taste for these things since the very beginning.

Other Reasons

General debility has also its ill effect on the children's teeth. During the pre-natal period, mother's bad health affects the milk teeth of the baby.

Their teeth become weak. Every kind of indisposition affects the child's teeth. Sound sleep, exercise, fresh air inhaled through nostrils also prove beneficial in respect of teeth as well.

Besides the above factors there are some other causes for poor teeth. Not cleaning well the mouth after meals, leaves behind starchy matter. Starchy food or sweet if accumulated in the teeth gaps prove very harmful. Bacteria thrive on it. The reminants of these edibles in the mouth produce lactic acid due to the action of bacterias which dissolve the teeth enamel and so the entire enamel is lost. After the destruction of enamel, the germs attack the dentine. Being soft it is easily destroyed. If no care is taken of the teeth the central cavity gets affected and pain is felt in the teeth. The teeth roots become hollow and rotten. Blood capillaries and nerves are then affected and get destroyed. At this time pain is caused in the teeth. The pain automatically disappears when blood capillaries are totally destroyed. The teeth begin to shake in the absence of life in it, because with the loss of blood capillaries necessary nourishment stops. Nerves of the teeth, too, are destroyed. One diseased tooth affects the others and in this way the entire teeth-set is affected. Pus is formed and there is every likelihood of wounds and boils appearing on the gums.

The Outcome

A man whose teeth are diseased cannot properly chew the food. The stomach, therefore, has to do extra labour in digesting the food. It becomes impossible for the stomach to discharge its function properly and timely. Consequently the food remains in the stomach for a longer period. Under these circumstances, the food begins to rot in the stomach causing the formation of harmful and disease-producing gases. Sometimes there is an attack of colic pain in the stomach. The pus of the teeth mixes in the food and enters the stomach. It gets mixed in the blood and causes many kinds of impurities there. This results into headache and skin diseases. The lymphatic glands in the neck, too, are affected and sometimes these are inflammated. Bad teeth adversely affect the tonsils and the throat also becomes bad. Foul smell comes out of the mouth. People do not like to stand near such persons and maintain distance while talking with them.

The Precautions

The teeth should be thoroughly cleaned before and after taking meals as a safeguard against teeth worms. Sticky food with generous proportion of carbohydrate and soft food due to remaining in contact with teeth for a long time becomes yeast-like. Pieces of bread, biscuits, potatoes, pastries etc., are food of this type. Their particles enter the teeth gaps and decompose there. Sticky sweets should also be avoided being taken in the night because some of its portion sticks or fills in the gaps and serves as food for the bacterias for the rest of the night. It is very necessary to clean the mouth before going to sleep.

The use of fresh fruits and green vegetables thoroughly cleans the teeth. It also gives exercise to the gums and removes .the panicles lying in the teeth gaps. Besides, being useful for the body they also prove beneficial to the teeth. The children should, therefore, be made to develop the habit of eating green vegetables and fresh fruits. The children should be given well-cooked bread. This is also useful for the teeth.

For protecting-the teeth from germs, food should be properly chewed. This not only proves of help to the digestive function of the stomach but gives exercise to the gums and jaws and provides also enough nourishing matter.

Hard Neem and Babul 'Datuns' or hard brushes should not be used for cleaning the teeth. This causes scratches on the gums resulting into bleeding. They should, therefore, be avoided. Soft twigs of Neem, Babul or Maulsri may be used as 'Datuns'. These have germ-killing qualities. Before cleaning the teeth with 'Datuns' its one end should be crushed and formed into a soft brush. The use of soft brushes is also useful. Chewing of green guava leaves and cleaning the teeth with the finger and mustard oil is very useful for the teeth and gums.

While cleaning the teeth, the 'Datun' should be moved upwards and downwards (i.e, vertical) direction and not sideways or horizontally. In this manner, the particles lying in the gaps get removed. Moving the 'Datun' or brush sideways or horizontally causes sacratches on the gums. Occasionally, the brush should be cleaned in hot water in order to destroy the germs which might have crept into it. If the food panicles are not removed by brush, they should be removed by some harder thing like toothpick. If the food particles are not removed-from the gaps it would produce germ and the teeth would consequently get weak.

Some people are of the opinion that the use of tooth-paste or powder is useful as a dentifrice. The powder enters the teeth gaps and thoroughly cleans them. The foam produced by tooth-paste, too, has the same action but their effect is not lasting. The fact is that these things do not possess those qualities which are present in such things as 'Datuns' of Neem, Babul or Maulsri or in the green leaves of guava. These powders or pastes are costly. 'Datuns' and guava leaves have qualities bestowed by nature. Their use gives exercise to the gums and jaws, cleans them and kills the germs. It is, therefore, advisable especially in tropical countries to form the habit of using 'Datuns' and guava leaves for cleaning the teeth as far as possible.

Another thing which proves of use to teeth is the mixture of common salt and mustard oil applied to them. It should be applied like a dentifrice. It must be used at least once a week. The examination of children's teeth by a physician or dentist twice a year is necessary in as much as early detection of defects in the teeth would result in early and proper treatment. Cavity in teeth should immediately be filled.

Irregular and haphazard cutting of teeth needs proper and early treatment. If one tooth cuts on the other it should immediately be removed so that the rest may come up properly. Care of teeth should start from the time the milk or the temporary teeth cut. If neglected in the early stages, it is difficult to correct them later.

Breathing through mouth is harmful. This habit of children should be discouraged. Inhaling air through mouth makes the cold air enter and warm air exit through it. The cold and warm air contacting the teeth at a time fell adversely on the enamel. It develops cracks and the teeth are destroyed. It is also harmful to take cold water just after drinking hot tea. Sudden change in the temperature causes trouble in the teeth. Children should, therefore be discouraged from doing these harmful things.

The use of very hard thing like betel nut, too, adversely affects the teeth. Their chewing can cause injury to the teeth enamel and thus cause destruction of the teeth.

People are sometimes observed using pins or wooden picks in the teeth. This is a dangerous practice and causes gaps between the teeth. The food particles enter these gaps and decompose, causing defects in the teeth.

This is a teeth disease found more commonly in adults than in children. In this disease, bleeding takes place in the gums. Small capillaries are formed near the teeth which serve as living places for bacteria. Foul smell starts coming from the mouth and the teeth become loose.

Pyorrhoea is caused by the following reasons :

(1) Uncleanliness of teeth, and (2) unhealthy gums.

Uncleanliness of Teeth—In the absence of proper cleaning of the teeth, particles of food remain in the teeth gaps which when decomposed cause bacterias. These bacterias weaken the teeth roots. The roots become hollow and more tooth particles begin to accumulate and decompose there. The teeth become loose and the pus formed there becomes the root cause of any diseases.

Unhealthy Gums—Pyorrhoea is caused when gums become unhealthy and weak. Lack of vitamins 'A' and 'C' make the gums weak and unhealthy. In the absence of the vitamin 'A' their resistance power against diseases diminishes and the lack of vitamin 'C' turns them soft. In these conditions they are attacked by germs and are destroyed.

At the first symptom of this disease, a dentist should be consulted. Cavities should be got filled. Instead of protein dominated food preference should be given to vitamin 'C' dominated food. Gums should be properly massaged. The cleanliness of teeth can cure these diseases.

Kinds of Teeth

Teeth are of four kinds : (1) Incisors, (2) Canine, (3) Premolars or Bicuspids and (4) Molars or grinding teeth. According to structure, the teeth may be divided into three parts—Root or fang, neck and crown. Their development is divided into two parts. Milk teeth or temporary teeth and permanent teeth. Milk teeth are 20 and the permanent ones are 32 in number. Carries and Pyorrhoea. Cause : lack of nourishing food, heredity, lack of hard food and general indisposition.

Treatment—Regular cleaning is absolutely necessary.

QUESTIONS

1. "Health of a man depends on healthy teeth." Comment.
2. Write a short note on the construction of teeth.
3. What do you know about teeth diseases ? How will you prevent them?
4. How can you keep the teeth clean ?

11

Circulation Setup

Circulation System

Blood is a glossy liquid which carries nutrition and oxygen to every part of the body and expells the fould matter produced in them. Whenever any part of the body gets a cut, a bright deep-red coloured liquid starts flowing from the cut part of the body. This bright deep-red coloured object is called 'blood'. Our body thrives on blood. The total amount of blood found in a person is one-twentieth part of the body weight. The blood coagulates after flowing out of the body. It is not entirely solid. It has a yellow tinged liquid in it which is called blood. Besides, there is a solid part, too, which is made of minute fibres. It is a net-like object in which suspend disc-like small particles which are known as corpuscles. The fibres are made of a thing called fibrine. It is a kind of protein. The blood corpuscles coagulate because being suspended in this net.

The blood on being seen through a microscope reveals the presence of four different substances in it. These are as under :

(1) Red corpuscles or Erythrocytes.

(2) White corpuscles or Leucocytes.

(3) Platelets and

(4) Plasma.

Red Corpuscles—The red corpuscles are like small round tablets. These are hollow on both sides. They are so small that if they are put side by side they will total to 100 million in a square inch. When seen through a microscope, each single corpuscle appears yellow coloured but when put together they appear red. It is because of this that the blood, too, seems red.

The structure of red blood corpuscles is sponge-like. There is a flexible cover on them. They are filled with red colour which is called haemoglobin. Haemoglobin is a kind of protein in which oxygen, hydrogen, sulphur, nitrogen and iron are present. The unique feature of this object is that it mixes itself with the oxygen. In mixing with the oxygen its colour turns brighter. The blood during circulation reaches the lungs and there it comes in contact with the inhaled oxygen. The haemoglobin immediately takes the oxygen and the oxygen in turn dissolves it. When the blood reaches the various body parts the haemoglobin leaves the oxygen. This oxygen keeps the cells in a healthy condition and helps their proper functioning. Haemoglobin and oxygen combine to form oxyhaemoglobin. Taking oxygen from the lungs and carrying it to be the body cells is the function of haemoglobin. Then the cells take oxygen from oxyhaemoglobin only haemoglobin is left. With the going out of oxygen the colour of the haemoglobin turns dull and it goes back to lungs to get oxygen again. This is a continuing process and in this way the blood takes oxygen from inspiration and carries it to the bodily cells.

During the pre-natal period, the red corpuscles are formed in the liver and spleen of the child but after birth they are formed in flesh and bones.

White Corpuscles—In comparison, the number of white cells is lesser than red corpuscles. These are in proportion of 1 to 500, that is, after each white corpuscle there are 500 red corpuscles. Different kinds of cores are found in the white corpuscles. Their shape is amoeba-like and they differ with the red corpuscles in form. Their shape continuously changes. Sometimes they are disc-like, sometimes they are triangular and on some occasions, they appear projecting like fingers. They are extremely small and are equal to 1/2500 inch. It is because of their size that they pass through the walls of even small blood veins.

The white corpuscles are of various categories. When some foreign elements enter the body, a category of these cropuscles fights and tries to destroy them. In the case of their failure, the man falls ill. If they succeed, the man escapes the illness. The germs thus destroy by this category of white corpuscles are eaten up by another category known as phagocytes.

The main functions of white corpuscles in this way are:

1. To fight and destroy the germs of disease:,
2. To eat up the destroyed germs, and
3. To keep a safe zone for the protection of the body.

Platelets—Platelets are even smaller then blood corpuscles. They are formed as a result of fatty food and sunlight. They play a prominent part in protecting the body against various diseases. They develop a different kind of swelling when their number in body decreases and consequently the body becomes weak.

Plasma—Plasma is a red liquid with yellowish tinge in which float both red and white corpuscles. It is formed by 90 per cent of water and 10 per cent of solid substance. These substances are as under:

(1) There are three types of proteins in the body out of which fibrinogen is the most important.

(2) Oxygen, carbon di-oxide and nitrogen gases, too, are present in it.

(3) Urea and uric acid are continuously formed in body and come out of it in the shape of perspiration and urine.

(4) Fat or carbohyrate.

(5) Glucose.

(6) Common and other salts.

(7) Different kinds of antidotes of poison and other substances that fight the foreign elements and undesirable germs entering the body.

(8) Glycogen : Changes in glycogen form glucose.

Functions of Blood

(1) It carries the oxygen mixed with haemoglobin to the various parts of the body.

(2) It carries foul air and other harmful products formed in the body to lungs, kidneys and skin through which these undesirable products are thrown out of the body.

(3) It carries nuitrition to every part of the body which helps its growth, for example, protein helps the development of muscles, fat produces energy in the body, sugar makes the muscles active, minerals help the formation of body cells and vitamins protect them.

(4) The body temperature remains uniform through blood.

(5) The white corpuscles protect the body and fight against the invasion of harmful germs like soldiers.

(6) If a part of the body gets cut, the blood flowing out coagulates and covers that portion of the body and its outflow is automatically stopped.

As has been stated, the blood circulates throughout the body. This action of the blood is known as blood circulation The question arises naturally as to how this process of circulation takes place.

There are two main parts of the circulatory system : (1) the heart and (2) blood vessels. Blood vessels are of two kinds. The first category with thick walls are known as arteries and the second one with thin walls and carrying foul blood are known as veins.

Heart—The form of man's heart is like a mango or a clenched first. It is covered by a membrane. This cover is made of fibrous matter.

The cover is sack-like, the heart lies safe in this cover. This cover is called paricardium. The walls of this cover are thin but have two layers. A liquid continuous to come out of this cover and keeps the heart wet or rather lubricated. This helps the smooth functioning of the heart. When the heart is relaxed this liquid protects the cover-walls from striking as against each other.

The heart which is made up of muscles, lies in the left side of the chest and is placed in the middle. Its lower portion named ventricle projects on the left side. The lower part is conical, while the upper is broad. A young man's heart is 4.5 inches long and 3.5 inches broad. Its thickness is 2.5 inches and weights about ten ounces.

The heart is like hollow lumps of flesh which in the inner side is divided into two upright parts by a strong fibrous partition. These two parts are independent of each other. Each part is further divided into two parts horizontally. Thus, a heart is divided into four parts. The upper parts are known as auricles and the lower ones as ventricles. The auricles are smaller in size in comparison to ventricles. An artery, comes out from the right ventricle and goes to the lungs and another big artery coming out of left ventricles sends the blood to every part of the body.

Each auricle is joined to the ventricle on its side through an auricle-ventricle door. The two doors on both sides are protected by valves. These valves are so formed by fibrous matter that they only open downwards and never upwards. They only allow blood from auricles to ventricle but not vice versa. These valves may be compared with tube valves of a bicycle or a mouse-trap. The air can only pass into the bicycle tube, but cannot come out, as the mouse can only enter the mouse-trap but cannot come out, so is the function of these valves of the heart.

The right side valve is called tricuspid and left side one is known as bicuspid because they are made up of three and two flaps respectively. From valves to ventricles there are flesh bonds which holds the valves so tightly that'-they cannot open towards auricles. These valves separate when cells in auricles contract and allow the blood an easy passage to ventricles. These ends of the valves rise upwards and meet together again when the blood flows out of ventricles. As the results of this the blood cannot flow back from ventricle to the auricle. There could have been a possibility of flaps instead of meeting each other moving towards the auricles and remain open thus allowing the blood to travel back from ventricle to auricle but because of the above described arrangements the blood cannot move towards the auricle. The result is that the blood cannot travel from ventricle.

The Heart

The function of the auricles is to take in the blood and that of ventricles is to let out the blood. These are thus formed according to the need. The walls of ventricles are thicker than those of auricles so that more blood may come in. Each ventricles can accommodate about two to three ounces of blood. The auricles can take in lesser quantity of blood,

The entire impure blood of the human body enters the right auricle-through the superior and inferior veins. When the blood is accumulated in it, contraction takes place as the result of which blood goes to the right ventricle. The right ventricle, too, contracts on the arrival of blood and the blood thus reaches the lungs through lung's arteries. In the lungs the blood comes into contact with the oxygen and is purified. This purified blood goes to the left auricle. Four arteries carry this purified blood to the left auricle. These are known as pulmonary veins. When the blood flowing through these four pulmonary veins accumulates in the left auricle, the function of contraction starts and the blood then is allowed to go to the left ventricle.

From here the blood goes to every part of the body through small arteries. For the performance of this difficult function there is a big artery coming out from behind the left ventricle. This thick artery is called systemic aorta. At the root of systemic aorta are semicircular valves. The blood flows from systemic aorta on the opening of these valves. These valves are similar to cell valves in heart. They only allow the blood to flow out from the left ventricle in the systemic aorta, but the blood cannot flow back from the systemic aorta to the left ventricle. The blood then flows into many small arteries from the aorta part of the body carrying oxygen and nutrition to each. After performing this function, the blood becomes impure and reaches the veins through capillaries. It again enters the right auricle and this cycle goes on again and again.

The heart beats automatically. It is not motivated or put into action by any other power. The beats at times increase and decrease. The heart beats due to the following nerves : (1) Vagus and (2) Sympathetic. Vagus decrease the heart-beats while sympathetic increases it. The heart-beats produce a sound which is clearly audible. It sounds like 'Lav Dhab'. When the heart relaxed the sound is 'Lav' and when it expands the sound is 'Dhab'. The heart-beats of a child are 120 per minute. In the case of an adult, the heart-beats are 70 times a minute and 80 times in the case of old persons.

Artery—It has already been said earlier that arteries circulate the blood in the body. The tubes that carry blood from heart are called arteries and those which carry blood to heart are called viens. Arteries carry deep-red coloured purified blood from the heart. Only one artery does not carry purified blood. This artery is known as pulmonary artery. The only function of pulmonary artery is to carry impure blood from the right ventricle to the lungs. Arteries are the very important part of the human body. If somehow they are cut, the man will die Immediately. It is because of this that they are placed in safe positions. They lie between the thick flesh walls and bones.

Arteries rise and fall down continuously. With the relaxation of the left ventricle chamber the blood rushes into these arteries. With the rushing in of the blood the arteries expand and with its moving forward they relax and come to their original condition. The expansion and relaxation of the arteries is called the pulse. There is a sort of vibration in them which can be felt by the finger. These vibrations occur at 13 places in the body. These places are called pressure points. When an artery is cut, the blood spurts out. Under such conditions, torniquet should be used to stop bleeding. The knowledge of using torniquet is necessary for the teachers as well as the students.

There is an artery called aorta that carries pure blood from the right side of the heart. The artery gets divided into two parts after proceeding to same distance. The one part carries blood towards the neck and the head and the other part to the hands. The aorta turns downwards. It supplies blood to various parts and again gets subdivided into two parts. Each part goes down towards each leg and supplies pure blood. These parts are known as lower arteries. For providing blood to the muscles situated in the middle part of the body, stomach and other extremities, many branches shoot out from the main aorta. A smaller artery sub-dividing itself into three branches supplies blood to stomach, liver and spleen. Two other arteries provide blood to various parts of the thigh. Two arteries supply blood to both the kidneys. The main artery after going down the kidneys is further sub-divided into two branches. Its one branch supplies blood to the pelvic girdle and the other branch again dividing itself into two parts supplies blood to the thighs. Many of its branches supply blood to the various parts of the leg.

Capillaries—The above description of the aorta shows that dividing itself into many branches it supplies blood to the entire body. The blood during this process flows through very narrow and small arteries. These very small arteries are called capillaries. Through these capillaries the blood reaches and supplies oxygen and nutrition to the various parts of this body. During the process of supplying oxygen and nutrition, it collects and absorbs the foul matter.

Capillaries are made like cells. Some of them are so narrow that only one blood corpuscle can move in it. The network of capillaries is extended all over the body. The walls of these capillaries remain just near the cells. The result is that some portion of the blood flowing in the capillaries seeps down through the walls and reaches the cells and the cells in this way get nutrition. Besides, these cells take oxygen from it. During this process the foul air carbon di-oxide of the cells dissolves in this blood. The colour of the blood in the capillaries thus becomes dirty.

Veins—The impure and dirty blood of the capillaries returns to the heart through the veins. After giving oxygen and nutrition to the body-cells and absorbing the carbon di-oxide, the capillaries join each other. This joining process results into the creation of pipes or tubes which are called veins. This impure blood reaches the right auricle-chamber passing through smaller and bigger veins for purification. The purification process starts as soon as ttie blood reaches there.

Veins are of two different categories. The viens in the first category are known as inferior vena cava. The others are known as superior vena cava. The joining of the two viens of both the lower parts of the leg and of the veins of pelvic girdle form two major veins and when these two combine a big vein is formed below the meeting point. As this vein proceeds upwards it becomes thicker because the smaller veins of the stomach region, too. join it. It passes through a hole in the chest diaphragm and enters the lower part of the right auricle. In this way, this vein carries the impure blood of the lower part of the body for purification in the heart.

The upper major vein performs the function of bringing the impure blood of the head, neck, both the arms and the chest for purification into the heart. It enters the upper part of the right auricle-chamber. In this way. whatever quantity of the pure blood flows out of the left ventricle-chamber into the arteries for providing oxygen and nutrition to the various parts of the body returns impure through these big veins into the right auricle-chamber. From there passing through the right ventricle-chamber it reaches the lungs through pulmonary arteries for purification. After purification, the blood flowing through two pulmonary veins passes through the left auricle-chamber and reaches the left ventricle-chamber from where it goes to the aorta. In this way, this cycle of blood circulation continues day and night.

Expansion and Relaxation of Chamber—The important aspect of the blood circulation is that the relaxation of chambers move the blood forward. After forcing the blood to move forward through relaxation, the chamber starts expanding and again is filled with blood. To move the new accumulated blood the chamber .again relaxes. This process of expansion and relaxation of chamber continues non-stop throughout the life. Both the auricle-chambers are filled with blood at the same time and they, too, relax simultaneously allowing the blood to pass to the ventricles. In the same way, the ventricles, too, are filled with blood at the same time. They also relax and push the blood forward at the same time. The auricles relax first and the ventricles later. Afterwards all chambers of auricle and ventricle relax giving the heart time to relax. Then again all the four chambers expand and relax. The heart thus expands and relaxes 70 times during a minute.

Proofs of Blood Circulation—William Harvey, the first man proved during the seventeenth century the theory of circulation of blood. The following proofs are particularly important in this respect:

(1) The blood rushes out at a high speed when an artery is cut. The only reason for this high speed of the rushing out .blood is the beating of the heart.

(2) The valves are so made that they allow blood in one direction only.

(3) Poison in a blood vessel reaches the entire body.

(4) If the artery of a living man is tied up, it expands towards the heart and narrows in the other direction due to the stopped flow of blood.

(5) During the time of the artery-cut pressure applied towards the direction of the heart stops the flow of the blood.

Lymphatic System—It has been already stated earlier that at the time of blood flowing in the capillaries, a water-like liquid from the blood seeps down through their thin walls and reaches the cells. This liquid is known as plasma. This liquid is not a coloured one. In it are present nutritious substances for the cells, like water, protein, sugar, fat and mineral salts. There are also present in some white blood corpuscles which had come out of the walls of capillaries. The walls of capillaries between the blood and cells in this way supply nutrition to cells through plasma. The plasma absorbs the foul matter produced by the actions of tissues.

Besides the blood capillaries, there are other varieties of capillaries known as lymph capillaries. After giving the nutritious matter and taking the foul matter, some portion of plasma flows back in the capillaries. The remaining very small portion of the lymph flows at the place from where the lymph capillaries start. These tiny capillaries join to make bigger lymph carrying capillaries. There are two capillaries of this kind. The smaller and the bigger one. The bigger one is 15 to 18 inches long and starting in front of the second vertebra of the stomach and waist region it passes through the middle stomach muscle and reaches the chest. From the chest it proceeds above the left collar-bone and joins the branches of. the chin and upper veins. It is called thoracioduct lymph capillary. The blood flows in it from the major part of the chest, left arm, chin and the left part of the head. The upper tube joins the lymph capillary with the blood of the veins below the right collar-bone below the right part of the chin. In this way, the plasma or lymph comes out of the blood from the whole body, is collected and again is mixed in the blood, through these two capillaries.

Lymph capillaries are generally like veins in appearance. The walls of these capillaries are thinner than those of viens. It is because of this fact that they remain flat when empty and are difficult to trace. These capillaries generally pass through glands. One capillary is joined at one end of the gland, while the other at the other end. Lymphatic capillary enters the gland through the first end of the gland and goes out from the other end. These glands are found in arm-pits, neck, thigh-pits and other similar places. These glands are called lymphatic glands. These laymphatic glands are oval in shape like an egg and vary in size from a mustard seed to beans. In these lymphatic glands exists a fibrous network and those phagocytes or blood corpuscles that fight the germs of various diseases and protect the body from them remain suspended in this network. These glands serve the purpose of filter for the lymph. It separates the germs and other foul matter which are destroyed by phagocytes. When phagocytes turn weak and germs of the various diseases' prove stronger to them there appears pain in these lymphatic glands.

The Defects

(1) Inflammation in the neck glands due to measles.

(2) Inflammation in the lymphatic glands of the neck due to poison produced from bad teeth.

(3) Injury in the hand causes swelling in the arm-pit glands.

(4) Injury in the leg causes swelling in the thigh-pit glands.

(5) Tuberculosis also affects the glands.

Due to the above causes, defects arise in the glands and besides swelling pus is also formed and it opens causing pus to flow.

Inflamed glands should be fomented. Poultice also proves useful. Such children who have inflamed glands should be advised to go through medical examination.

Anaemia—Anaemia is caused by the change in the form, number and action of the red corpuscles. This falls into two categories, primary anaemia and secondary anaemia. In the primary stage of anaemia, the bone marrow stops its function of producing red corpuscles as the result of which body turns anaemic. Chlorosis and pernicious are the outstanding examples of this category of anaemia. The other category of anaemia is ordinary and is caused by defect in the blood.

Anaemia is caused by excessive bleed from any part of the body, lack of food, lack of iron, salt or vitamins in the diet, lack of sun-light and fresh air, germs in the stomach or intestines etc. Anaemia is also found in persons suffering from diptheria, rheumatism, inflammation of kidneys or defects in the diet, lack of sun-light and fresh air, germs in the stomach or intestines etc.

The lips of the children who suffer from anaemia are not reddish. Such children turn yellow and are lazy. They suffer from headache and get exhausted after a little labour. They do not feel hunger and food becomes tasteless for them. Such children should immediately be examined by some physician and rest should be provided to them. Efforts should be made to remove the deficiency of iron and salts in the haemoglobins. Open and fresh air is very beneficial to persons suffering from anaemia.

Heart Diseases—The diseases of heart may be divided into three categories—(1) Congenital, (2) Acquired and (3) Functional (creating disturbance in the functioning of the heart).

Congenital Diseases—Due to narrow passage of the pulmonary artery in the right ventricle or the defective division of the chambers of right or left ventricle less blood mixes and this causes anaemia. The mixing of blood depends on the small or large size of the fibrous division.

Acquired Diseases—This is caused due to the valves or the muscles being affected by rheumatism, diptheria, scarlet fever, measles. Some other diseases also give rise to this trouble. When the valves do not function properly, it results into additional pressure on the heart: Consequently, the heart becomes weak. Those children who are the victims of this trouble are soon exhausted and their respiration considerably increases. Swelling also develops in their feet.

Functional Diseases—This trouble appears when the functioning of the heart gets irregular. The heart-beats sometimes either increases or decrease considerably. "The digestive system, as a result, becomes irregular and the man becomes anaemic.

Children suffering from heart diseases should not be made to work hard. Provision should be made to give them as much rest as possible.

The blood is divided into four categories : red corpuscles, white corpuscles, platelets and plasma. The number of red corpuscles is considerably high as compared with that of the white corpuscles. White corpuscles are the protectors of body. Platelets, too, perform this function. It is produced by fatty food. In the plasma protein, carbon di-oxide and oxygen exist.

The main function of the blood is to carry oxyhaemoglobin from the lungs "every part of the body and also to carry foul air and other foreign and harmful products of kidneys and skin for being expelled out from the body.

The heart has four parts, the two chambers of the upper part are known as auricles and the lower ones as ventricles. The auricles take in the blood and let in go into the various parts of the body.

The impure blood travels from the right chamber'of the auricle to the right chamber of the ventricle and from there through two pulmonary veins to lungs where it comes in contact with oxygen and gets purified and travels back through two pulmonary arteries to the left chamber of the auricle, from there to the left chamber of the ventricle and then to the aorta. From aorta to smaller arteries then to capillaries. From capillaries to superior and inferior veins and then again to the right chamber of the auricle. This is the cycle of the circulatory system.

The tubes that carry blood from the heart to the various parts of the body are called arteries. From small and narrow arteries blood travels into still narrower and smaller ones called capillaries. The foul blood from capillaries is earned by tubes called veins. It is through veins that the blood returns to the right chamber of the auricle.

From this blood comes out a liquid through the capillary walls. This liquid is known as plasma. The tubes that carry plasma are called lymphatic capillaries.

Anaemia, and congenital, acquired and functional diseases of the heart come under the disease of the circulatory system.

QUESTIONS

1. Describe the blood circulation in the body with the help of a sketch.
2. Prove that the white blood corpuscles are the protectors of the body.
3. Discribe in short the human heart.
4. What do you know about artery, capillary and vein ? Explain in detail.

12

Respiratory Setup

Respiration, the chief work of the respiratory system, is that function of the body through which we inhale fresh air and exhale foul air. This process of breathing fresh air is known as inspiration and exhaling the foul air is called expiration.

Many gases are mixed up in the air and their proportion is as follows:

(a) Oxygen	approximately	24 per cent.
(b) Carbon di-oxide	approximately	04 per cent.
(c) Nitrogen	approximately	79 per cent.

Besides, dust particles and some other gases are also present. The air exhaled out through expiration has the following proportions of various gases:

(a) Oxygen	16.50 per cent.
(b) Carbon di-oxide	4.04 per cent.
(c) Nitrogen	79.00 per cent.

The above figures show that some part of oxygen is left in the body and in its place 4 per cent more carbon di-oxide comes out. This means that leaving of fresh air in the body and throwing out of foul air is necessary in the interest of human body. Blood absorbs oxygen and gets purified thereby. This process is very necessary in order to keep the body strong and active. The oxygen after entering the body bums the foul matter. It creates heat and energy in the body in combination with other substances. This indicates the importance of oxygen for us. If fresh air is not available, the blood will not be purified. Consequently, the body will fall victim to many diseases. We should, therefore, inhale as much fresh air as possible and try to live in places where fresh air is in abundance.

All the body functions result into the breaking up of many body cells and this produces carbon di-oxide. Through expiration carbon di-oxide is exhaled out from the body.

We inhale at a time about 30 cubic inches of fresh air into our lungs and during expiration the same quantity of air is thrown out. During long breathing as much as 130 cubic inches of air reaches the lung at a time and same amount of air is exhaled out also during expiration. In this condition 100 cubic inches of and unexpected injuries cause difficulty in inspiration, suffocation is felt and it becomes impossible to laugh heartily or weep loudly. This situation arises when the stock of reserve air in the lungs exhausts and until that loss is recouped, a hearty laughter or a loud weeping is not possible.

Main Organs

The passage through which the air enters the body is known as air-passage. This passage is divided into five parts:

(1) Nostrils, (2) Throat, (3) Larynx, (4) Trachea and (5) Lungs.

The air enters the body through nostrils. There are two holes in the nose which have hairs. The entry of dust particles and other small germs into the body is checked by these hairs. These holes are surrounded by cartilages which have a number of holes. They are covered by mucous membrane. A number of capillaries are spread over it. The contact of cold air with them turns it warm and we do not catch chill. Their contact makes the air moist and dust particles and other germs get separated here from the air. Whenever any germ or particle processes its way, these capillaries get irritated and cause sneezing. The unwanted particle or germ is thus thrown out forcibly.

Some people are used to breathing through mouth. This is wrong and harmful. Breathing through mouth does not allow the air to be subjected to the same check and safeguarding process which occurs during inspiration through the nose. This causes many ills. It is, therefore, advisable to breath through the nose only. Mouth is for eating purposes, it must not, therefore, be used for inspiration. There are two reasons why some people adopt this unnatural method. One is the habit formed during childhood. It is the sacred duty of the teacher and parents to make the child to give up this habit. The other reason is that sometimes some defects or diseases of the nose compel the child to breathe through the mouth. In such cases some physician should immediately be consulted for giving proper treatment to the child.

In the process of inspiration through nose, the air reaches the throat through nostrils and then enters the larynx and trachea. When inhaled through nose, the air passes through a valley-like place-Here is situated the larynx which is made up of cartilages. Its mouth is covered by two pairs of cartilages. There is a hole in its centre. When a man tries to speak loudly, the hole shortens and causes loud voice. But when we speak in a low tone the holes enlarge and low voice comes out. At the mouth of the air-passage above the larynx there is a cartilage cover. This is known as epiglottis. The epiglottis opens during inspiration but closes when a man drinks water or takes food, and as such, water of food does nto enter the windpipe. It stops water and food from entering the windpipe. It is never advisable to speak or laugh while eating, because during conversation or act of laughing the epiglottis remains open and there is always the risk of water or food entering the windpipe and causing a violent spasm of coughing. Often this may create serious consequences. One should, therefore, never speak or laugh while taking food. Larynx have vocal cords. Their friction causes sound. These are made up of cartilages.

The pipe below the larynx is called trachea. Its length is about five inches and diameter about an inch. It is not particularly very circular. Its front is no doubt circular but the lower part which is joined with the alimentary canal is plain. This pipe cannot be flattened because there are rings inside make up of cartilages. It is round for the free passage of air. The air reaches the trachea through larynx. There is a layer of mucous membrane in the tube. In the inner layer of this membrane there are very thin hair-like wires. These wires are known as cilia. These remain in action continuously. Their main function is to separate the dust particles from the inhaled air. The windpipe reaches the chest from the neck and is divided there into two parts. The right one goes to the right lung and the left one to left lung. These two parts are further sub-divided into a number of small pipes. This structure of the respiratory system resembles a tree which has two thick branches with a number of smaller ones shooting out from the main branches. The leaves on these small branches can be compared with air-cells. The air inhaled fills in these cells. The air here mixes with the blood and after absorbing the foul matter goes out.

The two lungs situated in the chest are the most important organs of the respiratory system. The lungs are protected in the front by the chest bones or sternum, on the back by the vertebral column and by the diaphragm from the below. The colour of the lungs is brown with a slight shade of blue colour. The colour of the lungs of a child before the birth is blood-red and rosy. The right lung is heavier and broader as compared to the left one. Both the lungs are smooth and bright and are like spunge. Each lung is covered with a membrane which keeps it safe. The membrane is two-fold. Its one layer sticks with the back of the lung and the other with the inner chest wall. This membrane is known as pleural and the space between the two pleurals is known as pleural cavity. Pleurisy is caused when water fills this pleural cavity.

The Setup

The process of inspiration and expirations is a continuing one. If the process stops, the oxygen in the lungs will exhaust and the lungs will be filled in by carbon di-oxide. This function of the lungs is divided into two categories : (1) inspiration and (2) expiration. During inspiration the chest expands. There are two reasons why the chest increases—the first being that the semi-circular diaphragm contracts and takes the shape of a straight line towards the stomach. In this way, some cavity is formed between the lungs and the diaphragm. In this cavity, the lungs expand and are filled in with air. The other reason is that when the muscles between the ribs contract, all the ribs rise upwards. This porcess creates enough space for the lungs to expand. This expansion of the chest is upwards and not forward or back-ward. In this way the air enters the lungs and they expand. At this place, the tiny blood vessels of the lungs take oxygen from the air and leave out carbon di-oxide.

After this process, the air is thrown out through nostrils. The reason is that the nerves between the diaphragm and the ribs expand. The space reduces and due to the pressure thus applied, the lungs contract As a result, the air goes out taking with it all the foul matter. This process of exhaling out of the air from the lungs is called expiration. It is worth remembering at this stage that enough air remains in the lungs even after expiration. Only a small portion of the air goes out.

One inspiration and expiration complete the process of respiration. A healthy person inhales and discharges air sixteen or seventeen times a minute.

There is a difference between deep and ordinary breathing. Through deep breathing the quantity of the oxygen that reaches the lungs is larger. How many cubic inches of air a normal man ordinarily inhales at a time and how much air remains in the lungs has already been stated earlier. But during deep breathing, a man inhales about 100 cubic inches of air and discharges the same quantity. Deep breathing is very useful because the blood is fully purified thereby. We should, therefore, develop the habit of deep breathing.

During hard labour or vigorous exercise, the respiration increases. On such occasions, the muscles absorb more oxygen, and carbon di-oxide, too, is produced in a larger quantity. This foul air need to be discharged. It is because of this that the mechanism of respiration works faster. Exercise of hard labour is beneficial in two respects. First, the larger amount of oxygen inhaled purifies more blood; secondly, the blood circulation, too, increases.

The mechanism of respiration is controlled by respiration centre in the medulla oblongata. The respiration increases when the quantity of oxygen diminishes in the blood and carbon di-oxide increases.

The Challenges

The following are the common diseases of the respiratory system:

(1) Bronchitis, (2) Inflammation of Tonsils, (3) Adenoids, (4) Cold and (5) Sore throat.

Bronchitis—The respiratory tubes get inflamed when germs enter the mucous membrane or during small-pox, influenza, whooping cough etc. Children suffering from rickets, tonsilitis, or adenoids get their mucous membrane inflamed. In tonsilitis, a gland-like abcess is formed behind the soft part of the throat. This compels the child to breathe through mouth. The air inhaled through mouth does not become warm like that inhaled through nose. The respiratory tubes, as a result, catch cold. During winter season, the trouble increases because during that part of the year the resistance power of the mucous membrane against the disease decreases.

Inflammation of the respiratory tubes should immediately be treated, as there is always the risk of getting branchopneumonia. The children suffering from it should be advised complete rest.

Inflammation of Tonsils or Tonsilitis—Inside the throat on its both sides are two lumps of flesh. In between them is suspended a very soft piece of flesh. This is known as uvula. Its inflammation can cause the following diseases : (1) bronchitis, (2) asthma, (3) dip-theria, (4) bad throat, (5) cough, (6) common cold, (7) headache and giddiness and (8) general debility. Unhealthy and irregular diet, unhygienic conditions of the house, breathing through mouth, defects in the mouth, teeth and nose are some of the factors that cause the inflammation of tonsils.

As a safeguard against these diseases, the inflamed part of the tonsil should be removed through operation. Children should be taught to breathe through nose. Children suffering from these diseases- should be sent to a physician for proper treatment.

Adenoids—The inflamed flesh joined by a membrane behind the nose cavity is called adenoid. The disease generally occurs during infancy. Chill, cold or measles cause the inflammation of the nasal mucous membrane, as the result of which children fall victim to adenoids. Unhealthy atmosphere, lack of fresh air and sunshine in the rooms or too hot rooms are some of the factors responsible for causing adenoids. Children who breathe through mouth also generally suffer from this.

Those children who suffer from this disease are always in a state of restlessness and worry. Their pronunciation is defective. They cannot pronounce properly those words which have nasal accents. In such cases, the nostrils contract The nose turns flat. The upper teeth bulge out a little. The mouth remains open. Their hearing becomes defective and pus is formed in the ears which flows outside. Eyes, too, become dull and eyelids expand unusually covering the pupils. Children suffering from these diseases give a lethargic and foolish look. Their mental development is retarded and they are weak in studies. They lack concentration power. Simple mental exercises tire them out and they generally complain of headache.

The parents of children suffering from adenoids should get them operated. It is the duty of the teacher to inform the parents and advise them about proper treatment of their children. They should encourage their children to develop the habit of breathing through the nose. The-nasal and the throat membrane remain in a healthy state in breathing through the nose.

Common Cold—Common cold is caused by the germs which live in the outer passage of the respiratory tract. The resistance to cold in the body decreases by the inspiration of foul air, by catching cold or by living in damp or dark places. In these circumstances there is the risk of falling prey to common cold.

The symptom of the disease appear after two days. Body shivers, mucous flows out through the nose, eyes get inflamed and turn red, head becomes heavy and every pan of the body experiences pain.

This is an infectious disease. The child suffering from it should be given leave and sent home. He should be encouraged to inhale fresh air through the nose. Such children should be advised to sleep in open and keep their feet warm. Massage of mustard oil in the feet proves of great help in this trouble.

Sore Throat—Inflammation in the throat causes this trouble. The throat also becomes sore before the attack of measles, scarlet fever and diptheria. The glands become harder and cause trouble in eating food. Even it is painful to let the saliva go down the throat.

This is also an infectious disease. The child suffering from it should be isolated. A physician should examine those boys whose glands have turned harder. Sputum should also be examined. Through this check-up, dangerous diseases like diptheria may be prevented well in advance.

Oxygen, carbon di-oxide, nitrogen, steam, dust particles and some other gases are present in the air. During expiration, the quantity of oxygen decreases and that of carbon di-oxide increases. Respiratory mechanism has various organs like nostrils, throat, larynx, tranca and lungs.

It is necessary to breathe through the nose only. It has two benefits :

(1) The air is warmed with the contact of nose-hairs, and

(2) Foul matter, if any, irritates the mucous membrane and it is thrown out through sneezing. These things do not happen when air is inhaled through die mouth.

The air after entering the nostrils, passes through the throat, larynx and teachea; and then reaches the lungs. There in the lungs it fills in the air-cells. Respiration includes both inspiration and expiration. A healthy person's inspiration is normally 16 or 17 times a minutes.

The following diseases are related to the mechanism of respiration:

(1) Bronchitis, (2) Tonsilitis, (3) Adenoids, (4) Common cold, (5) Sore throat.

It is necessary to breathe through the nostrils as the preventive measure against the above diseases.

QUESTIONS

1. What do you mean by mechanism of respiration ? Describe some diseases of the respiratory system.
2. What do you understand by fresh air ? How does it affect the health ?
3. Describe briefly the various organs of the respiratory system.

13

Secretionary Setup

There are some glands in our body that secrete juices which are of use to the entire body. This means that secretion from these glands is not of local importance but important for the whole body. There are no ducts in these glands to carry the secretion to a particular spot in the body. 'It is because of this characteristic that these glands are named ductless glands. The secretion produced by these glands mixes in the blood of lymph and reaches every corner of the body. This secretion is called hormone. Their proper functioning keeps the body in a healthy state. These are, therefore, very important for the body. The following glands are particularly worth mentioning:

(1) Pituitary gland, (2) Thyroid gland, (3) Parathyroid gland, (4) Thymus gland, (5) Adrenal gland, (6) Islets of langerhans, and (7) Gonads.

The Organs

The gland that suspends by the lower duct of the brain is called pituitary gland. It is a small reddish brown gland. It has two lumps that secrete juice that helps the development of bones and keeps the body in good health. This secretion controls the large limbs. The height of man increases due to excess of this juice. The head and hands of such men become larger. Lack of secretion from this bone checks the development of bones. Consequently, the individual becomes dwarf. Such children are also not fully mentally developed.

The secretion from the rear gland controls the movement of intestines, blood pressure and blood sugar. Lack of this juice results into inadequate heat and energy in the white element of edibles. These turn into fat as the result of which the child becomes fat and his appetite increases. He loves to eat sweet things and turn lazy. Besides, the secretion from this juice also affects other ductless glands like thyroid, adrenal and gonad gland. The secretion from this gland also helps in the proper functioning of other body organs.

This important ductless gland is brownish red. It is throat gland and is divided into two parts. One part lies on one side of the trache while the other in another side. The secretion from this gland affects the entire chemical reactions of the body which helps the full development of the body. It is nourishing. Lack of this juice turns the child weak, his intelligence, too, becomes feeble and the shape of his head and face are deformed. This secretion is iodine mixed. The production of this juice is less in men living in places that lack iodine. Consequently, persons residing in such places fall victim to goitre. To remove this iodine or 'extract from the hormones of sheep glands' should be used.

Excessive activity of thyroid gland results into a condition. This disease reduces the weight of the body and the person dies prematurely.

These pea-shaped glands are attached to the left and right of the back part of thyroid gland. Parathyroid glands control calcium and metabolism. If these are removed from the body, deficiency of calcium occurs, tetany appears in the neck and the muscles automatically contract. If these glands are more active, too, much calcium is produced in the body and the muscles turn weak.

This rosy grey coloured gland lies behind the chest bones below the neck. Its functions are yet to be determined. However, at present it is thought that it is related to sexual growth. Its functioning stops at the age of 14 or 15. Although after this age it is sometimes found in some persons but they are physically and mentally weak.

These two lumped glands like just above the kidneys. The secretion from these glands keeps the blood circulation in order and maintains the correct proportion of sugar in it. Besides, it also controls the blood pressure. It also removes fatigue and helps the sexual development.

The secretion created by adrenal glands, is called adrenalin. This secretion activates the limbs at the time of fear. A strange excitement is produced in the organs. The same action takes place at the time of sudden accidents or happenings. Consequently, with the secretion of juice the heart-beatings increase and muscles become strong and powerful. The man sweats and he is excited.'During this time, the man's face becomes fierce and looking at this face it appears that either he is determined to give a fight or preparing for a fight.

Small divided cells in the pancreas are called langerhans islet glands. These glands produce insulin which by burning the starch helps the tissues in making it useful for the body. In the absence of sufficient quantity of insulin in the blood, the quantity of sugar increases which causes diabetes. Injection of insulin cures this disease.

The System

There is a difference between the reproductive glands of male and female. The reproductive glands in man are known as sperm glands, while the glands of woman are called ovaries. Besides producing semen and ovum respectively, these glands also produce a special type of juice that creates the distinguishing feature in male and female. This secretion is responsible for the hoarse voice, beard and moustaches in man and development of breasts and sweet voice in women. These glands affect the personality of human beings, because they are connected with the mental and physical development. If these glands are not active in a balanced proportion disorders appear in he body and the consequences are very severe. Proper treatment should immediately be started as soon as symptoms of any disorder appear.

Those glands which have no canals emanating from them are called ductless glands. These are seven in number : (1) Pituitary glands, (2) Thyroid glands, (3) Parathyroid glands, (4) Thymus glands, (5) Adrenal, (6) Islets of langerhans, and (7) Gonads. The personality of a person depends on these glands. These glands are responsible for distinction between male and female.

The organs that produce a child are called reproductory oragns. The reproductory organs of male and female differ in shape and formation.

The Reproduction

The male reproductory or genital organ is divided into two parts. One is the external organ which comprises of penis and testicles and the other is internal organ which lies in the pelvic girdle. The second part is not visible from outside. This part comprises of spermary; vasa efferentia, penis root gland etc.

Penis—Penis is the main genital organ through which the male sperm reaches in the female vagina and the act of copulation is performed. Urine comes out of the body through this very organ. Ordinarily the penis is three to four inches long but becomes longer, thicker and stiffer when the desire for intercourse is excited. In this state it penetrates the vagina and measure four to six inches in length. This state of penis is called the erection state.

The front part of the penis is called glans penis. This part has a hole in it through which both semen and urine pass. this is called urinary passage. The penis has a skin cover over it. This foreskin may be stretched forward or backward whenever desired. This foreskin is called glans penis skin cover. The skin is hairless. When this skin is narrow and does not stretch upwards it produces pain during intercourse or during urination.

There is a cavity near the glans penis where a white smooth matter is accumulated. The matter is produced by certain glands of the glans penis. If this matter is produced in greater quantity and this part of the penis is not kept properly cleaned, small boil are likely to appear over it. It is, therefore, necessary that this part is kept well cleaned. The latter part of the penis is its root which is covered by testicles.'Penis has no hair on it.

Inner Structure of Penis—Penis is formed of fibrous tissues and involuntary muscles. It has three cylinder-like parts. Two out of these are on the upper part just near each other. These .are called penis columns. The third part is situated in between the two parts and is known as urinary column. The third part is hollow inside. The urinary passage tube lie in the lower portion of this hollow part.

As already stated, the penis columns are cylinder-like in shape and it is because of this that there is some gap in their upper, lower and middle parts. In the upper gap there are two arteries, two nerves and one vein. The lower gap is deep where lies the urinary tube. All the three columns are made of white and yellow fibrous tissues with the involuntary muscles. There are small cells which are filled with blood during erection of penis. This causes stiffening of the penis. As soon as after the intercourse these cells become empty, the penis becomes soft and inactive. The penis columns end before the glans penis. The glans penis is like a cover on their pointed end. The three column separate with each other after reaching the root.

In the rear portion of the urinary column there is a muscle attached to it. The urine flows out when it contracts. This muscle also contracts during the outflow of semen. Consequently, the penis becomes stiffer during semen discharge.

Testicles—The sack suspending below the penis is called scrotum. In the thin skin of scrotum there is a layer of involuntary flesh. This skin expands and contracts which causes the scrotum, too, the increase and decrease in size. Cold contracts the skin while heat or warmth expands it. The scortum is divided into two parts. Each part has a testicle in it. These testicles are known as right and left testicles. The testicles are like an egg in shape. They suspend a bit slantingly. The testicles in normal condition is 1.5" long, 1" wide and 1" thick.

Sperm Glands—The sperm gland contains two to three hundred cells which have eight to nine hundred tubes as thin as hair. These hairlike thin tubes are joined with each other by means of fibrous tissues. A big tube is thus formed by their joining together. This tube is called sperm duct. It goes upto the lower edge of the testicles. The tube is so zigzag that when straightened it measures 20 feet in length. Semen is produced in sperm glands and spermatozoon is its main constituent.

Spermary—Behind the ureter and in front of rectum in the pelvic girdle there are two bladders about two to three inches in length. The upper end of these bladders is wide while the lower end is narrow. The sperm duct is joined with these bladders. This junction is the starting point of vasa efferentia which joins the urinary passage after passing through the prostate glands.

The matter that is produced in sperm glands is known as semen. It accumulates in spermary through sperm duct and after some time goes from here to the urinary passage through vasa efferentia.

Semen is a thick, white and gelatinous fluid, it has got a peculiar smell. When examined through a microscope, countles of spermatozoa are seen swimming in it in all directions. The presence of spermatozoa in semen are essential for producing a child. The healthy spermatozoa are active and fast while the unhealthy ones are slow and less sctive. Those persons whose sperm glands do not produce semen with spermatozoa are incapable of procreation. The oval-shaped thick front of the spermatozoa is known as its head while the rear part is called the neck. After the neck there comes its body and tail. The production of spermatozoa in the human body begins as early as the age of fourteen or fifteen years, but at that age they are not capable of proceration. Healthy and capable of procreating spermatozoa are born in the human body between the age of twenty to twenty-five years. Spermatozoa are born in sperm glands only. The Semen which passes from sperm glands to sperm duct is so thick that sperma tozoa cannot move freely in the semen thinner. The secretion of sperm makes the semen still thinner. Secretion from prostate and penis rooting and also mix in it at the time of copulation. In this way, it will be seen that semen consists of many kinds of secretions.

Prostate—This lies in the pelvic girdle below the urinary bladder and parallel to rectum. The prostate glands are covered with a lining of fibrous cells. The secretion produced in the prostate glands mixes with the semen in the urinary passage through its thin veins. Enlargement of prostate glands in the old age block the urinary passage and cause the trouble during urination.

The female genital organs may be classified into two categories like the male genital organs.

(1) Those visible from outside—like vagina.

(2) Those in the pelvic region, not visible from outside, like ovaries, ovary ducts, uterus etc.

Vagina—Whereas a man has penis and testicles, the woman has vagina. In the middle of vagina there is a canal on both sides of which are labiums. There are two passages inside the vagina. The bigger passage is known as vaginal canal. The blood comes out of this passage during menses. The child is born through this passage. The male organ penetrates through this very passage during cohabition. Half inch deep inside the vagina is another passage with smaller mouth. This is the urinary passage. Urine comes out through this passage.

There is a thin membrane with a hole on it which covers the vaginal orifice of a maiden. This membrane is torn when for the first time the erected penis enters the vagina with force as the result of which a little blood also comes out and there is some pain. This hole of the membrane is bigger in size in case of some maidens and the man with a penis of smaller diameter may perform the act of cohabition with such girls without tearing the membrane. The tearing of this membrane and the enlargement of the hole are generally regarded as indications of girls having sexual interocourse. But this'cannot be said to be a hard and fast rule because sometimes this membrane gets torn by an injury or hard physical labour.

Over the urethra there is a small organ called clitoris. It has two columns. Women have separate urinary passage. Blood flows in the clitoris making it stiff like penis at the time of intercourse. After the act of cohabition is complete, blood flows back from the clitoris and it also turns sluggish like the male penis.

Ovaries—A woman has two ovaries just as a man has sperm glands. Conception is caused when these meet spermatozoa. The two ovaries lie on the left and right side of the uterus. The ovaries are approximately equal in size to a pigeon's egg. These are an inch and a quarter long and quarter to an inch broad. There are about 72,000 ovary cells in these glands. As these cells increase in size a kind of liquid accumulates in them The ovary cells generally ripe at the time of menses. An yellow object begins accumulating inside the ovary cells when they reach the stage of bursting. The colour of ovary cells turns yellow on account of this yellow object. After some time, a yellow gland is formed. At the time of conception this yellow gland gets bigger in size.

Fallopian Tubes—There are two fallopian tubes. These start from uterus and reach the ovaries. The fallopian tubes are narrow at the uterus end and funnel-like at the ovary end. The ovum remains in the fallopian tube till reproductive power is attained by it. The spermatozoa meets the ovum after passing through the uterus. In case, the conception does not take place, the ovum goes out along with blood and mucous at the time of menses. Ovums are pin-like and come out from both the ovaries alternately.

Uterus—Uterus lies behind the urine bladder and in front of anus in the pelvic region. It is not in upright position, instead it appears to be bending forward. It resembles a pear in shape. On its both sides, there are the ovaries. The upper end of the uterus is broad. In its lower, there is a five inch long duct which opens in the outer direction. This is called vagina. Uterus is hollow inside and its walls touch each other. These separate after conception and the child grows in it.

Menses—When the girl attains puberty, a fluid flows out of vagina every month. This phenomenon is called menses. The appearance of menses is called menstruation. It indicates that the girl's genital organs are developing the power of reproduction. Besides menses, other symptoms indicating the advent of pubescence also appear for example, the development of breasts and hips and the appearance of pubic hairs, etc. In our country, the menstruation starts when the girl is between 12 to 14 years in age. The effect of climate, soical environments and other atmosphere and the standard of living are factors that are also responsible to some extent for an early or late start of menses. In hotter countries, menses start at an earlier age as compared to colder countries where menses start late. The menses start early in the girls that are prone to reading sex literature and lead luxurious life. Nourishing and rich food is another factor that affects the menses. In healthy women, the state of menopause appears between the age of 45 to 50 years. Before the menopause the healthy woman gets regular menses every month except during the period she is pregnant and a few months after the childbirth. The menses stop totally when the woman attains the age between 45 and 50 years. This state is called menopause.

Menses appear after every 28 days and mis state remains for a period of three to six days. A longer period of menses or its occurrence more than once a month is a symptom of some disease or disorder. During the period of menses, women appear lethargic and do not show interest in things or work.

The purpose of menses is to make the mucous membrane of uterus capable of reproduction. It also has some bearing with the maturity of the ovum. There are more chances of a woman getting conceived after menses. Menses is caused when the mature ovum reaches the fallopian tube. This happens every month. Conception is caused when the male spermatozoa meet the ovum at die proper moment. The ovum is lost if conception does not take place.

During the act of intercourse, the male organ rubs against the vaginal walls hitting clitoris. Both the man and woman experience great pleasure during the act. The glans penis reaches near the uterus and after some time it discharges semen. The semen comes out of the penis rushing and falls into the uterus. The act is complete after the discharge of semen and the male organ no longer remains stiff. At the completion of sex act both man and woman experience a peculiar satisfaction.

Conception—Spermatozoa remain alive for a number of days in the vagina and uterus. They have special attraction for ovum. Only a powerful spermatozoa can enter the ovum. The entry of spermatozoa in the ovum is called conception. The tail portion of the spermatozoa disappears when it enters the ovum and only the first half part mixes with the ovum. A single spermatozoa is capable of causing conception. Its stay, therefore, even for a moment in the uterus can cause conception. Conception takes place easily when both man and woman are healthy and are in the right age. After the conception occurs, the embryo cell leaves immediately the fallopian tubes and reaches the uterus. There in the uterus, it sticks to the mucous membrane and grows on the blood that is brought by the artery coming to the uterus. The conception thus taken place gradually develops in the womb and after a period of nine months, some baby is born.

Reproductive System

Male Genital Organs		Female Genital Organs	
External	*Internal*	*External*	*Internal*
Penis Scrotum	Penis root	Vagina	Ovaries
and testicle		Spennary	Uterus
Sperm duct			Gland
		Fallopian tubes	

QUESTIONS

1. What are the ductless glands ? Describe their structure and functions.
2. Draw a sketch of ductless glands and explain their utility to the human body.

14

Mental Fitness

We have already both implicily and explicitly hinted briefly at the nature and importance of mental health. However, for the convenience of the readers.we propose here to mention some essentials of mental health. In this connection, first of all, we shall refer to marks of bad and good mental health, then we shall refer to the nature of mental health from infancy to the end of life.

(i) To feel insulated and unhappiness on simple things which may be easily ignored.

(ii) To remain suspicious about others for no apparent reason.

(iii) To be self-centred and becoming inconsiderate about the feelings and conveniences of others.

(iv) To get enraged on simple things.

(v) To feel very much elated on very petty affairs.

(vi) To over-estimate onself and to be boasting about one's own false good points.

(vii) Uncertain ways of behaviours so much so that no one can rely on his words.

(viii) To formulate an opinion about others on the basis of inadequate informations.

(ix) To be in the habit of speaking ill of others.

Indications of Bad Health

Although just opposite to the marks of bad mental health we can easily perceive the status of good mental health, but it is necessary here to state some important marks which explicitly stand for good mental health. Below we come here on these:

1. To show no differences in words and deeds (i. e., in saying and actually doing).
2. Not to harbour ill will against any person, even when some one behaves adversely.
3. To be self-respectful.
4. Not to harm others for any gains—small or big.
5. To have a clear vision of one's ability and possible performance accordingly.
6. To realise one's inadequacies and to try to remove the same.
7. Not to get annoyed if some one points to his weaknesses.
8. To listen to other's points of view patiently and smilingly.
9. To be sweet in conversation. Harsh words must never be used against any one. It need be, a harsh suggestion to some other person may be given indirectly through projecting how he himself would have reacted in an identical situation.
10. To be respectful to others even when having differences with them.
11. To face a confronted problem squarely.
12. To be able to adjust oneself according to circumstances and not to get perturbed and emotional.
13. To be determined to achieve one's pious goals for making life sublime.

Now we shall hint at the measures that should be adopted for acquiring good mental health.

The Strategies

In fact, avoiding the bad marks and imbibing the good ones of mental health are the two principal measures for ensuring good mental health. But for the benefit of readers we mention onwards about the measures to be adopted for acquiring good mental health.

Since physical health is the principal base on which everything in life hinges, good physical health is the first requisite for acquiring good mental health. For having good physical health, the contents of the various chapters of this book should be religiously followed.

The Journey

Development of mental health is a continuous process from infancy to grave. In other words mental health goes on developing through out the whole life. Just as at time some one falls ill due to some physical ailment and afterwards he gets well, similarly, the curb of mental health sometimes may be lower and sometimes higher but in totality it acquires a smooth straight line. We shall understnad the nature of development of mental health onwards in the different periods of life such as infancy, childhood, adolescence, adulthood and old age. Normally, the entire life of an individual may be divided into such phases. In each of these phases the mental health is of a different nature which must be understood correctly in order to ensure good mental health. Below we are hinting the main line of action that should be followed for good mental health in each phase of development.

Infancy—During this period the baby is almost self-centerd. He is neighter moral nor immoral. In fact, he is non-moral. The normal craze of the baby is towards obtaining physical well being. Further his phyiscal needs pertaining to food, normal exercise in the form of self-activity, rest and simple coloured and harmless toys should be arranged sympathetically from time to time. No over-attention should be given, otherwise the young child will want that the mother must always have him in her lap. The child should be protected from illness which may occur some time.

Childhood—During this period of 6 to 12 years of age, the child becomes conscious of many of his surroundings which manifest themselves through his questioning which must be answered sympathetically and correctly. The good arrangement for his playful activities with other children of his age should be made along with his schooling in basic rudiments of knowledge. It should be seen that the child does not fall into company of undesirable children. He must be sent to school and needful should be done for his good physical and mental health. All his legitimate demands must be met sympathetically.

Adolescence—Adolesence (the age group between 13 to 19 years) is a period of great stress and strain. An adolescence is full of various ideas and notions and he wants to give expression to the same at times. He wants that his personality should be recognised and his points-of-view must be listened to sympathetically. If this is done and his reasonable demands are fulfilled many of his emotional upheavals will be cooled down and he will proceed towards obtaining good mental health.

Adulthood—During adulthood (the age group between 20 to 45 or so) the individual is generally married and he gets busy in raising his own family. He has to take up some job. He should be guided to strive hard for his optimum level of growth. A person during adulthood has normally a friend-circle. This circle should consist of good persons who also believe in effecting social happiness everywhere. The adult shall be able to earn enough in order to have both the ends meet in relation to his wife, a number of children and old parents, if any. If an adult is always busy in doing his best in all situations of life, he is sure to be happy and make others happy in his association.

Old Age—Old age is a period of inabilities and weaknesses of various kinds. So one must be prepared for the same. Like a bee he should be careful to preserve something for a rainy day (i.e., during old age). If this is not done the individual will feel frustrated and many kinds of physical and mental illness will encircle him. For ensuring one's old age secure and happy, proper attention should always be given on physical health along with having satisfaction that he has fulfilled his duties to all concerned faithfully. If all these are honestly done an individual is sure to be happy during old age also. N.B.—For obvious reasons, no summary is needed for this chapter.

Mentally Retarded Children

Except the backward and dull children, the remaining four categories belong to those children who suffer from some mental defect. Defects in the brain are caused when the brain has not fully developed or something has retarded its development. Heredity is one of the main causes. Heredity is .the cause of mental defect in about 25 percent of children with mental defects. A scrutiny of their family history may reveal that their parents suffered from diseases like, epilepsy, hysteria, syphlis etc. Their mind too, was weak. Children born with mental defects have a lesser number of cells as compared to a normal child and their brain, too, is not properly developed.

Besides heredity, this defect may also be caused by any of the following reasons:

(a) An injury caused to the brain during the pre-natal or inter-natal period.

(b) Less secretion by thyroid glands.

(c) Defects since birth in sensory organs like eye, ear, nose etc. retard the development of brain cells. Consequently, the brain is not fully developed and defects arise in it.

(d) Inflammation in brain nerves during childhood. Excessive sleeping also cause defects in the brain cells.

It should be properly understood that treatment of this defect is possible in special circumstances only. Ordinarily, it is not possible to remove these defects. Such children may be divided into four categories according to the defects.

This category of defect is either since birth or since childhood but it does not come in the category of idiocy. Such persons depend on others for their protection but they should not be entrusted with either their own or other person's safety. Arrangements for their education should be made in special institutions. They are incapable of learning in ordinary schools. The mental age of such children is generally three years below that of an average child.

Such children are either born with this defect or develop it during childhood. The mental defect in this category of children does not reach the idiocy stage. These children cannot look after their own safety. They are not capable of learning, reading and writing.

This is the lowest category of children with mental defects. They are completely unfit for education. They even cannot express themselves through speaking. Their mental derangement reaches a stage where they cannot even protect themselves against ordinary physical dangers.

Such children have weak moral character since childhood. Criminal tendencies develop in them. Lying, theft or violating law becomes an ordinary thing for them. Punishment has no effect on them.

The symptoms may be divided in two categories:

Mental symptoms, and Physical symptoms.

Mental Symptoms

(1) The will and thinking power of such children lack determination.

(2) Their memory is weak because of the lack of concentration. Such children develop mechanical memory by doing a work repeatedly, but if there is a slight change in the routine their memory fails them.

(3) The mentally retarded child cannot discuss a subject and support it on the basis of reasons. He is neither able to establish relationship between two objects on the basis of reason nor can he put to action what he has learnt. For example, if he knows mathematical tables he will not be able to use them in additions and subtractions.

(4) Such children, cannot of their own accord, concentrate on a problem for a considerable period. Their concentration power is weak. They have blank looks.

(5) The power of establishing relationship between two objects is lacking in these children. Their imagination and reasoning power is weak.

(6) The speaking of these children is also defective, because they start speaking at a late stage.

(7) Their imitating power is generally very strong. They learn through imitation.

Physical Symptoms—The teeth of children of this category cut late. They start speaking and walking late. Their excretory organs are also not fully under control.

(1) Their facial expression and physical movement are lethargic. They also appear to be unable to control their muscles.

(2) The development of such children is retarded. So the development also does not take place properly and systematically. Such children are generally short-statured. Their blood circulation too does not function properly.

(3) The shape of the ears of these children is uncommon. They have more hairs on their fingers and toes. Their skin is dry, thick and rough.

Role of Education

The teachers should find out such children in the class and the school, doctor's attention should be drawn towards them. If the doctor finds them mentally defective they should be transferred to special schools. In these schools attention should mostly be concentrated in developing their mental faculties.

These special institutions should be located in spacious places where open air and sunshine are available in abundance and there is enough land for gardening and other things. A class should not contain more than 25 students. Physical training, vocational training, sports, hygiene etc., are subjects in which education may be of more help to them. Being mentally below par these children should not be given intellectual education directly. In special conditions, they should be taught reading, writing and speaking correctly. Simple arithmetic, painting, natural science and music are some of the subjects that may be taught to them. Gardening, leather work, tailoring, cooking, carpentry, etc., may be taught to them. They should be encouraged to do such work which may arouse interest in them and develop their mental faculties.

Sensory training will prove more beneficial to them. Models, charts, toys and machines, etc., are good mediums for training them. Montessori toys, constructive sports, designing on bed-sheets and paper work are some of the mediums of their education in the early stage. Later on, the children should be taught leather work, tailoring and card-board works. Further, they should be given training in carpentry, tool repairing and making of metal wires. Such practical training will afford opportunity for roll development of the sensory organs.

Social education is also important for them. They should be taught manners, cleanliness, virtuous living and protection of others' properties. Opportunities should be afforded to them so that sense of responsibility, duty and doing good to others may arise in them. They should be encouraged to participate in organisations like girl guides and scouts.

The Cure

At the slightest suspicion of mental defects in a child, the first thing to do is to get him mentally and physically examined. The parents should always be present during the medical check up so that they may be readily available to supply all detailed and relevant informations the physician might need. Such children should be taken from the common schools and admitted into special ones. It is also good to send these children to the places of treatment. If it is, however, felt that their proper care is needed in the house, the home atmosphere should then be made congenial. Doctors should always be consulted about the child's progress and conditions.

Precautionary Steps

To check the growth of mentally dearanged persons, it is desirable to that their marriages should be banned. They should be sterilized and should be placed in mental asylums.

The Diseases

This is a dangerous nerve disease. There is a possibility of the patient becoming a victim of heart disease too. The attack of this disease generally occurs between the age of seven and fourteen years. Sometimes, whooping cough, scarlet fever, high fever, fear, excessive worry and too much of work cause these diseases.

At the initial stage, the child appears lazy. His face is deformed. The actions of his muscles suddenly become irreguair and aimless. This disease can easily be diagnosed from tongue. The children, suffering from it cannot keep their tongue steady if once they take it out. The tongue appears shivering and the child loses control over it.

Different body parts show different symptoms. The attack of this disease on face causes the muscles go out of child's control. The muscles of lips, cheeks, eyes and nose shiver continuously in a manner that gives the child the appearance of a naughty boy making faces. The speech is also affected. If the hand is affected, it continues to shiver. Consequently, it is not possible to hold things in the hand and these always fall down. Continuous contraction of hand muscles produce only one kind of movement which is aimless, as the result of which the writing becomes bad. As the disease develops, the restlessness in the child, too, develops. His concentration power becomes weak. He feels headache and becomes short-tempered.

The child suffering from this disease should be given full rest and allowed to go to school only when he recovers. If the child stops taking rest while some symptoms of disease remain, there is always a possibility of the disease relapsing and grave situation may arise.

Doctor's supervision is essential till his absolute recovery. Proper medical treatment should be provided to the child and he should remain in health surroundings. He should be given nourishing diet at regular intervals, suitable clothes, sufficient rest as well as regular exercise. Particular attention should be paid in keeping the child clean. Sufficient improvement will take place if the child is looked after in the above manner.

Stammering causes defective pronunciation. This defect is caused by various irregularities of the muscles that control speaking. When the child while speaking pays undue attention to the muscles concerning mouth, tongue, lips, etc., and less attention to respiration then more energy is lost on muscles not relating to speech than on other. Consequently, pronunciation becomes defective and obstructions in speech are caused. Stammering is divided into two categories :

Initial Stammering—This causes trouble in pronouncing the first word.

Stammering—In this repeated obstructions appear either in the beginning of the speech or in the middle whenever consonants are spoken.

The defect is caused by the following :

(I) Tonsilitis or Adenoids, (2) Sudden accidents, (3) Serious illness, (4) Imitation, (5) Perturbation, (6) Unusual excitement, (7) Hesitation, (8) Emotion, (9) Worry or troubles, (10) Hereditary nerve disease.

It is necessary to pay attention to the mental state of the child for removing this defect. The child should be made free from worry, hesitation and perturbation. Enlarged tonsils should be operated upon. Nourishing and balanced diet should be given to the child. They should not be asked to labour hard and rest should be provided to them. The services of a child psychologist should be utilised for the proper care of children suffering from the above defects. He should be admitted in a class where there are only ten or twelve students. The personality of the teacher has an important place in the treatment of children. The feeling of self-confidence should be aroused in such children. They should be asked to give exercise to'their tongue, lips and respiratory organs. The .co-operation of parents is necessary for speedy improvement. Children should be made to practise in the home what they learn in school. The teacher and parents should see that the child should speak slowly and inhale enough air in lungs with each word.

Mental irregularities cause hysteria. The fit is caused when the patient tries to attract others' attention or is filled with a particular emotion. There is no change visible in the body during this fit. Girls suffer more from this disease. The girls with unbalanced emotions suffer more from this disease during adolscence.

During the fit the patient either cries or laughs or indulges in other exciting actions. Afterwards he heaves a sigh, falls down and turns unconscious. The face of the patient does not turn yellow during the state of unconsciousness. The pulse also remains regular. His or her consciousness is not lost fully. It is due to this that while falling, the patient manages to escape injuries.

The patient should not be shown any sympathy durig the fit. After preparing the parents history he should be advised psychological treatment. Cold water should be sprinkled over the face The patient becomes all right when left alone.

Epilepsy–Disorder in the nervous system is the cause of epilepsy. The disease is divided into two categories—(1) Major epilepsy, and (2) Minor epilepsy. In the major epilepsy the body contracts besides occuring of unconsciousness. The patient appears lethargic and restless before the attack. His face turns yellow. Sometimes, no symptoms appear beforehand and the child all of a sudden cries and becomes unconscious. During the fit, all the muscles contract and the body becomes stiff; The patient contracts his body during the first two or three minutes and begins to throw his hands and feet hastily. The mouth throws foam. He also emnates during the fit. The eyes move in a corner. When the contraction stops, the body becomes dull as the result of which the patient remains unconscious for a time and then falis asleep, it is possible that after the fit his mental condition may not remain normal. In this condition, he has no feeling of responsibility towards his duties.

The fit in a patient suffering from minor epilepsy is ordinary and the duration is short. There is no contraction in the body. The patient becomes unconscious for a short period. Some sweat also appears on the body during the attack. His body turns yellow and become stiff for a time. There are possibilities of major accidents during an epileptic fit.

After a fit of minor epilepsy, the patient generally becomes normal and performs his work as usual. But sometimes it also happens that his mental condition remains disturbed and he is not in a position to decide as what to do and what not to do. In this state of mind. he is not responsible for what he does.

Care should be taken to protect the patient from injury during the attack of epilepsy. If bleeding starts due to injury it should be stopped. The patient should be made to sleep on his back and his clothes be- removed. Everything likely to cause injury to the patient should be removed from his surroundings. Care should be taken to see that the patient does not bite his tongue. Something should be placed in the mouth so that he may not be able to bite his tongue. He should be allowed to do whatever he please.:;. During the attack, cold water should not be sprinkled over his face. He should be allowed to sleep undisturbed and soundly.

The daily routine of the patient should be regularised as the first precautions against recurrence of the attack. He should be given light and easily digestible food, at proper intervals. He should sleep as much as possible. He should not be excited. He should live in a place where fresh air and sunshine are in abundance. Such children should be sent to special institutions, where they may get education according to their mental state.

Special Centres—Main four : (1) Auditory word centre, (2) Visual word centre, (3) Motor speech centre, (4) Writing centre. Word deafness is caused when auditory word centre is not fully developed and when visual word centre is not developed word blindness occurs.

Mentally, deranged children—(1) Backward child, (2) Dull child, (3) Feeble-minded child, (4) Imbecile, (5) Idiot, and (6) Morally defective child. These children should be imparted vocational training under the guidance of specialists.

Diseases of Nervous system—(1) Chorea or St. Vitus, Dance, (2) Stammering, (3) Hysteria, (4) Epilepsy.

QUESTIONS

1. Explain the principal marks of bad and good mental health.
2. Hint briefly at the measures to be adopted for acquiring good mental health.
3. What are the specific periods of life ? Hint at the essentials that should be taken into consideration for ensuring good mental health in each period ?
4. Describe briefly the various parts of the brain and their functions.
5. Draw a sketch of the brain and spinal cord and show how and with which body parts they are connected.
6. How does narcotic drugs or alcoholic drinks affect the nervous system ?
7. Prove that the functioning of nervous system depends upon the movement of body parts.
8. What do you mean by 'Mentally defective children' ? Write short notes about them.
9. What do you know about the diseases of nervous system ? Give a detailed account of the same.

15

Digestion Setup

When we take food it goes down the stomach through a long tube. This tube is known as the alimentary canal. Starting from the mouth it travels to the rectum. It is 28 or 29 feet in length. Some part of the alimentary canal ties in the neck and the chest. The remaining lies in the stomach. This alimentary canal is wide, thin and narrow at places. This is also called the food passage.

The alimentary canal is divided into the following parts : (1) Mouth Cavity, (2) Digestive System, (3) Stomach and (4) Intestines.

The Door

Mouth cavity is the upper part of the alimentary canal. It is open in the front. Its inner part is covered by a smooth membrane starting from the lips. This part is made of a strong and hard bone. Its name is palate. On its right and left sides are cheeks which are made of soft pieces of flesh. Beyond the cheeks lies the pharynx. On both sides of the pharynx are small lumps of flesh known as tonsils. There are teeth whose main function is to chew food in the upper and lower jaws of the mouth. There is also a tongue in the mouth. It performs two functions. It indicates the taste and carries the food this way or that way when it is being chewed. When after chewing the food becomes pulp-like and ready for being swallowed the tongue helps it to go down the alimentary canal.

The Stages

The real work of the digestion begins with the teeth. When we chew the food with teeth the saliva mixes with it and the food becomes pulp-like. In this way, it easily goes down in the alimentary canal with the help of the tongue.

Saliva is produced by six glands in the mouth. Three of these are in the right side and three on the left. There is a gland in the cheek just opposite the ear. This gland is called parotid gland. The other is below the ear. The other is below the jaw and is named the sub-maxillary gland. The third lies below the tongue and is known as sublingual gland. The saliva comes from these glands through small tubes and mixes with the food. The'food becomes soft and smooth with the help of saliva and easily goes down. Saliva is an alkaline liquid which is thick and sticky and active tissues exists in it. These active tissues are known as ptyalin. It is a kind of ferment which turns the starchy objects like rice, wheat, potatoes into sugar. It is because of this that these things give us a sweet taste. This affects only things having alkaline in them. The things with acid in them remain unaffected by ptyalin. It is, therefore, not advisable to eat edibles with acid side by side with wheat and rice. When these objects change into sugar, they reach the blood and get dissolved in it and provide nutrition to the body. In this way, the over produced sugar turns into glycogen and is accumulated in the liver and when needed again turns into sugar. Ptyalin is not present in the saliva of young children. It is due to this reason that young children are unable to digest the starchy food properly.

The food reaches the alimentary canal after being chewed in the mouth. The first part of the alimentary canal is called Oesophagus. This part is made up of muscles. It is flat like a deflated cycle tube. It is inflated when the food enters it and again deflates. The epiglottis does not allow the food to enter the windpipe because it closes the upper part of the larynx. The food in this way straight goes down in the alimentary canal and reaches the stomach. The alimentary canal goes down the neck just behind the windpipe.

From here proceeding through the middle portion of the chest it penetrates the diaphragm and goes still down. Finally, it reaches the stomach. The food reaches the stomach through this alimentary canal. In the stomach the alimentary canal takes the shape of sack. This sack is about ten inches in length. There is a hole made by the muscles at the place where alimentary canal joins the stomach. This is known as cardiac opening. The cardiac opening changes its size on expansion and relaxation of the muscles. The broader part of the stomach called fundus lies beneath the cardiac opening. The last portion of the stomach is narrow. Here also there is an opening or hole made by muscles which changes size on the expansion and relaxations of muscles. This opening is called pyloric. The expansion power of the stomach is high. When the food is collected in the stomach it expands.

In the inner part of stomach there is a lining of mucous membrance which has a number of glands in it. A particular type of juice is produced by them. This juice is called the gastric juice. It has got hydrochloric acid and two varieties of yeast called renin and pepsin. The food in the stomach gets digested with the help of these juices. These juices easily digest fish, egg, pulse and meat. Renin curdles the milk. Pepsin turns the protein into peptones. It then turns it into amino acid and mixes it in the blood for digestion. Water is necessary for all these chemical actions. The unique feature of renin is that it separates water and coagulates milk. The curdling of milk in the stomach is a natural process and is an indication of the healthy working of the digestive system.

Pepsin affects the protein and separates it into smaller parts. It functions only in the presence of hydrochloric acid. Protein is not fully digested in the stomach. The remaining portion is digested when it reaches in small intestine and then only it becomes fit to be absorbed in the blood.

The starch found in the food remains unaffected by the gastirc juice. Sugar and glucose are affected by it and therefore, they change.

Fat also remains unaffected by the gastric juice. This is fully digested in the small intestine.

The gastric juice falls in the stomach only when food reaches there or when hunger is felt. The gastric juice is not produced when the mind is in a state of fear because the digestive system at that time does not function properly. it is, therefore, necessary that we should be calm and peaceful at the time of taking food. The gastric juice is capable of killing germs. It kills the germs which reach along with die food.

The digestion periods of different foods vary. Ordinarily it take four hours to digest food. After the food is fully affected by the gastric juice, the following products remain:

1. Starch turned into sugar, 2. Some unchanged starch, 3. Peptones, 4. Liquid fat, 5. Portion of the food of no use to the body and unfit for digestion, 6. Water and 7. Salt.

The above parts of the food reach the doudenum in a liquid form. Duodenum starts from the lower part of the stomach. It is a small part of the small intestine and is 12 inches long. It is a narrow tube and is semi-circular in shape like the English letter 'C'. In its lining are chamber-like glands. The gall tube originating from the liver and the pancreas tube each other in the lower portion of duodenum. The juice coming out of both the tubes mixed with the food juice and helps in its digestion. In this way, both the organs, the liver and the pancreas have got an important place in the digestive system.

Liver is the biggest gland of the body which lies in the upper part of the stomach and below the muscle in the middle of sternum. It is reddish brown in colour and weighs about quarter to two kilograms. The liver is divided into two parts by a deep cut. There are five cavities in its lower layer. The gall-bladder which resembles a pear in shape lies in one of those cavities. Coming out of the liver the bile is collected in this bladder and reaches the duodenum according to the need.

The colour of bile is greenish yellow. This is a sticky liquid and tastes bitter. There are minerals and bile pigments in it. The blood, when it enters the liver, has many food tissues in it. The liver takes the excessive part of the sugar from blood and leaves only the necessary quantity in the blood. The sugar creates heat and energy in the body. The liver also supplies the sugar to the body when it falls short of it. The bile coming out of the liver helps in the digestion of food. It has its effect on fat which, as the result of bile-action, is dissolved. The bile also kills the instestinal germs. It also removes the effect of poison on the intestine. The bile returns to the liver when its entering into duodenum is stopped and get mixed with the blood. This causes the dreaded disease of jaundice.

During the action of cells the protein breaks and produced liver urea which mixes up with blood and enters the kidneys. From there it it expelled out of the body through urine.

The gland called pancreas is below the stomach near the linings of the stomach. It is a long and narrow gland. It is pistol-like in shape. Its broder right part is called the head and the narrow left part called the tail. It is about six or seven inches in length. A number of tube comes out of it and this network is called the pancreatic system.

The juice secreted by this gland is called pancreatic juice. It is thin, clean and sour. It has no colour. Secreting from the pancreatic system it mixes with the juice of gall system (bile) and in this way, juices of both the systems reach the duodenum.

The following things are present in this juice:

1. Amylopsin — It digest the starchy food.
2. Tripsin — It digests the protein.
3. Lipes — It digests the fat. It turns the fat into fato-acid and again into glycerine which reaches the body through blood.
4. Insulin — This insulin keeps the sugar in control and checks the sugar going out of the body with urine. Lack of insulin in the body causes diabetes. Therefore, the diabetic person is given insulin injections.

The above descriptions show that the digestion begins with the food reaching the mouth and is almost over when the food reaches the doudenum. The last action is completed by the juice of smaller intestines.

Last Phase

It is muscular tube about 12 feet in length covered with mucous membrane. There are a number of projections in this membrane. They are from 1/48 inch to 1/8 inches in length. There are about 12,000 projections in a square inch of the membrane. A big lymphatic capillary is placed between each projection. This is surrounded by blood capillaries and flesh. The relaxation of flesh caused movement of projection and these generally remain shaking.

In the lining of the lower part of smaller intestines there are groups of a special type of glands. Wounds appear on them during the period of typhoid fever. This condition is also present in the cases of intestinal tuberculosis.

The last part of digestive action is performed by the juice produced in the intestine. The intestinal juice has elements possessing a number of qualities out of which the following three are particularly worth mentioning:

Pancreas exciting element—This element is called enterokinase. It affects trypsinogen secreted by pancreas due to which trypsinogen turns into active trypsine.

Protein disintegrating element—This element affects the protein. It disintegrates substances produced by pepsin and dripsine and provides them the simple form.

Sugar changing element—This element affects the sugar produced from starch and turns it into glucose.

The remaining part of the so far digested food enters the large intestines in a semi-liquid form.

This is comparatively broader than the smaller intestine but only five Feet in length. There is a door at the junction of smaller intestine and larger intestine in which are fixed valves made by mucous. These valves remain shut so that food may not return to smaller intestine. The beginning part of the larger intestine is like a bladder.

Larger intestine starts from the right region and goes upto the lower part of the liver. After reaching there it turns towards left and is spread upto the spleen. After reaching the spleen it again truns and goes upto the left region. It again turns and enters the pelvic girdle. It ends at the anus. The upper part of the anus is called rectum.

The linings of she larger intestine are also of fleshy fibrous tissues and mucous. But there are no projections in it. In the outer fleshy fibrous tissues there are a number of smaller glands but the glands found in the smaller intestine are not present here. In these linings there are many wrinkles as on a bladder No particular digestive juice is produced by these glands. The food juice that comes from smaller intestine to larger intestine looses its watery part as it proceeds towards pelvic girdle. This water goes in the blood and plasma. In this way the excreta in the larger Intenstine dries and goes out of the body through the anus. When the excreta reaches the rectum, the man feels the need of easing himself. At the time of expelling die stool, the anus opens up due to expansion of the muscle and the stool goes out.

Generally, the stool contains the undigested part of the food, spent up tissues, small germs called bacteria and other harmful and waste substances. There is also some part of bile in it. Bacteria produces many harmful things which cause foul odour in the stool. Due to decomposition many gases, too, are produced. An advance stage of decomposition of stool produces harmful and poisonous germs. It is, therefore, necessary that stool should pass daily.

The digestion of food is one process, while the abosrption of food is another. This process helps the food to be able to supply blood and lymph to the body. The process of food reaching the blood and lymph is called absorption.

When the food changes into soluble matter it, after being absorbed by various organs, mixes in. the blood. The process of absorbing food takes place in every part of the canal in a more or less measure. This action takes place mure prominently in smaller intestine. While describing the smaller intestine earlier it has been stated that the linings inside the smaller intestine are made up of mucous membrane. There are projections or villis in it. These villis are also surrounded by the layers of cells. In them lie the lymphatic capillaries, nerves and the blood capillaries.

The villis suck a major portion of the digested food. The blood capillaries absorb the sugar and the amino-acid while the lymphatic capillaries absorb the fat. The cells of the villis are so formed that they take from the intestines the ready elements which are easily absorbed in the blood. After taking these substances they mix it with the blood. They reach every part of the body through arteries from here. The blood capillaries of villis join and take the form of veins. When these veins join, a major vein called the portal vein is formed. This portal vein enters the liver and disintegrate into small blood capillaries. Parts of the food containing starch and protein reach bigger blood capillaries from the liver. Unnecessary part remains in the liver. Here it turns into glycogen and reach the blood.

While the digested starchy and protein bearing food flows in the small capillarries of villis the fatty goes in the lacteal capillaries. These lacteal capillaries join to form lymphatic capillaries. In this way the fatty part gradually moving towards the upper part of the body reaches a major vein on the left side of the body near the neck. After reaching this place this part of fat mixes with the blood stream.

The non-digestion of food causes many diseases in the body. Out of these some will be discussed below:

The following are the reasons that cause this disease :

1. Continuously taking such food that abounds in fat and carbohydrate cuases dyspepsia.
2. Over-eating, too, causes this disease.
3. Bad teeth are also a factor in causing dyspepsia, because the food cannot be chewed properly if the teeth are in a bad condition. The poison from the gums mixes with the food

and enters the stomach. In this way, the food not chewed properly and the poison mixed due to bad gums obstructs the smooth functioning of the digestive system causing dyspepsia.

During dyspepsia, a particular type of acid is produced by the undigested part of food which causes stomach-ache. Sometimes vomitting and motions start. Giddiness is also indicative of dyspepsia. There is burning sensation in the stomach and the mouth feels a strange sour taste. Dyspepsia can result in anaemia, headache, dysentery etc. Children suffering from dyspepsia are liable to fall prey to number of diseases.

As a safeguard against this disease, one should regularly take limited food at a fixed hour. Children should particularly be given food that is easily digestible. Large quantities of warm water taken during this disease proves beneficial. It causes vomitting which clears the stomach. Sometimes, laxatives or purgatives, too, prove helpful. By so doing he stool comes out and the intestines become clean.

The Diseases

Indigestion also causes diarrhoea. Germ-laden food, half-ripe fruits or the use of bad and dirty water causes this disease. This disease spreads through flies. They carry the germs in their legs and leave them on the food while sitting on it. Eating the food where flies have left germs causes diarrhoea. Sometimes this disease attacks when the stomach catches cold. As a safeguard against this disease one should drink boiled water and protect food from flies by keeping it always covered. Fresh and light food should always be taken. Use of curd may protect one from this disease.

Constipation is caused when reasonable quantity of stool does not pass out regularly. The factors causing constipation are more than one. When the food is fried in fat, a very small part of its reaches the rectum. As the result of this the urge to excrete is not strong and constipation is caused. Suppressing the desire of passing motion also cause constipation. When due to bad and defective teeth food is affected with poison and germs reach stomach constipation is the result.

One feels headache, fatigue, lack of hunger, dullness and depression during constipation. Some mild natured poison is likely to be produced in the rectum due to non-passing of the stool. Chronic constipation cause ulcers and appendicitis. These are the diseases of stomach and intestines.

Green and leafy vegetables like spinach, bathua, raddish, tomatoes, lady-finger, parwal and cauliflower are good for cleaning the bowels. It is very necessary to eat fruits. Sufficient quantity of water should also be taken. These edibles cause excitement of the rectum as the result of which stool passes easily. One should regularly pass stool. The desire to pass stool should never be suppressed. Physical exercises also prove helpful in cleaning the bowels. People take purgatives and laxative in order to remove constipation. These things do give relief at the time, but their effect is not lasting. Too much use of purgatives tells adversely on functions of digestive organs. For lasting and effective cure one should take recourse to the above described measures.

Alimentary canal has four parts : (1) The mouth cavity, (2) Digestive system, (3) Stomach and (4) Intestines.

The food after entering the mouth proceeds to the stomach, then to duodenum, smaller intestine, larger intestine, rectum, and then passes out as stool through the anus.

The digestion starts with the teeth. Saliva helps the digestion. Salvia is produced by six glands. The stomach is like a bladder in shape. Food is digested here with the help of gastric juices. The food containing protein is not digested here. It is digested in the smaller intestines.

Food passes from duodenum to smaller intestine. Bile and pancreatic juice is produced in the duodenum which also help in digesting the food. The bile juice digestes the fat. The digestive action is almost completed by the juice produced in the smaller intestine. The remaining food in liquid form enters the larger intestine. After reaching here the watery part of the digested food is left behind and the dried up stool goes out of the body through the rectum.

Constipations, dyspepsia and diarrhoea are caused when the food is not properly digested. As a safeguard against these diseases, one should take reasonable quantity of food regularly at a fixed hour. One should also develop the habit of passing the motion regularly.

QUESTIONS

1. Describe the digestive organs.
2. Explain in detail with the help of a sketch the changes that appear in the food after entering the mouth and subsequently reaching smaller intestine.
3. Describe the structure of the alimentary canal.
4. Throw light on the structure of intestines and describe their functions in the digestion of food.
5. What diseases are caused by non-digestion of food ? What are their symptoms and how to safeguard against them ?

16

Disposal of Refuse

Due to activities in the body some useless matters are produced throughout. The waste and harmful matters should expelled out of the body; otherwise due to them poison is likely to spread in the body. The process of expelling of these waste and harmful substances out of the body is known as excretion and the system is called excretory system. The organs that take part in this process are known as excretory organs. The following are these organs:

(1) Kidneys, (2) Skin, (3) Lungs, (4) Bowel.

The Setup

The part of body where urine is produced is called kidney. There are two kidneys in the body—the right one and the left one. These ase situated in front of the last ribs.

Kidneys are deep-brown in colour. These are surrounded all round particularly in the rear with fat. There is a small gland on the upper part of each kidney. The shape of the kidney is like a bean. Kidneys are four inches long and two and a half inches broad.

Like the bean the back portion of the kidneys are projecting. Their outer edge, too, is projecting. The inner portion of the kidney near the vertebral column is pressed inwards. In this part the artery enters and the vein comes out. This part of the kidney is known as its mouth. The ureter also originates from here and goes down to the bladder. There are two ureters; each coming out of a kidney. The length of the;ureter is about 15 inches. They are just like rubber tubes in shape. The urine flowing through these tubes (ureters) is collected in the bladder. The bladder is a sack made of muscles and lies in the pelvic girdle. When the bladder is filled with urine it contracts and the urine goes out through urethra. The action of urethra is controlled by voluntary muscles. A person feels the need of urinating when about six or seven ounce of urine is collected inside the bladder. At the mouth of urethra the flesh of kidney wall contracts and blocks the outlet of urine but when a man wants to urinate the walls loosen up and the obstruction at the mouth of urethres is removed. At this time, the urine comes out of the bladder and passing through urethra goes out. The major protion of the urine is water and the rest comprises of some chemicals. These chemicals remain dissolved in the water in the following proportion :

The urine of a healthy person is free of sugar and protein, but in a sick one these things are found in larger or smaller quantities. The urine of a healthy man is wheatish in colour, in the sick one the colour becomes yellowish. Sometimes it turns reddish as well.

Kidney is surrounded by a membrane. This membrane cover is called kidney bladder. Fat also covers it from all sides. If the kidney is cut through from one end to the other by a knife, the colour of the cut portion would appear to be black. Its formation is crystal-like or granular. Its inner portion is comparatively of lighter colour. The formation of kidney's middle part is stripe-like and is constituted of very thin capillaries. These very thin capillaries join together and become tower-like. These tower or minarets have small holes at the end. These holes are called mouths of bigger' capillaries of the kidneys.

Kidneys are the lumps formed by the collection of groups of small and thin capillaries. Besides, the kidney have nerves, arteries, veins and lymphatic capillaries. The top part of the capillaries is disc-like and thick. It is situated in the back of the kidney. This portion is flat in the centre where there are blood capillaries. Each capillary passing through this swelled portion joins the other capillary. When a number of smaller capillarie join this, a big capillary is formed. The minarets of the liver are formed of such bigger capillaries. The urine comes out of the mouth of these capillaries and reaches urethra.

The Working

Blood reaches the kidney through the branches of aorta. This artery is divided here into many branches. These smaller branches of the artery enter the mouth of each capillary. Through it blood reaches the capillaries. The plasma come out of the walls of these arteries, and reaches capillaries through their walls. The inflamed part of the capillary serves the purpose of a filter. Some part of the plasma is filtered through them.

The blood comes out of the groups of the capillaries through a tube. Coming out the blood from here spreads itself in the network of capillaries in the remaining portion of the tube. These capillaries lie besides the cells and take in the seeped urea and uric acid, etc. form the lymph and then carry in to the tube. These substances (the uria and uric acid, etc.) mix up in the tube with that water which seeps from the rear inflated part of the tube. This water flows through small tubes and reaches the bigger tubes of the minarets. Coming out of the holes of these minarets the water reaches the-upper portion of the ureter. This water-like object is urine. It is thus clear that the blood reaching the kidneys gets purified and leaves the foul matter in the shape of urine which flow out of the body from there, A healthy and normal man urinates about a quarter and seer to a seer and half urine during twenty-four hours.

The skin protects the body like an armour. Its cells are continuously damaged and formed as well. It has got two layers (1) Epidermis, and (2) Dermis.

Epidermis is that covering part of the body which separates from the body where a hot liquid falls on the body or where some strong medicine is applied on the skin. The thickness of epidermis is not uniform throughout the body. Its thickness is 1/24 inch at the sole and 1/200 inch on the face. The epidermis is comparatively harder than dermis. This is made up of many layers of epithelial cells. Its cells are thinner and flatter than the lower cells but they are hard like the cells of the heart. They protect the lower cells and continuously get emaciated.

In the lower cell of the epidermis there are colour producing particles. It is these particles which give white, black, brown, or wheatish complexion to the skin. These are found in abundance in the skins of Africans while they are found in lesser number in those of Europeans. It is because of the large number of these colour particles that Africans have black complexion. These colour-producing particles are changeable. Their number increases or decreases according to the climatic conditions. The colour particles are found in large numbers in the inhabitants of hot regions, because the colour particles help the body to resist the heat. The man faces the climate of the hot countries with the help of these colour particles.

There are no blood-carrying capillaries in the epidermis. The cells in it get nutrition from the lymph. It seeps from the dermis. There are no nerves in the epidermis. It is because of this that man does not feel pain if these are cut.

There are a number of pores in the epidermis which could be seen through microscope. Some foul matter of the body seeps out of these pores in the form of perspiration.

On the walls of the inner cavities of the body (mouth etc.) there is a thing rosy mucous membrane. The uniqueness of this membrane lies in the fact that it soon absorbs the dissolved substances. There is no such thing in the epidermis.

The real skin lies beneath the epidermis which is made of connective tissues. It is thicker and stronger than the epidermis. The connecting tissues are joined strongly in the upper part, but are loose in the lower part. There is a lot of fat in it. The projecting parts of the body are filled up by this fat and it makes the body fleshy. It also keeps the body hot and checks heat from escaping out of the body. In the dermis are present the nerves, lymphatic capillaries and veins.

In the outer part of the skin are the projection of fingers. These projections are called papillae. They are situated like parallel lines. In the centre of a papillae is a bunch of blood capillaries and oval part of flesh which is called touch corpuscle. We feel the touch, pain and temperature through them.

Two varieties of glands are found in the skin (1) sebaceous glands and (2) the sweat glands.

These are small sack-like objects from which comes out oil-like smooth liquid. The liquid coming out of each sack through a capillary reaches the hair root. The hair and the skin remain glossy due to this liquid. These glands are not found in the palm or the sole of the foot.

Role of Glands

These glands are found in the lower pan of the dermis. They lie like snakes in the lower tissues of the dermis. These are tubes-like and are surrounded on all sides by the blood capillaries. When the blood flows through the capillaries, the cells of these glands take from the seeped plasma water, urea and other harmful products. This water is known as perspiration. It evaporates out of the body through the pores of the epidermis. If it is in large quantity it is changed into drops and does not evaporate. Sweat is of two kinds. One which is invisible and evaporates as soon as it comes out of the body. The other kind of sweat in the form of sweat is visible and appears on the body. The quantity of sweat coming out of the body depends on the climate and hard work.

Perspiration is useful in more than one respect. It keeps the body at a uniform temperature. During the summer season or during hard work when heat is generated in the body perspiration starts. It causes the body to remain cool. In this way perspiration keeps the body cool in summer.

Hair and Nails

Epidermis produces nails and hairs. When the cells of epidermis become hard these two things are formed. In the roots of nails there are a number of blood capillaries which are covered by the cell of epidermis. These cells grow rapidly. On coming outside, these turn hard. The nail grows in this fashion.

Hairs are the projections of epidermis. In the root of each hair is a deep and very narrow pore. There is a gland in its root which is called sebacious gland. This gland produces oil-like liquid which keeps the hair soft and glossy. Each hair has a muscle in its root. The hair stands when this muscle relaxes.

Significance of Skin

(1) The skin covers the entire body and protects the muslces beneath it.

(2) Keeps the body temperature at a uniform level by expelling the heat through sweat.

(3) Makes the body feel a touch and heat.

(4) Foul matter is thrown out of the body through the skin.

Protection of Skin and Hair—The body if not kept clean in a regular way begins to emit foul smell. The dust particles and the foul matter of the sweat sticks to the body causing obstruction in the outlet of harmful matter through the innumerable pores on the skin. This state of affaris fells adversely on the health of the individual and numerous boils appear on the body. The body falls victim to a number of skin diseases. It is, therefore, necessary to teach the child the importance of cleanliness of the body.

If the skin remain unclean and dirty, a number of infectious skin diseases take root on the body. Sometimes, the results are serious. A brief description of some of the skin diseases is given below :

Impetigo—This disease is generally found among children of poor families. It is caused by a particular germ. In this disease many small red rashes appear on the face, chin, head, hand and other parts of the body. Sometimes, blisters also appear on these rashes. When the rashes dry, yellow hard crusts are formed and there is etching in them. When children use their dirty nails over the itching parts, the germs, enter into nails and other children may also catch the infection.

Children suffering from impetigo should be isolated and other children should not be allowed to touch their things. Other children should be examined to find out if they, too, are suffering from this disease. The lavatories and the bathrooms of the institution should be examined and kept clean. The useless part of the nail should be cut so that it may not be used in irritating the affected part. The yellow hard crust should be removed first of all. The affected parts should be washed with boric acid mixed with hot water. Sulphonamide ointment should then be applied. The ointment prepared with mercury also may be applied.

Itch—This is an infectious disease which is caused by a particular type of germ. The germ penetrates the epidermis. It generally affects calves, leg, wrist and in the space between two fingures.

In this disease small patches appear on the affected part. Gradually, they develop in bigger ones and cause itching. Pus is also formed and sometimes the patches form abscess.

One should avoid the company of a man suffering from this highly contagious disease in order to save himself from falling a victim to the same. All the things used by the patient should be disinfected. The children suffering from this disease should be granted leave of absence. Proper treatment should be given in consultation with the physician.

Hot water bath and rubbing of effected part destroys the germs. After the hot bath, an application of sulphur on the whole body proves beneficial. Bensoyl Benosnate is also useful. Its solution should be applied on the affected part and allowed to be dried up. The process should again be repeated. On its being dried up, the patient should take a good bath with germ-killing soap. This process will destroy the germs and the patient would soon recover. The clothes of children suffering from this disease should daily be disinfected.

Eczema—In eczema the red rashes appear in the beginning as the result of which the skin turns rough, watery and thick. Later on, hard crusts are formed on the rashes. Children of about five years in age commonly suffer from it. Such children should be given leave and advised proper treatment.

Ringworm—It is of four categories : (1) Skull ringworm, (2) Leg of thigh ringworm, (3) Chin ringworm and (4) Body ringworm,

Particular germs in the above-mentioned parts of the body cause ringworm of the part concerned. Tinea Tonsuraus in the skull. Tinea Morginate in the legs of thighs. Tinea Sycosis in the chin and Tinea Circinate cause ringworm in the body. These germs attack the skin at the root of the hair. This is also a contagious disease.

First of all, a red patch appears on the affected part. The rash is generally one and half inch in diameter. It is circular and projecting. In the centre it is all-right but spreads towards the edges. Irritation is felt in the affected part at times.

Children suffereing from ringworm should be given leave to avoid contagion to others. The disease is cured by applying tincture of some suitable ointment at the affected part.

Skull Ringworm—As a result of ringworm on the skull, round patches appear over the head causing the affected part in order to give a rosy appearance. The affected part also appears to be covered with scales. There is some inflammation too. The germs in this case penetrate the hair-root and make them weak so that hairs begin to fall. Gradually, these germs attack the nearby hairs and destroy them as well. This affects the entire head as the result of which new rashes appear over the entire head.

No sooner the first symptoms of head ringworm appear on the head of the child, it should immediately be examined by a physician. He should be granted leave from the school till he fully recovers. The clothings of such children particularly the cap should not be given for use to other children. It is advisable to put a paper in the cap before putting it on the head. This paper should be changed daily and the old one should be burnt. The comb, pillow, hair-brush of the diseased child should be kept aside and other healthy children should not be allowed to use them.

Proper treatment should immediately be started on the appearance of the first symptom because at later stages the cure becomes difficult. Accordingly to some medical doctors X-ray is its effective treatment. The effect of the X-ray is that all the hairs fall down and the germs are destroyed when the new hairs grow.

Leg and Thigh Ringworm—This kind of ringworm generally occurs in toes, between the fingers and in the joint of the thigh. This is also a contagious disease. It is, therefore, not desirable to use the clothes of the person suffering from it. Cotton socks prove beneficial in this disease.

Sulphur ointment should be used in the affected part and the other bodily parts should be kept clean. The disease is soon cured by applying ointment and keeping the various parts clean.

Chin Ringworm—This disease attackes the roots of the hair in chin. There is inflammation in the affected part and the hairs fall down. The treatment of this kind of ringworm is the same which is prescribed for the skull ringworm. The same precautions and care should be taken in this case also.

Alupicia or Baldness—This disease affects the hair of head and they fall down. Some people wrongly consider it a kind of ringworm. This disease is caused by some defects in the nerves. The hair on the head fall and the affected portion becomes glossy and smooth.

This is not a contagious disease. It is 'the opinion of some persons that artificail sunlight proves helpful in the disease.

Pediculosis—The head and sometimes the entire body is filled with louses. It is because of the uncleanliness that louses are born. A louse has six feet. The skin of this insect is thick and its claws strong. Louses live in the roots of hairs and thrive on blood. Blood is their only diet. The grown up louse daily lays eight to ten eggs. These eggs stick to hair and are yellowish-white in colour. The germs on the body are like the ones that are on the head. They live in the roots of hairs or in the corners of clothes. Their diet is human blood. They cause restlessness in the body and sometimes one becomes very much restless. Itching, insomnia, restlessness and irritation are some of the symptoms that indicate the presence of louses on the body. It becomes difficult for the child affected by louses to concentrate on studies. He is always found scratching. This presence of louses is harmful, because other infectious and contagious diseases also may attack. A person can become anaemic, too, and there is always a fear of being affected by typhoid fever.

Special attention should be paid towards keeping the hair clean in order to get rid of louses. Spray of D. D. T. powder in the hairs kills the louses. After the spray, hairs should be thoroughly cleaned so that louses are rooted out along with the dirt that gave birth to them. The solution of Bensoyl Bensonate is also helpful in removing louses. This solution, too, kills louses. Equal quantities of kerosene and coconut oil and hot vinegar applied to hairs kill louses as well. After applying this mixture, the head should be washed with soap and lethane oil applied on the whole body. The remaining louses are thus killed by this oil. Combing the hairs also removes the louses.

The clothes of the children having louses on their head and body should be boiled in hot water and thoroughly cleaned. They should be ironed when dry. This process kills the louses along with their eggs. Children should regularly be given bath.

Role of Lungs

Although the Lungs comes direct under the category of respiratory organs even then they may be included in the excretory organs because foul gases are expelled out of the body through lungs. This has already been stated in the chapter dealing with respiratory system.

The bowel is also included in the excretory organs of the body because undigested part of the food comes out through it. Besides, the activities of body cells create many useless and harmful things. These things go out of the body through the bowel.

Kidneys, skin, lungs and bowel are the main excretory organs of the body.

Kidneys—They are two—the right one and the left one. They lie on the back portion on both sides below the last ribs. They are bean like in shape. The ureter originates from the kidneys and urine brought by ureter is collected in the bladder. Urine contains 95.6% of water, 2% uria, 60% salt and 8% other chemicals.

Kidneys purify the blood and throw out the foul matter in the shape of urine.

Skin is of two categories : (1) epidermis and (2) dermis. Epidermis is the protector of the body. There are innumberable pores in it that expell the foul substance out of the body in the shape of sweat.

Dermis is the real skin which keeps the body temperature uniform throughout. In this there are also situated nerves, lymphatic capillaries, arteries and veins. There are two kinds of glands in it (1) Sebaceous glands and (2) the sweat glands. The first one, keeps the skin and hairs smooth and glossy. The cells of the other glands absorbs the foul matter of the body.

The following are the common skin diseases :

(1) Impetigo, (2) Itch, (3) Ringworm, (4) Baldness and Louses, (5) Louses on the head and body.

The bowel expells the undigested part of the food out of the body and the lungs throw out the foul air out of the body.

QUESTIONS

1. Explain through a sketch the various activities of the different parts of the skin.
2. Describe the various diseases related to skin.
3. Give a detailed account of the skin diseases that occur in children.
4. Explain the structure and function of kidneys.

17

The Diseases

Infectious diseases may be classified into two categories : (1) Simple infectious diseases and (2) Serious infectious diseases. Infectious diseases reach from one person to another in two ways—directly and indirectly.

The Roots

Very small germs like a curve snail which may be seen only through a powerful microscope, cause infectious diseases. These germs multiply in number and try to establish themselves in the body as soon as they enter it. There are many mediums through which they travel and enter the body.

Through Air—These germs come out of the body of a patient with the air exhaled through nose or mouth and get mixed in the outside air. They enter the body of a healthy person when he breathes fresh air. That is why such an infection is called droplet infection, because the germs are formed in the droplets or infected sprays from the nose or mouth of the person suffering from the disease. The infectious diseases that spread through air are small pox, measles, cough, influenza, tuberculosis etc.

Through Contact—These germs enter the body even of a healthy person when he comes in contact with a patient suffering from infectious diseases. Not only his direct contact causes infections but even a healthy person catches "infection when he comes in contact with the clothes, books, chairs, tables etc. of the diseased person.

Through Edibles—The germs also spread through food and water. When a healthy person takes food that had come in contact with a diseased person the germs enter his body and he falls ill. The germs of tuberculosis which are present in milk may cause tuberculosis.

Through Insects—Insects like mosquitoes, flies, bugs and lice also serve as germ carriers. When these insects suck the blood of a patient, the germs stick to their trunks or stings and when the same insect bites a healthy person the germs are left in his body. Mosquito bites causes the dreaded diseases of malaria. Flies are the repository of diseases. They cause many serious diseases.

Through Skin—Skin prevents the growth of germs but rubbing of skin causes germs to enter through it. Germs of Fetanus and Anthrax reach the body in this manner.

Through Genital Organs—Dangerous diseases like syphlis and gonorrhoea reach from one person to another through intercourse when penis contacts vagina.

Through Carrier—The infection spreads through a certain type of persons who although possess infectious germs in the body, remain healthy. The symptoms of diseases do not appear in such persons but when they come in contact with other persons, they (the other persons) catch infection. Such persons are called disease carriers. Blood dysentery, typhoid, diptheria etc., are diseases that spread through persons who are disease carriers.

Factors at Work

(1) Each infectious disease has a fixed time limit during which the man remains ill.

(2) It spreads from one persons to another.

(3) A person suffers only once from one type of infectious disease, because once he is attacked, he becomes immune from it. Influenza and diptheria are exceptions to this general rule.

(4) Each infectious disease is caused by a different kind of germs. For example, plague is caused by plague bacillus, measles by measles virus and so on. These germs multiply in number as soon as they enter the body and produce poison. The poison produced by one particular type of germ differs from that produced by another.

(5) The first stage of an infectious disease is called incubation period. During this period neither the symptoms appear nor can it be said that a particular person is affected by a particular disease. The ill effect of the disease is not visible till their number multiplies and they gain in strength. The incubation period of each infectious disease differs, but it is fixed in each case. After the incubation period comes the onset period during which the symptoms of disease appear.

Indications

(1) First of all, a person's temperature rises which produces poison in the body. Consequently, the heat producing and heat discharging arrangements in the body become inactive.

(2) The man feels cold even in high temperature and his entire body shivers.

(3) Small red rashes appear over the body which indicate the functional inactivity of the skin.

(4) Indisposition, headache, throat troubles in children are also indications of infectious diseases.

The Precautions

(1) For preventing the outbreak of infectious diseases a physician should be infromed first of all so that he may make efforts to check the outbreak of the disease.

(2) The victim should be isolated from healthy persons in the house.

(3) As a preventive measure, persons should get themselves inoculated or vaccinated. This may prevent the outbreak of disease.

(4) At the slightest suspicion of catching infection, the man should be isolated during incubation period and symptoms should be carefully observed. During this period either symptoms will appear or the disease will end.

(5) The things used by the patient should be throughly disinfected so that the germs may be completely destroyed.

Measles. Measles is a very common infectious disease. Its consequences are grave. Generally, small children fall victims to this disease. If careful and proper treatment is not given, many serious complications arise and sometimes the patient dies. The incubation period in this disease is of a week's duration.

Symptoms—The patient first of all complains about cold and headache. Then the temperature arises high along with cough and sneezing. Water flows from eyes and nose. The correct diagnosis is possible only when small rashes appear over the body. The coarse blotchy rashes are visible on or after the fourth day. These small rashes are first of all visible on the forehead, temple and behind the ear. In the early stage these are of dusky red colour. These remain prominent for two days then start drying. The fever, too, shows a downward trend. Within eight or ten days, they dry up complety and the patient recovers.

Treatment—In the absence of careful treatment, the disease takes a serious turn. The patient should always be saved from catching cold because slightest cold may cause bronchitis and pneumonia.

The incubation period of measles is very dangerous because infection generally spreads during this period. If any symptoms of the disease are observed in a fluid in the school, he should immediately be sent home. The child who had an attack of measles should not be permitted to attend school for at least three weeks.

This disease is not dangerous like measles. The germs in this disease affect the gland below the ear as a result of which it swells. Sometimes, the glands at the angles of the jaws in front of the ears are also affected. This causes swelling and difficulty arises in taking food.

The incubation period of this disease lasts from two to four weeks. The onset of the disease produces pain at the end of the lower jaw below the ear. Besides, there is stiffness and tenderness at the affected spot. Gradually, it spreads upto the neck which makes it difficult to open the mouth and eat anything. The swelling, pain and stiffness, generally subside in a week or two.

The germs of the disease are found in the sputum, saliva and the air exhaled by the patient. The disease spreads when other persons come near the patient or through sputum. The effect of the disease lasts for four weeks.

The child suffering from this-disease should be kept warm in the bed and light food should be given to him till the swelling completely subsides. He should be isolated in order that other persons may not catch infection.

The Complaints

Whooping Cough. This disease spreads from one person to another through a special type of germ that travels in air. This infectious disease of the child is the most harmful one. Its incubation period lasts for 18 days.

In the beginning, the child is attacked with cold. Secretion comes out of his nose. He sneezes and water flows from his eyes. Besides, coughing starts at short intervals. Every attack of coughing lasts for many minutes and the face turns red during coughing. Vomiting generally follows every attack of cough. Whooping cough affects the lungs and there is always a possibility of defects arising in the lungs. This disease reduces the resisting power of lung's tissues. Consequntly, there is always a danger of the child falling victim to dreaded diseases like pneumonia, tuberculosis etc.

The children suffering from this disease should be kept in a warm place. He should be saved from dampness and humid atmosphere. Sufficient fresh air should be available to him. The food should be light and easily digestible.

Such children should be granted leave of absence from the school till they are completely free from the disease. Other children should not be allowed to come in their contact for at least six weeks.

Scarlet Fever. This disease is caused by a germ named streptococens scarlatinae which enters the body through tonsils. Generally, this disease attacks children in the age group of five to ten years. The incubation period in this disease lasts from two to eight days.

The patient feels shivering at the start of disease. He vomits and feels pain in the throat. The face turns red and he feels heat and roughness in the skin. Small rashes appear over the neck and chest. Later on, these small rashes appear on legs and stomach. These rashes appear like deep-red dots over a red skin. They disappear on the seventh day. The dry scabs start leaving the body on the sixth day and within two days the dry covers are completely removed.

The infection in such cases reaches from one person to another through the patient's sputum and ear and nose discharge. It also spreads through the utensils, clothes and books used by the patient.

The children who had an attack of the disease, should not be permitted to go to school till their skin becomes free of the traces of rashes.

Diptheria. The symptoms of this disease are very much similar to measles and scarlet fever, but it is not dangerous like any of them. Its incubation period is of about 19 days' duration. Small rashes appear in this disease as in scariet fever. But these begin to dry on the third day. The symptoms of cold and cough are not present. The lymphatic gland of the thigh generally becomes large and stiff. This is the difference between measles and scarlet fever on one hand, and German measles on the other. It is ascertained by this difference. There is a possibility of the glands being affected by tuberculosis due to this disease. The effect of German measles stays for seven days. The patient should be isolated from healthy persons even after a week of his being cured. The infection in this case spreads through germs in the sputum.

Children in the age group of two to five years generally suffer from this disease. It is a dangerous, fatal and highly infectious disease. Its incubation period lasts for three days.

Swelling in the throat, formation of a brownish-white membranes over the tonsils and throat tissues and the enlargement of neck glands are some of the main symptoms of this disease. Larynx is also affected and the membranes creates obstruction in respiration. Many parts of the body are paralysed. The heart muscles lose their power of functioning which may cause death.

The germs of diptheria spread in air when the patient speaks, coughs or sneezes. Eating in the same utensils used by the patient or coming in contact with the patient affects other healthy children. The germs also enter the body through milk. These germs affect the throat, larynx, windpipe and the nostrils.

For curing the disease, it is necessary to take the injection particularly prepared for it. It does not allow the disease to take a serious turn and the patient's muscles are saved from being paralysed.

As a safeguard against the disease, children should be examined on the basis of Shick test and resistance power against this disease should be developed in them.

Chicken Pox is a disease that generally attacks a large number of children. It is not very serious. Like small pox rashes also appear on the body in this disease. The incubation period lasts from 12 to 19 days while onset period is 21 days duration.

First of all rashes appear on the trunk and there is some light fever. In two days there appear ail over the body. These begin to dry after three or four days and scabs are formed over them. In few days, the scabs dry and start falling. The germs of this disease spread through the sputum or by contact with the patient. The germs are also found- in the scabs. The possibility of infection remains till the scabs dry and fall from the body.

As a precaution, the patient should be got examined through a physician so that the identity of the disease is established. There is always a chance of error in diagnosis by a layman as chicken pox and small pox differ little and misunderstanding may create a bad situation. The patient should be isolated for 21 days.

Other Diseases

This is a very dangerous and highly infectious disease. The incubation period in this case lasts for 14 days.

At the outset of the disease body shivers, vomiting starts, temperature rises high, face turns red and the patient feels pain in head and back. On the third day, red rashes appear over the forehead and wrists. Gradually, they appear over the entire body. The rashes are blister-like and are full of liquid.

The small pox germs spread through the exhaled air and the secretion from nose and mouth of the patient. The scabs from the skin and patient's contact with others also contribute to the spread of the disease. The possibility of infection remains for a month and a half.

As a safeguard against this disease, small pox vaccination should always be taken. If small pox appears even after the person has been vaccinated, the disease will not be so serious. At the slightest suspicion of the disease, the child should immediately be isolated. Other children of the family, besides the patient, should also not be allowed to go to school.

Definite causes responsible for the outbreak of influenza have not yet been established. Many germs cause this disease. The incubation period of this disease is of some hours' duration. Sometimes, the incubation period lasts for some days as well.

The symptoms of the disease are rise in temperature, headache, pain in limbs, shivering due to cold, watery discharge from eyes and nose and sneezing. The attack is sudden and the symptoms immediately appear.

This infectious disease spreads through the patient's exhaled air, cough, mouth and nose discharge. The germs enter the body of a healthy person through his eyes, nose and mouth.

As a precautionary measure, children suffering from cold should be given leave from the school and the school, too, should be closed for some days so that the outbreak may not take the form of an epidemic. In ordinary cases, children having an attack of influenza should not be allowed to go to school for a period of ten days. In extraordinary cases, they should be given 21 days' leave from the school.

Cleaning the nose and throat with common salt solution is helpful. The patient should be given complete rest after the temperature comes to normal. He should also be saved from cold, otherwise he is likely to catch bronchitis and pneumonia.

The nervous system is particularly affected by this disease. This infection spreads through a poisonous germ. Its incubation period lasts from 2 days to 14 days.

The child suffering from this disease remains lethargic and gradually this lethargy turns into unconsciousness. At the onset of the diseases, inflammation is caused in the throat, eyes feel a burning sensation and the eyesight is affected. Difficulty is experienced in speaking. There is headache and sometimes there is an attack of paralysis on the tongue which may become very serious. The brain is dearranged and the nature of the person is affected. He changes all of a sudden.

Contact with the patient or the germ carrier causes the germs to enter the body of a healthy person through eyes, ear, nose or throat and so he falls ill.

As a safeguard against the spreading of diseases, the patient should be isolated. These children who had come is contact with the patient, should not be allowed to go to school for a period of at least 21 days.

Children between one and five years of age fall prey to this disease. In this disease a particular type of germ affects the grey maueron the chest and waist region as a result of which some of the nerve centres are destroyed, and the connected muscles are paralysed. The incubation period of this disease lasts for ten days.

The patient suffers from cold at the onset of the disease. Inflammation is caused in the throat, temperature rises and the patient experiences a peculiar type of restlessness. The muscles become inactive and this stage remains for some time, but if the effect of disease becomes permanent, the patient's limbs become deformed for the rest of the life.

The infection spreads through the urine, stool, throat and nose secretion and the sputum of the patient. The precaution to be taken for checking the infection of concephalitis lethargica should also be taken in this disease.

The brain and the spinal membranes of the children suffering from this disease become affected. Generally, children below five years of age fall victims to this disease. There is headache and high fever at the onset of the disease. The entire body feels stiffness. The brain also becomes senseless as a result of which there is a possibility of delirium. Rashes appear over the body. Therefore, it is also called spotted fever. Many physical defromities are left behind when the disease subsides. There is a possibility of the mind being affected as a result of these deformities. It takes at least two week's time for the patient to recover completely.

The infection spreads when the patient speaks, exhales air or blows his nose. The germs of this disease remain present in the sputum and in the nasal discharge of the patient. It also spreads through carriers.

The patient in the disease should be isolated. Fresh air and sufficient rest are required for the recovery of the patient.

Infectious diseases are of two categories:

(1) Simple infectious diseases and (2) Serious infectious disease. These spread through contact, air, edibles, germs, skin and genital organs. These disease have a fixed duration and are caused by different germs. The incubation period differs in each disease.

At the onset of the disease, temperature rises, red rashes appear over the skin and headache is felt by the patient. The germs should be completely destroyed as a measure of safeguard against them.

Amongst the infectious diseases measles, mumps, whooping cough, scarlet fever, German measles, diptheria, chicken pox, small pox, influenza, tuberculosis, infantile paralysis and meningitis are worth-mentioning.

QUESTIONS

1. How do the infectious diseases spread ? What precautions should be taken as a safeguard against them ?
2. Give a detailed account of the symptoms of infectious diseases.
3. Write brief notes on the following diseases:

   Measles, Smallpox, Whooping Cough, Diptheria.
4. How does influenza spread ? What are its symptoms ? What precautionary measures should be taken as a safeguard against this disease?

18

Treatment Facilities

We have already discussed the problem of school health education programme. But in the present chapter some other related matter in the same context and also about the duties of the government medical doctor are being discussed.

Medical examination of students in school is of great importance, because it may reveal the various types of students having some ailments which need immediate care and treatment. In this examination it may be found out that there are several students suffering from some kind of disease pertaining to ears, teeth, eyes, spinal-cord, nose, skin and other ailments which play a vital role not only in their physical and mental well being but they also in turn affect their studies. Several children are having some types of the physical difficulties. But the parents are prone to ignore them till they assume serious shapes. In our country the school does not at all care about the physical fitness of its students. Whether the school happens to be big or small, it is better if each child is medically examined each year at least once, if not more if need be. It will be excellent if some dispensaries are organised only for looking after the common ailments of school children in simple cases. These dispensaries may be set up on a co-operative basis with the government assistance and nominal donations from willing parents in specific areas. Thus there may be a number of such dispensaries, in an area depending upon its size.

Doctors' Responsibility

For obvious reasons, the school doctor cannot take up serious cases. In fact, his main function should be limited to casual examination of each child at least once a year on an appointed day and specific time. The main duty of the school doctor should be limited to point out the specific trouble, if there is any in case of some child. On the advice of the doctor the parents will become careful for doing the needful by consulting some specialist of the disease concerned. Some students may have some problems about their teeth, some about their eyes or ears or some other difficults. The school doctor will make his report in a specially prepared booklet. On the basis of this report parents or guardians will consult a specialist as advised. For obvious reasons, the school doctor cannot suggest any treatment. He has just to suggest the general nature of the trouble in some specific parts of the body, namely, ears, eyes, teeth, throat or any other trouble that is likely to hamper with the normal growth of children. It will be better if different types of medical doctors are invited at different times during a year. Specialists of ear, nose, throat and eyes may be invited at times at least once a year to examine some particular students suffering from some specific troubles. The advice of such a specialist will be of great help in the maintenance of the health of school children.

At the time of visit of a doctor there should be a band of other workers, in order to assist him. Among these workers, some teachers may be requested to help and the services of some trained nurses may also be hired for the appointed hour.

Inspection by the medical doctor is quite helpful to the Public Health Department. The doctor may advise the health department regarding the steps to be taken for the proper verification in the school. It may point out about the measures to be adopted for adequate sunlight and fresh air necessary for school children. In some of our densely populated cities the school buildings have been so constructed as to deprive the children, teachers and others concerned of fresh air and adequate sunlight. In this connection the doctor may suggest some suitable manners to be adopted for minimising the inadequacies.

Through the medical examination of children the doctor may detect cases of certain infectious diseases to be reported to the parents, who in their turn, will do the needful for the care of their wards. If the schools happen to have some clinics for sick children suffering from infectious disease then they (children) may be admitted there for some time. Through this measure the other children will be saved from the infectious diseases. Needless to mention that medical examination in a school is to educate the parents also in some way because many of them happen to be quite ignorant about many common ailments which impair the health of their children.

The school authorities should be very careful about the general cleanliness in the school and its immediate surroundings at the time of medical inspection. If need be, the help of the Health Department of concerned government may also be sought. It is always better, if in case of very young children within 12 or 13 years of age, the medical examination is done in the presence of their parents (either the father or the mother). This measure is necessary because the father or the mother will be better able to explain the specific difficulties that are troubling the child. In case of older children of high school and intermediate classes the presence of parents may not be very necessary.

In the school medical examination primarily the following items are specially measured:

1. Height.

2. Weight.

3. Measurement of the chest and waist.

Along with the above, it should be clearly ascertained if the general development of the child is going on well or not. In this connection the child's vision and hearing power should also be carefully examined. In this relation ear, nose and throat should be carefully examined. If any ailment in these organs of the body are perceptible the same should be specifically noted down. These points about various children should be carefully examined by class teacher and the typical cases needed for special treatment showed be brought to the notice of parents or guardian for required treatment by some specialist.

Doctor in School

1. On request, from the head of a school, the medical doctor should examine the concerned children.
2. Those children should be re-examined who need some special type of medical treatment.
3. Those children should be particularly examined who have been sent by some parents for specific medical advice.
4. The medical doctor should make a list of those students who need some special type of food or particular nourishment.
5. Without any hesitation, the medical doctor should suggest for the segregetion of some children who happen to be suffering from some infectious diseases.
6. The doctor may choose to frankly advise the head of the institution or parents to transfer the child to some other school where he or she can be better educated because of his/her some mental or physical inadequacies.
7. The doctor should carefully inspect the work of the school nurse if, there is some one appointed for infant classes.
8. With the co-operation of the head of the institution it is also the duty of the doctor to maintain a full medical report of each child of the school. Of course, the report will be kept in the school, but on each one of the same, the signature of the doctor must be there.
9. The school nurse of infant classes is supposed to maintain a complete record of the previous illness, if any, of each child and to explain the same to the doctor at the time of his visit.

10. The school nurse meant for infant classes should make occasional visits to the children houses and in order to find out from their parents about their physical welfare.

Teachers' Role

The co-operation of some teachers may be very helpful in selecting those types of students who need some specific medical examination. In this way he will be able to present such students before the doctor for advice when he comes to visit the school. The teachers may also be of great help in taking measuıement of height, and weight and also tell about those students who should be segregated for some time because of certain temporary infectious diseases.

The Personnel

1. This officer is at the head of the Department which is responsible for prevention and cure of infectious and other simple diseases of the common people. He is supported to be a friend of each at an hour. This government officer inspite of being a medical man is supposed to work as a social worker as well. His main work is supposed to be devoted to public service, wherever it is need in their specified area. In this manner he tries to offer as good a help as possible to the affected people within his zone.
2. The government medical officer is fully responsible to see that the assistants under his charge do not show any slackness in rendering the needed medical services within their jurisdiction. The medical officer has to see that the infectious disease in his area is not spread. He has to adopt measures for its immediate prevention and render immediate help to those who are actually affected. Malaria, and chicken-pox section and maternity department should be separately located in the building, if a separate building is not available. A lady doctor should take care of the maternity centre with the help of some nurses.

3. The chief government officer has to see that all the persons under his charge fulfil their duties sincerely to the satisfaction of all concerned:
4. On the basis of past experiences, the previous carelessness showed should be particularly avoided and wherever required the necessary injection and inoculation should be carefully given in a scientific manner.
5. The dispensaries established for the immediate help of some patients and new entrants should be carefully seen and any difficulty with regard to any function should be broughtout to the notice of the Chief Medical Officer for removal.
6. The Chief Medical Officer must see himself without any pre-information given to him, that all the necessary medicines and the implements are ready at hand in order to meet any emergency.
7. The Chief Government Officer is also chiefly responsible for the medical check up of each student brought to him for the purpose.
8. He should carefully examine the admitted students and the particular medicines needed for them must be immediately procured.
9. The Chief Medical Government Officer should encourage the concerned public of the immediate vicinity regarding the measures to be adopted at the time of epidemics.
10. The Chief Medical Officer should assign various duties to the concerned workers at least a week in advacne, but for some emergency case a band of some workers should be ever-ready to render any prompt service wherever necessary.
11. The Chief Medical Officer has to see that the medical store is carefully maintained in a systematic order and no emergency medicine necessary for injection and inoculation are lacking.

12. The nurses employed at the various health centres within the jurisdiction of the Medical Officer must be required to be alert for giving any needed service at the request of the Chief or any medical assistant concerned.
13. Daily supervision of the zone under him (the doctor), should be made in order to examine the working of the same.

The medical social workers also, like the general Health Officer, has some chief duties. He is to assist the health officer according to his insturction. Besides he also looks after some of the personal and social problems of certain patients and brings the same to the notice of the Chief Medical Officer for help.

1. The basic health worker applies medicines and helps to make bandages on the specific affected parts of the patients in the health centre.
2. The basic health worker has to tour around in his area in order to find out if there is any danger of spread of any epidemic.
3. The basic health worker has to maintain a note-book for each village under his care for entering any detail about any person who needs some medical attention. At the appointed hour he should bring such persons to the health centre for the necessary medical assistance.

Sanitation

1. The sanitary inspector helps the chief medical officer in ascertaining any difficulty pertaining to the sanitation of the area under his jurisdiction,
2. The sanitary worker is also supposed to prepare a programme for family hygiene and also in relation to the problem of population control.

Female Functionary

1. The lady health worker should try to inform each family within her area for the measure that should be taken for the sanitation of the village surroundings.

2. She may also encourage the women folk of her area for adopting suitable measures for control of the expanding family.
3. The lady of the health centre will work under the control of the chief medical officer.
4. She will maintain a record of the various babies born on particular days and she will also report about their general welfare.
5. She has to send some particular patients to the lady doctor present in the centre for giving the necessary treatment.
6. Lady of the health centre is chiefly responsible for general cleanliness of the surrounding of the clinic and any specific sanitary problem must be immediately attended to by her assistants.
7. After the delivery of a child, the lady of the health centre is usually expected to visit the house of the nursing mother and give her the needed assistance from time to time.

First Aid

Sometimes, accidents like fracture of bones, injuries, burn, sprain etc., occur in schools while the students are playing, doing wood-work, taking exercises or making experiments in laboratory. The teacher should possess knowledge of these every-day accidents and render immediate first aid relief. The teacher should not only have knowledge of the above but should be efficient in the job of rendering first aid. Students involved in serious accidents should be sent to some medical doctor for proper treatment.

Fracture of Bone

The causes of bone fractures of children may be many. Fracture along with the external wound is called compound fracture but when there is no external wound, the condition is called simple fracture. Sometimes, complications arise when the simple fracture is neglected and proper treatment is not provided. Occasionally, bone fracture happens along with the internal injury. This condition is called complicated fracture. The bones of children are soft as compared to an adult's bone and easily bend aside. This condition is called green-stick fracture. The bone in this type of fracture bends like a green twig of a tree. Serious injury sometimes breaks the bone in many parts and splinters scatter. This kind of bone fracture is called complex fracture..

Symptoms—During fracture, the affected part gets swollen, severe pain is felt in moving the affected part, chattering sound is produced by the friction of one bone part against the other, and the larger bones become shorter.

Treatment

(1) Great care has to be taken in the treatment of fractures so that the trouble may not increase.

(2) Fracture should be treated as far as possible on the spot. The situation may worsen if the patieni is removed from one place to another, because it involves the movement of the patient.

(3) The patient should not be allowed to move unless the broken bone has been set. If this care is not taken, complications may arise later.

(4) If during the fracture bleeding also starts, attempts should be made first to stop the bleeding. In an extraordinary situation, the wound should be cleaned with water and germicidal soap and bandage with soft pad be tied over it.

(5) For setting the broken bones and bringing them in the normal position, splinters and bandages should be used. The splinter should be tied by bandages by applying reef-knots so that the broken bones may not be displaced.

(6) The patient should be kept warm in order to ward off the effect of shock.

(7) The injured person should be laid on a stretcher and carried to the doctor for further treatment and advice.

Every joint remains in its position as it is bound to ligament fibrous bonds. These joints' bonds sometimes either get broken or stretched during a sudden jerk. This condition is called sprain.

Symptoms

(1) The joints lose their power of movement.

(2) Inflammation appears on the affected part.

(3) Severe pain is experienced in that part.

(4) The colour of the skin changes.

Treatment

(1) The affected parts should be given complete rest and movements should be stopped for some days.

(2) The affected part should be thoroughly massaged with mustard oil.

(3) The affected part should be tightly bandaged and put in ice-water. Use of opium also gives relief.

(4) If the above treatments do not relieve pain the sprained part should be washed with hot water. This is likely to reduce the pain.

(5) The affected part should be tightly bandaged with a water-soaked bandage. This fully tightens the affected part. The affected part should not be used for work.

The displacement of a bone from its joint is called the dislocation of bone. Generally knee, elbow, shoulder, lower jaw or feet bones get dislocated.

Symptoms

(1) Dislocation of bone causes severe pain.

(2) The affected part gets swollen.

(3) The affected part loses its power of functioning.

(4) The part is deformed.

(5) The part becomes motionless.

Treatment

(1) This part should be tightened with a cold water-soaked bandage.

(2) If the cold water-soaked bandage does not relieve the pain, the affected part should be fomented

(3) If even the fomentation does not prove of any use in relieving the pain, a doctor should be consulted.

Cut and Bleeding

Injury to blood vessels causes bleeding. Before attemping to stop bleeding, it is necessary to know which kind of the blood vessel is bleeding, whether it is an artery, vein or capillary. A knowledge of various types of blood vessels helps in the treatment of stopping bleeding.

Symptoms of Capillary Bleeding—Blood flows slowly from a capillary, this is an ordinary bleeding.

Treatment—To stop the capillary bleeding, the affected part should be put into cold water or a water-soaked pad should be put on the bleeding spot and tied with a bandage. This should be dipped into cold water.

Symptoms of Venous Bleeding

(1) The bleeding part should be raised upwards and a pressure should be applied below.

(2) A tourniquet should be tied below the bleeding part.

(3) A water-soaked clean pad should be put on the affected part and a bandage tightened around it.

(4) The injured hand or leg should be suspended downwards.

Symptoms of Arterial Bleeding—

(1) The blood spurts out like the beating of heart.

(2) It is deep-red.

(3) It is very bright too.

(4) This blood always flow in the opposite direction of the heart. If the bigger artery of hand or feet is cut, the man dies in a minute and a half.

Treatment—Bleeding from the artery is a very serious matter. Immediate efforts should be made to stop it. It is not an ordinary matter to stop arterial bleeding. For stopping the bleeding, pressure through a cloth should be applied over the wound. Mostly the bleeding stops with this action.

If the bleeding does not stop by the above treatment, the thumb pressure should be applied at the nearest pressure point about the heart. There are 13 such pressure points in the body. This has earlier been discussed in the preceding pages.

Besides, the bleeding may also be stopped by applying tourniquets. Raising the bleeding part upwards also does good because much of the blood goes back and only a little comes out. Doctor's consulation is very necessary in this case, because applying pressure for a long period affects adversely the nerves. A stimulating beverage should be given to the injured person only after the bleeding stops.

Nose Bleeding—An injury caused to the nose or the appearance or a boil causes rupture of blood capillaries of the nose. Consequently, bleeding starts. Sometimes, strong sneeze also injures the blood capillaries with the result that bleeding starts.

Treatment—Children bleeding from the nose should be made to sit on a chair with head hanging backward. They should sit in the direction of blowing air. Raising of both hands above the head also helps. By so doing, the flow of blood towards head slows down. The clothes on the neck should be loosened, and a cold water-soaked pad of clean cloth should be placed behind the neck or on the nose bone. The feet of the patient should be placed in hot water. He should neither be allowed to sneeze nor breathe through mouth. Alum solution in cold water may also be used. If these treatments fail, a doctor should immediately be consulted and treatment should be given accordingly.

Wounds are caused when body nerves break down and cause bleeding. Disease spreading germs and other poisonous matters enter the body through wounds.

Treatment—The first aid rendered to a wound has two objects : Stoppage of bleeding, and Stopping the poisonous matter to enter the body.

(1) The treatment for stopping bleeding as described above, should be attempted for stopping the flow of blood from a wound.

(2) The coagulated blood on the wound should not be disturbed as a precaution against contagion.

(3) The wound should be cleaned with lukewarm water in order to remove the dirt etc. The wound should then be allowed to dry for some time. When it dries, a gauze dipped in tincture iodine or spirit should be placed on the wound.

(4) A bandage should be tightened over the wound when a gauze dipped in tincture iodine or spirit has been placed over it after it has been cleaned with clean and warm water. This protects the wound for germs. A gauze or a pad is most suitable for this purpose.

An injury, pressure or a fall causes the blood vessels beneath the skin to break as the result of which the injured part turns blue.

Symptoms—Pain is felt in the spot that has turned blue. Its colour also changes and it swells.

Treatment—

(1) A cloth soaked in ice cold water applied to the injured place gives relief.

(2) Fomentation is also beneficial.

(3) The injured part should be given sufficient rest.

Wounds are sometimes caused through an insect sting or bite. Although only a little bleeding takes place, but there is a likelihood of poison spreading in the body.

Treatment—

(1) Sometimes, the sting is left at the place where the insect strikes. The sting should be taken out with the help of a forcep or a disinfected needle and blood allowed to flow for sometime. Later on, the wound should be cleaned with clean warm water and soap and mercury iodine applied over it.

(2) Applying ammonia, spirit or a strong solution of soda bi-carbonate at the affected part also reduces pain.

A man turns unconscious due to the following reasons:

(1) Effect of some poison,

(2) Sun-stroke or heat-stroke,

(3) Too much bleeding from the head,

(4) Serious mental shock due to injury on head,

(5) Hun and

(6) Hysteria, epilepsy of unconsciousness caused by profuse bleeding.

Intake of Poison

Although there exist a number of poisonous matters in the world, but from the first aid point of view these are divided into two categories: In one category fall those which burn the body tissues and are called corrosive poisons. The second category is of those poisons that do not burn the tissues. These are called non-corrosive poisons.

In both the cases of poisoning a physicain should immediately be contacted and should be informed of the category of poison. The patient should not be allowed to sleep. Different poisons need different treatment.

Non-corrosive Poisons—These poisons do not burn the lips or mouth or any other part of the body. The patient should, therefore, be made to vomit in these poisoning cases. The following methods should be used for vomiting:

(1) Two spoonful of salt mixed in a glass of cold water taken by the patient enables him to vomit.

(2) A spoonful of powdered mustard seeds mixed in a glass of water taken by the patient also enable him to vomit.

(3) The above described two processes should be repeated every five minutes till vomiting starts.

(4) Vomiting also starts when fingers are put into throat.

(5) The vomited substance should be kept for chemical examination.

(6) A drink having cooling effect should be given to the patient after vomiting.

Heat Assaults

During the summer season sun-stroke or heat-stroke is caused due to exposure in bright sunshine. This produces restlessness, headache and giddiness. The person feels like vomiting and his temperature rises high. His respiration increases and he feels thirst. His face turns red and sometimes he becomes unconscious.

Treatment—The first treatment of such a person suffering from sun-stroke is to reduce the temperature. His clothes should, therefore, be loosened and he should be kept in a cool place. His head and neck should be washed with cold water and ice be placed over his head and neck. This gives sufficient relief to the victim. The patient should be given cold water to drink. If all this treatment does not reduce his suffering, sandal paste be applied on his body. If even this fails to give relief he should be taken to a physician for proper treatment.

Sometimes foreign matters enter into children's ear, nose or throat which, though do not give much trouble at the time, should immediately be taken out. Generally, people try to take them out with the help of crude instruments by their own hands which are not used for doing such delicate jobs. The results sometimes are very serious. This should never be done under any circumstances, instead a physician should be consulted.

Small insects, dust particles or thin blades of grass sometimes fall in the eyes while the child is playing, walking or running. This is very painful. Efforts should immediately be made to remove them.

The victim should repeatedly open and close his eyes in clean water. Washing the eye with water or boric solution is also helpful. Blowing the air from mouth to the eye also proves useful and relieves the pain. If the foreign matter is in the upper lid, the upper eyelid should be stretched over the lower one. This will enable the eyelashes of the lower lid to remove that substance. This process should continue till the matter is removed.

Sometimes flies, small seeds, insects or blades of grass, etc. enter the ear which besides being painful also produces deafness. This causes swelling in the ear. There is always a fear of this swelling reaching the brain as well.

In this condition putting some oil in the ear is very helpful. The matter in the ear leaves its place and floats on the oil thus coming out of the ear. If the oil treatment fails, the child should be taken to an ear specialist.

Sometimes things like-beans, peas and grass blades enter the nose of children and create trouble. In such conditions, the child should be made to smell things that produce sneezing. The nostril that is inhaling air should be closed and efforts should be made to sneeze through the blocked nostril. The child at this time should be advised to breathe through mouth. If these methods fail to remove the matter from the nose, a doctor should be approached.

An obstruction created into the throat by foreign matter also creates a troublesome situation. The face turns bluish, throat is choked, eyes appear to be coming out ef their sockets and the victim turns senseless. In this conditon efforts should be made to remove the obstruction by putting the finger in the throat. This could cause vomiting and the obstructing matter would come out. If this fails, the back in between the shoulders should be patted, forcefully. If even this method fails to produce the desire effect, artificial respiration should be resorted to. A physician should immediately be called and the victim should be made to stand on his head by raising his legs towards the sky. There is a possibility of achieving success by so doing.

One becomes unconscious when he drowns in water, because the water enters the windpipe creating obstruction in his respiration. He feels cold. In this condition efforts should be made to bring him to senses. Immediate help of a doctor should be sought. All the tight-fitting clothes of the drowned man should be loosened carefully. His legs should be raised upwards for

taking out the water from his body. Artificial respiration should be continued till he begins to breathe air of his own accord. When the victim regains breathing he should be covered with blanket and hot-water-rubber bottles be paced by his sides. If he is able to drink, hot drinks like tea or coffee should be given to him.

Fire Assaults

Burns are caused when one's skin comes in contact with fire, electric current, hot metal or acid. When the skin is burnt by a-liquid or steam, it is called scalds.

Symptoms—The skin turns red when it burns or scalds. There is unbearable pain and the clothes stick to the "burnt spot. The burning sensation caused by the formation of blisters is extremely painful. Sometimes, besides the skin, the flesh below it, too, is burnt.

Severe burning produces shock as the result of which one may die. His face turns yellow, he feels cold, his respiration and heart-beatings slow down due to shock.

Treatment—

1. The clothes from the burnt spot should be removed carefully. The cloth should be cut if it sticks to the wound. Some kind of oil should be applied over the burnt spot.
2. A solution containing a spoon of soda bi-carbonate in about a pound of water should be applied on burnt places with the help of cotton or piece of clean cloth.
3. The burnt spot should be put in water having body temperature.

4. Blisters should not be opened, because by so doing there is a possibility of catching contagion.
5. Tannic acid jelly ointment should be applied over the wound. It produces cooling effect and cures the destroyed tissues, lodex or Repento ointment, too, is useful.
6. After applying these ointments, clean cotton should be placed over the wounds and it should be bandaged.
7. Efforts should be made to overcome the shock. The patient should be kept warm by covering him with blankets and by keeping hot-water bottle besides him. He should be given hot milk, tea, coffee of half a glass of clean water with a spoon of ammonium carbonate or the solution of vanishing salt.
8. Solution of soda bi-carbonate applied over the wounds through a gauze also relieves pain in the case of acid burns.
9. Vinegar of lemon juice solution made in water proves beneficial in the case of burns caused by alkalines.
10. The person should immediately lie down on the floor when the clothes catch fire and he should continue to roll till the fire is extinguished completely. The fire also extinguishes if the victim is covered by a piece of blanket.

Fracture are of four categories : (1) Simple fracture, (2) Compound fracture, (3) Complicated fracture and (4) Green-stick fracture. Besides, dislocation of bones and sprains are also related to it.

Bleeding can be divided into three categories : (1) Cutting of limb or any body part, (2) Bruises and (3) Insect sting or bite.

Unconsciousness is caused by the following factors:

(1) Poison, (2) Sun-stroke or heat stroke, (3) Bleeding from head, (4) Injury or concussion, (5) Shock and (6) Hysteria, epilepsy or unconsciousness from blood.

Care should be taken when foreign matter enters eye, ear, nose, throat or stomach and also during burns or scalds.

QUESTIONS

1. Describe the main duties of the Medical Doctor in the school medical examination.
2. What are the duites of the government medical centre?
3. What are the different kinds of bone fractures ? What are their symptoms and how should they be treated ?
4. Give a brief account of bleeding.
5. What causes unconsciousness ? How is it removed ?
6. What should be done when foreign matter enters eyes, ears, nose, throat and stomach ?
7. What kind of treatment should be made when a child gets burns and scalds ?

19

Eating Stuff

Nutritive and balanced diet provides body with the required energy for doing every-day work. The food also makes good the energy lost in various activities. Besides, the responsibility of keeping the body temperature is that of the food. It is the food that helps the body to grow.

The quality and quantity of food taken by persons of different ages differ. That which is beneficial for children may prove harmful to adults. The variety of food needed for persons engaged in manual work differs from those doing mental work. Tissues in body continue to break during activities. The process through which tissues are formed is known as anabolism, while the process through which these are destroyed is called katabolism. The formation and destruction of tissues happen simuiata-neously. So the chemical reaction of the combined anabolism and katabolism is called metabolism. All the chemical reactions in the body produce heat.

Items for Diet

Different kinds of chemical substances are found in food. These are as follows:

Protein (vegatarian and non-vegetarian) : Tissues and muscles are produced by protein.

Protien

The substance formed by the combination of carbon, hydrogen, oxygen, nitrogen, sulphur and phosphorous is called protein. Protein is found in the shape of albumin in the egg, as myosin in meat, as casein in milk, as glutenin in wheat and as leguminin in various pulses and leafy vegetables. Ordinarily, the protein found in the vegetarian edibles as inferior to that found in non-vegetarian edibles or in other words protein derived from vegetation is inferior to that received from animals. The cells of animals are very much similar to those found in man, therefore, the protein derived from them is more useful. This is the reason why protein received from animals is comparatively superior.

Utility of Protein—(1) The protein helps the formation of new tissues replacing those which are destroyed during exertion. It produces protoplasm.

Because of this, protein is also called tissue producer. Protein is absolutely necessary for life. The growth of body is retarded in its absence and many diseases set in.

(2) When excessive protein is formed in the body, it is accumulated in the form of fat and produces heat and energy in the absence of carbohydrate.

(3) Protein produces in the body power to resist diseases.

(4) It helps in the production of digestive juices. It also helps the ductless glands to produce juices.

Carbohydrate. It combines in itself starch and sugar. Chemicals like carbon, hydrogen and oxygen are also found in it. This is necessary for the formation of fat.

Starch is found in potatoes, rice, wheat, corn, millet, sago, etc. Sugar is found in sugar-canes, beet and different fruits. Lactose is found in milk. Starch is also found in some non-vegetarian diets, but the vegetarian diet is its main source.

Utility—This is the main source of producing heat and energy. Muscles need it when a man puts in hard physical labour. The digestive system changes it into glucose which mixes with blood and reaches muscles and proves a very useful diet for them. The glucose in excess of body requirement collects in the liver in the shape of glycogen and when required again turns into glucose and supplies heat and energy to the muscles.

Fats. Carbon, hydrogen and oxygen are found in fats like carbohydrates but the proportion of these chemicals differ in them. Mixture of fatty acids and glycerine also exists in fats. Soap and glycerine are produced by the action of alkalies on the fat. The fat is divided into very small particles. The first action is called saponification and the other is called emulsification.

Utility—This produces heat in the body and energy for muscles. It produces more heat and energy as compared to starch. Excessive fat in relation to body requirement is deposited below the skin in the body. Consequently, the body becomes healthy and the bones, joints and other body parts get protection against external injuries. Fat produces smoothness in the skin which minimises the loss of body albumin. The fat below the skin protects the body from outside heat and cold. Fat collects below the skin consequently the body becomes healthy, symmetrical and good looking. The bones, joints and other body parts become safe from external injuries. Fat also produces smoothness in the body which prevent the loss of albumin.

Fat is Derived-from Two Types of Diets : (1) Non-vegetarian and (2) Vegetarian. Both produce heat and energy in equal proportion. The fat produced by non-vegetarian food has vitamin 'A' and 'D' as well. Ordinarily, fat is found in butter, cheese, ghee, pig's fat, mustard, coconut and til oils.

Useful Things

Mineral salts have their value, for the health of the body. Calcium, iron, iodine, phosphate, sodium, chloride, magnesium, sulphur and copper are important amongst the mineral salts. These fill up the twentieth part of the body. These contribute towards the general development of body and activate the digestive juices. The nerves, muscles and blood receive strength from them. These help in keeping the acids and alkalines in proper proportion.

Calcium is Found in Good Quantity in Edibles—Like milk, cheese, yolk, orange, fish and the green vegetables. It is needed most in the formation of teeth and bones. Tooth decay is the result of calcium deficiency. The growth of children is retarded and bone diseases appear when there is calcium deficiency in them. It controls the action of heart, blood and nerves. The muscles lose their activeness during calcium deficiency in the body. Asthma and skin diseases appear and the nerves become excited in the absence of adequate quantity of calcium in the body. Vitamin 'D' is necessary for calcium.

Quantity of Calcium Daily Required

(1)	Infants and babies	(1 year to 9 years)	1.0 gm
(2)	Children	(10 years to 12 years)	1.2 gm
(3)	Girls	(13 years to 15 years)	1.3 gm
(4)	Boys	(13 years to 15 years)	1.4 gm
(5)	Adults	(above 16 years)	1.0 gm
(6)	Expectant mothers		1.5gm
(7)	Women during Lactation Period		2.5 gm

Iron. Iron in body is produced by edibles like meat, eggs, carrots and green and leafy vegetables. These are, therefore, useful during anaemia. Iron is the main part of haemoglobin. This gives strength to blood corpuscles in carrying oxygen to the body parts. Lack of iron in the body causes anaemia. It is also useful for bile.

Iodine. Iodine is found in healthy food and some vegetables. It is also found in fish liver oil, water in some places and edibles got from sea.

It is useful for thyroid glands. Its deficiency retards the growth of body causing a serious disease called goitre. The brain also is not fully developed in its absence. Iodine is a necessary constituent of medicines prescribed for goitre.

Phosphate. Phosphate is found in meat, eggs, dry fruits, liver, milk and cheese. It is necessary for the growth of teeth, bones and nervous system. It is also useful for blood. Its deficiency retards the development of the body and teeth and bones become weak.

Sodium Chloride. This special type of salt is found in meat and milk. It may be mixed in any food separately. It is particuilarly useful for health. It is present through out the body tissues and is the main source of the hydrochloric acid found in digestive juices.

Magnesium. Bones and teeth are formed by magnesium. It helps the carbohydrate to become useful for the body. Its deficiency -like the calcium deficiency causes contraction of the muscles, of hands and legs. It functions as a digestive juice and expels the foul matter of the body through urinary passage. Magnesium is found in meat and vegetables.

Sulphur. Sulphur is also an important object that is needed for keeping the body healthy. This is a necessary part of the body ceils. It helps (in the formation of brain, nails and hairs. Sulphur deficiency is a cause of falling hairs and nail decay. The hairs remain glossy as long as sulphur remains in good proportion in the body. It also helps in the digestion of food. It reaches the body in adequate quantity through eggs, beans, radish, spinach, pulse, cabbage etc.

Fibrous Edibles. Fibrous edibles are also necessary for our body. The muscles of intestines get some useful matter from the fibrous edibles which help in passing out stool because this matter helps in contraction and relaxation of muscles. These edibles keep the digestive system in order. Constipation is caused in the absence of fibrous edibles in food. This matter is found in green vegetables, fish, meat and beet roots in sufficient quantities.

Other Elements

All the knowledge about the vitamins has been gained in the beginning of the twentieth century. Before this century, people had no knowledge about vitamins. It was in the year 1881 when an Englishman named Hopkins and two Americans experimented on rats and found out that the rats could not survive even when fat, protein, mineral salts and carbohydrates were given to them in proper proportion and quantity. In the year 1912, some important matter was discovered without which life was not possible. This matter was 'Vitamin'. These vitamins are known as life-giving matter. So far only six main varieties of vitamins have been discovered. There are named as A, B, C, D, E, K. The vitamins may be divided into two categories: Water-soluble and Fat-soluble.

Vitamin B and C belong to the water-soluble category while vitamin A, D, C and K belong to the fat-soluble category. All of them are important from the health point of view. Each vitamin has a separate action on the body. These are differ from each other. The vitamins are found in all the edibles. These are destroyed when cooked or kept for a long time. The vitamins found in vegetables are affected by time, place and circumstances.

Utility —(1) They produce disease resistant and destroying capacity. (2) They help in the proper growth of body. (3) They facilitate the digestive and nervous actions. (4) They help in producing healthy babies. (5) They help in making the carbohydrates and mineral salts useful for body.

Water-Soluble Vitamins : Vitamin 'A'—It is a combination of hydrogen, oxygen, carbon and sulphur. It has ten different varieties and collectively it is known as vitamin complex. In these varieties, vitamin B1 and vitamin B2 are particularly useful for the human body. These are crystal-like and soluble. They continue to exist in heat but are destroyed in high temperature. These may exist in acids but are destroyed in alkalies. These varieties of vitamins are found in sufficient quantity in seeds, plants, the yolk of eggs, wheat, rice, many fruits, vegetables, beans, fresh peas and milk.

Vitamin B' after reaching the body gives the heart, liver, stomach, kidneys and both the intestines matter that is required for keeping them in a good state of health. Its deficiency thins the intestine membrane, consequently, it does not function smoothly. It causes indigestion, constipation and many other stomach ailments. The deficiency of vitamin B1 is a cause for the heart weakness, eccentricity, lack of concentration and headache. The dangerous disease of Beri-Beri is also caused by its deficiency. In this disease nerves get inflammation, muscles become useless and the hands are paralysed. The development of body is checked and it becomes weak. Heat is also affected. Abortion, bleeding, trembling of hands and feet, duodenal ulcers and inflammation etc. are also caused due to the deficiency of this vitamin. In its absence, the ends of lips turn white and crack. Ulcer on the tongue, inflammation of palate, and buccal mucous membrane appear. The skin becomes thick. Small boils appear on the body and sleep is seldon sound. Vitamin B burns the carbohydrates and protects a person from the diseases of nervous system and heart. It helps the body growth and increases the digestive power. It saves one from skin diseases and helps vitamin 'A'.

Vitamin 'B' is found in large quantities in yeast, pulse, rice, wheat brown, leafy vegetables like turnips, radish, dry frutis, linseed, cabbages, onions, carrots, eggs, etc. It is also found in potatoes, grapes, bananas, orange, papayas, water-melon, melon and meat but in small quantities. It is destroyed when cooked in open utensil for a long time. The food, therefore, should be cooked in a closed utensil on medium fire. The deficiency of vitamin B tells more adversely on persons who do not work hard. Hard working persons are less affected by its deficiency.

Vitamin B2 —It helps to maintain youth. Its deficiency makes one prematurely old, and causes the skin and membrane to become unhealthy and eyes and eyelids feel pain. This vitamin is destroyed by sun-light. It is aslo destroyed when cooked. Vitamin B2 is found in yeast, green vegetables, meat, kidneys, liver; cheese, and the albumin of the egg.

Vitamin B—It-is also called P.P. or Pallegra Preventing. It is found in each live cell. Its deficiency causes the diseases of pallegra. The tongue, mucous membrane of the mouth, gums and palate get inflammation in this disease. Sometimes, the patient becomes senseless, paralysed or insane. This vitamin is also found in edibles that are rich in vitamin B and B2.

Vitamin 'C'—This vitamin is also called anti-scorbutic vitamin because it protects a man against the disease of scurvy. This disease reduces the strength of blood vessels. Consequently, these burst and start bleeding. In this condition blood generally flows from teeth gums. The deficiency of this vitamin produces excitement, teeth defects, fatigue, gum defects and anaemia in children.

Vitamin 'C' is destroyed when food containing it is cooked in open utensils. It is better to cook food in a short time than prolonging the process of cooking. The best way to cook vegetables is to prepare them with the help of steam in a short time. This vitamin is also destroyed when soda biocarbonate is mixed in vegetables.

Lemons, grapes, tomatoes, apples, cabbages, sprouty pulses and turnips are rich in vitamin 'C',

Fat-soluble Vitamins: Vitamin 'A'—Vitamin) 'A' is not destroyed by long exposure to sun-light or cooking. It also does not lose its properties when kept in sealed tins. This is very important for our body. It particularly affects the eyes, lungs, intestines, skin and soft membranes in the body. It provides the body organs with the necessary diet. It increases appetite and helps our digestive system to function properly. It increases the vitality and builds resistance capacity against diseases.

The deficiency of vitamin 'A' causes bronchitis, cold, cough, eye diseases, deafness and intestinal diseases. Its prolonged deficiency retards the growth of our body, because new cells are-not formed. Inflammation of body parts appears due to anaemia. Secretion stops from nose, ears, mouth, stomach, etc., consequently, dryness appears in these body parts. This causes mucous membranes and the skin to crack. Its continued deficiency produces stones in the kidneys. Serious diseases like chronic, bronchitis, branchopneumonia, etc., are caused due to vitamin 'A' deficiency in the body.

Fish liver oils, green vegetables, grain sprouts and leaves, cabbages, betel leaves, leafy vegetables, butter, milk, eggs, carrots, ripe tomatoes, millet and linseeds are rich in vitamin 'A'.

Vitamin D—This vitamin is found through two processes:

(a) By consuming things which are rich in this vitamin and

(b) Through sun-light. The body receives vitamin 'D' from sun-light when rays fall on the skin.

Vitamin 'D' is found like vitamin 'A' in fish liver oils, black 'tils', milk, butter, cream and yolk. This is not found in adequate quantity in any vegetable. It is produced when ultra violet rays fall'on the human skin. When the sun-rays fall on the ergosterol which lies in the body below the skin it changes into vitamin 'D'. It is because of this action of sun-rays that children after oil massage are made to lie for sometime in sun-light. The deficiency of this vitamin in poor children is made good by sun-light. This vitamin increases in edibles when these are exposed to sun-light for sometime.

Vitamin 'D' is also called anti-rickets vitamin because calcium and phosphorous—the two things needed most for the development of bones and teeth—require this vitamin. In the absence of vitamin 'D', phosphorous and calcium go out of the body without performing their function and without being digested. Its deficiency in children is most harmful because the proper development of bones and teeth takes place in this early age. In the absence of vitamin D the teeth of children cut late and not without trouble. Besides, the teeth are ill-shaped, either too close to each other or with abnormal gaps. Sometimes teeth appear to be over riding each other. Vitamin D is particularly needed in the diseases of rickets and soft bones. The bones become soft and easily bend on sides and delay in standing on legs in a child are symptoms of deficiency of vitamin 'D'. Diseases like small-pox, whooping cough, tuberculosis are likely to attack a person suffering from deficiency of this vitamin. The intake of this vitamin should be increased in children in order to cure bone and teeth diseases. They should be exposed to sunlight for long periods after oil massage.

Vitamin 'E'—This vitamin affects the reproductory power of the body and is called anti-sterility vitamin. Its deficiency renders person incapable of reproduction. Women, too, do not escape from its effect. Its deficiency causes death of the body, abortions and miscarriages happen with the result that the woman loses her reproductory capacity.

Sprouts of wheat, yolk, dry and fresh fruits and leafy vegetables are rich sources of this vitamin. Meat and milk are not rich in this respect. This vitamin has the power to bear heat.

Vitamin 'K'—It is soluble in fat. Its main function is to coagulate the blood. This vitamin is needed for coagulating the blood when bleeding starts due to injury. In the absence of this vitamin, blood does not coagulate. Vitamin 'K' produces prothrombin in the liver. The presence of this vitamin is essential in a woman during pre-natal and post-natal periods.

Vitamin 'K' is found in abundance in spinach, cabbages tomatoes, cauliflowers, potatoes, wheat, bean and yolk. Non-vegetarian diets are also rich in this respect.

Good Diet

It is necessary to pay attention to the following in respect of balanced diet :

(1) The human diet should contain all the essential ingredients like protein, fat, mineral salts, carbohydrates, vitamins, fibrous edibles and water.

(2) All the described things in the preceding pages should be present in an adequate proportion. These should be neither in excess nor in smaller quantities. Everyone should eat these things according to his age, sex and profession. One should also take into consideration the climatic conditions.

(3) Food should be light and easily digestable.

(4) The food should be served in a manner that one should automatically be attracted towards it. Food which is not tasteful and served in a bad manner does not stimulate the appetite. Consequently, one does not take it in the required quantity and the pleasant way in which it is served also has its adverse effect on the digestive system. Some house-wives shout or throw spoons and other utensils at the time of serving meals. Their temper, thus, spoils the efficancy of the diet. As a result of this it is not properly digested. The same menu should not be repealed everyday. It does not create interest in the food. The food which is not eaten with interest tells adversely on the digestive system inasmuch as

it does not help in producing reasonable quantity of gastric juices as the result of which constipation is caused.

(5) Carelessness while preparing food and carrying it from place to place causes many defects in the food. Dust and flies, too, spoil food. Consequently, it becomes harmful, when exposed to these. Stale food turns posisonous. This kind of food should not be taken in any circumstance.

The above factors should be kept in view while preparing food. The diet for a normal and healthy individual should consist of edibles in the following proportion :

Bread 15 oz Milk 16 oz Vegetables 40 oz Meat 6 oz Butter 1 oz Cereal 2 oz Sugar 1-l/2oz Fruits 4oz Liquids 3 pints

Changes should be made in the above list according to the profession, body built, sex, age and climatic conditions.

Profession—Those persons who are engaged in manual work need larger quantity of food as compared to those who do lighter work. Persons engaged in mental work need less carbohydrates but more protein. They should take food rich in protein.

Body Built—A fat person needs more food as compared to a lean and thin person with short stature. This is because more heat is lost in the person beloging to the first category as compared to the lean and thin one with short stature.

Sex—Women need less food as compared to men because of short stature and less body weight. They also put in less physical labour as compared to men.

Age—The quantity of food depends on the age factor. Children need more food for their body development. They need larger quantities of fat and protein.

Less quantity of food should be taken by old persons. In old age, one does not require enough food. The digestive system, too, becomes weak. Eating more food, therefore, proves harmful in old age.

Climatic Condition—Climatic condition also affects the quantity of food. Persons living in colder regions need more food than those living in hotter regions. For keeping up their body-heat, the people of colder place need food rich in proteins and fats. More hunger is felt during winter than in rainy season and as such, we need more heat during winter. Not only this, we need such food that produces more heat during winter. On the contrary, food producing cooling effect is neded during summer. Changes should be made in the food in view of the above condition.

Bad Diet

The following are the causes of malnutrition :

(a) Malnutrition is caused due to lack of sufficient balanced diet.

(b) Circumstances also cause malnutrition. Nutritions, under adverse circumstances, do not do good to the body and their food value is lost.

(c) Defective food is another cause of malnutrition. Despite favourable atomosphere and circumstances this kind of diet proves harmful.

Defective Atmosphere—Among the causes of malnutrition come lack of fresh air, sun-light and physical exercise. Unhealthy situation of school buildings, obstruction in the way of fresh air and big gatherings are also contributory factors.

Overwork—Overwork needs more food and the average intake of edibles generally prove insufficient to meet the greater demand of food. It adversely affects the health. Covering the long distance of school on foot and not getting appropriate diet proves harmful to the body. Foul and dirty atmosphere and circumstances also cause bad health.

Chronk Ill-Health—Long illness reduces the vitality to such an extent that the body finds itself unable to utilise all that is eaten.

Lack of Sleep—A person does not get sound sleep in absence of fresh air and proper sleeping arrangements. Overwork and noisy surroundings also disturb sleep proves harmful for health.

Lack of Sufficient and Proper Food—As has been stated above, the food requirements of individuals differ according to age, sex and nature of profession. When a person does not get proper food according to his age sex and nature of work and if this state of affairs persists for a long period, his health is adversely affected, and malnutrition is caused.

The development of body is checked in the absence of nourishing and balanced diet and one grows weak. This weakness may be caused by two factors. Either it is due to the lack of sufficient quantity of food or the lack of those things in the food that are necessary for the maintenance and development of body.

Improper Food—Obstructions are created in the way of the natural development of body due to improper food. It has been generally observed that some persons eat things that are hard to digest. Consequently, they fall victims to indigestion and become ill.

Those children who fail to get nourishing and balanced diet become weak, lean, thin and short-statured. Their face turns yellow, eyelids appear to be heavy and eyes give a dull expression. Lack of fat loosens the skin and wrinkles are formed on the body as well. The hairs lose their glossiness and become dry. Such children cut their teeth late and the teeth are generally defective. These children always face the risk of falling victims to rickets and other diseases. They do not get sound sleep and wake up many a time during sleep. They suffer from restlessness. They lack in concentration. They easily catch infections and are generally seen suffering from cold and cough.

The first thing to be done for improving health is to find out the causes responsible for bad health.

It is the duty of every teacher to find out such students who do not get nutritive and balanced diet. They should invite the attention of parents, school physician and nurse towards such students and get proper arrangement of food made. It is also the responsibility and duty of the government to provide nutritive food to such children.

The Ingredients. Protein, starch, fat, mineral salts and vitamins are the ingredients of food. Protein consists of carbon, hydrogen, oxygen , nitrogen, sulphur and phosphorous. It has the quality of forming tissues and producing heat and energy. Starch is needed most for producing fat. Carbohydrate is the mixture of fatty acids and glycerine. These are the essential constituents which must be present in food for good health.

Vitamins of Two Varieties—(i) Water-soluble and (ii) Fat-soluble. These are named A, B, C, D, E and K. These are absolutely necessary for health.

The man needs nutritive and balanced diet for good health. Food should be taken according to age, sex, profession and climatic conditions. Malnutrition is caused by insufficient food, adverse circumstances and defective food.

QUESTIONS

1. Describe the essential constituents of balanced food ?
2. What is the utility of protein for the body ? Discuss in brief.
3. Explain the nature and importance of vitamins ?

20

Body Care

Physical exercise is as necessary for health as is the nutritive and balanced diet. Physical exercise is related to the actions of muscles and it is necessary for the proper blood circulation so that the muscles should remain reasonably active. Muscles are controlled by the brain but the brain itself cannot remain in good health if the blood circulation is not proper. The muscles, brain and the blood circulation are, therefore, interdependent. Evidently, physical exercise is absolutely necessary for activising the muscles. It helps both the physical and the mental development. Those who are engaged in manual labour need mental exercise. Persons doing mental work need physical exercise. This helps the balanced development of the two fields of activity. In its absence only one-side development will take place. Exercise is, therefore, very necessary for healthy growth of body and mind.

Role of Physical Exercises

Regular exercise not only helps the muscles but also all the other organs of the body. It accelerates the function of heart as the result of which the heart muscles are put to more work. This makes them strong and these become capable of doing more work in case of emergency.

Physical exercise, besides making the muscles strong, also helps their growth. Consequently, these enlarge in size and come fully under the man's voluntary control. These muscles act according to one's desire and in this way greater co-ordination is established between the brain and muscles.

Exercise helps in overcoming the mental defects, because the brain becomes more powerful. Not only this but also the deformities of the body caused by the faulty postures are cured. The spinal curvature, obliqueness of shoulders, flatness of foot and other body deformities may be cured through these exercises.

Not only a person is physically, benefited by exercise but he also stands to gain educationally. Collective exercises or taking part in sports and games, helps children to develop the spirit of co-operation, quick decisions, discipline, control, self-support, determination etc.

The Guidelines

The following rules should be observed while doing exercises:

(1) The principle of 'proceed from easy to difficult' should be observed. Exercise should be done for a shorter duration in the beginning. Gradually, the duration should be increased. Exercises should be stopped when one feels tired. Tiredness is an indication of reaching the saturation point. It means no more further exercise at that time, because continuing the exercise even after that will harm the body.

(2) Exercises should be taken in open place where fresh air is available in abundance. The doors and the windows of the room should be wide opened.

(3) Exercises should be done regularly at a fixed time. Over-exercise for the sake of competition is harmful.

(4) Exercises should be taken according to age. Fifteen to twenty minutes light exercise is sufficient for adolescents. Over exercise is harmful. Young children should be asked to run, jump, glide, dance, sing and take Part in sports. This is the

best type of exercise for them. The Indian system of 'dand' and 'baithak' will prove harmful during early adolescence. This kind of exercise may adversely affect the- heart. It is, therefore, advisable to prescribe exercise after keeping the age in view.

(5) Weak children should not be subjected to hard exercises. Walking in fresh air, body massage and deep breathing exercises are enough for constitutionally weak children. Persons engaged in mental work, should play tennis, foot-ball or do horse-riding. This kind of entertaining exercises are beneficial for them.

(6) Exercises should not be taken with empty stomach or just after taking food. This is very harmful.

(7) Drill produces more fatigue as compared to exercises. Young children should not, therefore, be asked to perform drill. Drill also tires the brain along with the body. Attention should, therefore, be paid more to sports than to drill.

(8) The person taking regular exercise needs nourishing diet. His diet should necessarily include milk, almond, green vegetables and butter. Those who are non-vegetarian should eat meat, fish, egg etc. Granced-nut and germinated grams are also very wholesome.

After continuously doing a work, a stage is reached when a man feels overworked and likes to stop it. This state is called fatigue. Fatigue creates such a mental state that the desire to work disappears. The tired children will have their hands and the whole body inactive. Their shoulders will not be straight and their calves will be bent. Such children yawn and place their hand on forehead frequently. They cannot concentrate on work and they commit many mistakes.

Causes of Fatigue—Brain, spinal cord, nerves and muscles are responsible for keeping our body active. Brain and spinal cord produce impulses which are carried by nerves to muscles. On receiving these impulses, the muscles expand and contract. In this way, the causes of fatigue can be divided into two parts : (1) physical and (2) mental.

A chemical action takes place in the body when the various organs become active. This action produces lactic acid and carbon di-oxide etc., which are poisonous products. The body becomes inactive when these substances accumulate in larger quantity in it. The muslces and nervous tissues also lose the power to do a work at that time.

The nerves are comparatively less affected by fatigue and, therefore, they easily regain strength and become normal, but the brain and spinal cord tire in a shorter period. Their tiredness affects the muslces which are also tired as a result. Tiring of muscle due to physical exertion or fatigue and of brain due to mental exertion—both are related to nerves.

Beneficial Steps

Proper seating arrangement should be made for children. To many children should not sit in a single room. The rooms should be so built that sufficient light and air are available. Schools should he built in places where the atmosphere is peaceful. This will enable the children to concentrate on their lessons easily. The students reading in schools built in the heart of markets have to tax their energies more in concentrating over lessons. Consequently, they get tired in a shorter period as compared to those students who study in a peaceful atmosphere.

The teachers should keepin view factors that create fatigue in children. Efforts should be made so that the children who are afraid of their parents and examinations may gain self-confidence. Only those teachers who enjoy confidence of students can only succeed in this work.

Sound sleep is very necessary for removing fatigue. Children who do not sleep for sufficient time soundly, cannot do mental work efficiently. They appear restless and becomes short tempered. Sound sleep is absolutely necessary for overcoming mental fatigue. It provides that much needed rest which protects the body from those harmful products that are produced in the body as a result of fatigue. Besides, the children gain in height and weight while asleep.

While resting in-day one should lie on the back. It is more beneficial because in this manner the muscles get ample opportunity to relax. The heart also gets rest because the heatings decrease.

About twelve hours of sleep for children between four and eight years, eleven hours for those between eight and twelve year?, ten hours for boys between twelve and fourteen and nine hours sleep for boys between the age group of 14 to 16 years is necessary to ensure proper and healthy development. Provision for sleeping during day should exist in nursery schools. This is very useful. Children below the age of seven years should at least get 40 minutes' sleep in the day after meals.

Insomnia, that is, lack of sleep is also a problem. Mothers sometimes give narcotic drugs to children for making them sleep. But this should not be resorted to in any circumstance. These narcotic drugs tell adversely on health and particularly on the brain of children.

For preventing fatigue, one should change over from one work to another. This is entertaining, and provides rest also. Light and entertaining work like gardening, playing and walking are useful for those who are engaged in mental work. Similarly. Those who are engaged in physical labour, work like writing, reading or playing any game proves beneficial.

Gradual Steps

Exercise should be taken regularly and the principle of 'From Simple to Difficult' should be observed. Exercise should be taken at a fixed time daily in open air.

Lack of interest or disinclination towards work is a sign of fatigue. There are two causes of fatigue: (1) physical and (2) mental.

Extraordinary fatigue is also felt occasionally due to physical or mental disorder. Overwork also produces excessive fatigue. Sound sleep gives sufficient rest and removes fatigue.

Bodily posture means the balancing of body in a proper manner while sitting, standing, reading or writing or doing any other body action. In a proper posture, the whole body weight falls on the two legs without any effort and the entire body appers a vertical line. In this state, all the limbs perform their functions and do not tire easily. Proper body posture indicates a healthy and strong body, while improper faulty postures represent a sick and weak body. The proper posture also reveals a sound mind. Self-confidence, happiness and determination are the results of correct posture and on the contrary anxiety, unhappiniess and pessimism are the outcome of wrong posture.

The child should possess from the early days the knowledge of correct posture of standing, sitting and reading. In the absence of this knowledge, he adopts faulty postures as a result of which the backbone bends, the chest becomes like a pigeon-chest, the shoulders turn drapping, feet become flat, vision turns defective and many other deformities appear in the body. There are two reasons for faulty postures. One relates to home and the other to the school.

Domestic Factors

1. In the absence of nourishing and balanced diet, the bones and muscles of the child become weak and they tire in a short period. Consequently, the child adopts faulty postures.
2. Lack of fresh air, sufficient light, rest and sleep lead to developing wrong postures.
3. Improper physical exercise and dirty habits are also responsible for wrong postures.
4. Taking it a fashion, some children, particularly some girls adopt faulty postures and bring artificiality in their natural postures.
5. Dresses are also responsible for producing ill effects on the children and they develop wrong postures.

School Factors

1. In many schools the shape and size of desks and chairs are uniform as a result of which the students with different

physical standards cannot sit comfortably on them. Consequently, they occupy wrong positions while reading and writing and they develop the habit of sitting in faulty postures.

2. Lack of attention in school towards the fatigue and recreation of students develop in them faulty sitting habits.
3. Overlooking the habit of faulty postures also creates this defect.
4. Carrying the load of books continuously on one shoulder also influences the posture.
5. Children have to bend their body for seeing and listening to their mistakes. They have also to bend the body when defects appear in their vision. Consequnetly, they assume wrong postures.
6. Continuously doing the same work for a long time, tires the brain of the child. He, therefore, wants, to relax by changing the body position. In these circumstances also some posture defect may arise.

Defects of Posture

Attention should be paid on the following things for removing the defects of faulty posture :

1. The children should get nourishing and balanced diet so that they may develop enough strength to stand, sit or read for a long time in the same position.
2. Arrangement for suitable living accommodation should be made so that fresh air and sufficient light may be available in abundance.
3. They should be given opportunity for suitable physical exercise and of developing clean habits.
4. The dresses of children should not be very tight. They should be such-that physical development may not be hampered.
5. The desks and chairs should be so constructed as to give maximum comfort to the child.

6. The children should be told the necessary things about the body posture and whenever they default, they should be cautioned or warned.
7. Even if the desks and chairs are suitably made the children should not be allowed to sit for long one position. Changes in the sitting positions should be made at regular intervals.
8. Children should be made to undertake such physical exercise which may help them in removing the defects caused by faulty postures.
9. Children should be advised to go to hospitals for the treatment of complicated deformities.

The foregoing account makes it clear as to how important are the body postures for the physical and mental development of the children. Attention towards it should therefore, be paid since the very beginning. It is very necessary that the reading, writing and standing positions of students should be carefully watched.

Reading Posture

The children should sit in an upright position while reading. The book should be placed at a distance of at least twelve inches from the eyes. Myopia develops if the book is placed very near the eyes. An angle of 45° should be formed between the eyes and the hand holding the book. For keeping the head erect, the book should be placed much below. Very young children should be given books of bold prints. The vision becomes defective when books with small prints are read.

If adequate attention is not paid to the above, defects will arise in the sight, chest will become narrow and the bones in the backbone will become deformed while Reading.

Attention should be paid on the following while writing :

(a) The way of holding the pen.

(b) Position of the paper.

(c) The method of writing, and

(d) Form of hand-writing.

Position of Pen

The child should balance and keep his body in an upright position before starting writing. The chair should be pulled nearer the desks, the things kept straight and the lower limbs placed in a vertical position. The legs should rest on the ground and the left hand should keep the papers in order. This helps in writing and the hand does not remain idle.

The forearm should be rested on the elbow in a manner so that palm may remain continuously visible. The pen should be held by the thumb and the two fingers nearer it and the upper end of the pen should remain between the thumb and the finger adjoining it.

Place of Paper

The paper while writing should remain parallel to the edge of the desk. In this way, the hand-writing will be upright and the words also will be legible, regular and attractive. The body limbs, too, will remain in this manner at their proper place and function efficiently. By so doing, deformities will not appear in the body parts.

In order to teach writing the use of black wooden slate should be made first of all. Letters should be taught first and the words should follow next. It is always beneficial to write on the black wooden slate with a broad pointed wooden pen. A broad pointed pen should be made of reeds and the point should be bisected. The entire wooden blackboard should be lined and letters and words be written in between the lines. This helps the children in developing a good and beautiful hand-writing. The words thus written are regular and beautiful. This paractice of writing on black wooden boards is gradually vanishing these days. Consequently, the hand writing of people, too, is losing attraction. The student after doing sufficient practice on the wooden black-board, should switch over to slates. Writing on paper with ink should start in the fourth year. The old saying killing two birds with one stone, will thus be proved, i.e., the hand-writing of the child will become beautiful and expenses on ink and stationery will also be minimised.

Writing Methods

Children when sit in a wrong posture while writing, write slantingly and the lines are not straight. Slanting hand-writing never looks attractive. In this kind of hand writing the paper does not remain parrallel to the edge of the desk. The head bends towrards the left side and the right shoulder gets raised. The eyes, too, do not remain at an distance from the paper and the backbone also bends. The muscles and nerves are more strained in this posture of writing and they tire out within a short time.

The child should be encouraged to write in an upright manner, because he easily learns thus the method of writing. His sitting posture remains in the correct position and the paper being equi-distant from both the eyes, writing does not unnecessarily strain the eyes. He can sit upright on the chair and write with paper remaining parallel to the desk. No part of the body in this way is strained. He does not tire out easily.

Posture of Sitting

The correct sitting posture may be recognised by the following:

1. The hips region should be properly placed at the sitting place.
2. The head, shoulders and hips should be in a straight line.
3. Vertebral column should be straight.
4. Head should be upright so that the muscles behind may get some rest.
5. Both arms should be balanced.
6. Thighs should be straight.
7. Legs should be vertically resting on the feet.

It is very harmful to sit with a bent vertebral column. This causes extra strain on the connected limbs which tire out in a short period. Consequently, obstructions are caused in their functioning.

Posture of Standing

In the correct standing position, the body weight falls on both the legs equally. The heels should rest on the flat surface correctly and no muscle should be strained. In this position, the waist and the head should be straight, chest should bulge a little forward and the two shoulders should be in a straight line. The two arms should also rest on the thighs in a straight line. This position of attention should be adopted for a short time because the two legs tire out simultaneoulsy due to the body weight falling on them equally. It is advisable to stretch a leg forward in case one is required to stand for a longer time, because in so doing, the body weight will fall on the back leg and the front leg will get an opportunity for rest. The position of the leg may be changed when the back leg feels tired, in this way, both the legs rest in turn. This position is called the standing position at ease.

If the school-going children are examined in relation to body postures, at least fifty percent of them will be found adopting faulty postures in some way or other. These defects are of the following category:

Spinal Curvature—This defect is generally found in a large number of children. Excessive strain during childhood on the vertebral column makes it curve and the following defects arise. (1) Appearance ofKyphosis. (2) Lordosis- (3) Socialist Kyphosis.

The following deformities appear with the Kyphosis :

(1) Bending of head and body in the forward direction, (2) Round back, (3) flat chest, (4) Round shoulders, (5) Round hallow back, (6) Bulging out of the belly.

The above mentioned defects are caused by unnutritive and unbalanced diet, lack of fresh air and inadequate physical exercises. Besides, faulty desk sitting posture, myopia, excessive strain on shoulders, and rickets also deform the waist region. The teacher, in order to remove these defects, should impress upon the students the importance of adopting correct postures while standing, reading and writing. Boys with deformities should be advised to take proper physical exercises in order to remove their defects.

Other Factors

The defect causes the back to bend in either direction. Curvature also appears in the waist region. The shoulder bones in the back also seem to be bending towards the sides. Hips also bulge out. In this state of body, occasionally the child experiences pain in the back and walks like a lame person.

This defect is caused by the under-development of legs, disease of bone-joints, dislocation of hips or infantile paralysis. Faulty standing posture, too, causes this defect. In this condition the body lets the body weight fall on one leg. Consequently, .the vertebral column takes the shape of the English letter 'C'. The habit of standing on one leg also causes this defect.

For removing this defect, the child should be made to stand in the correct posture and to do special physical exercise, too, cure this defect. In severe and complicated cases, proper treatment should be undertaken on the expert advise of a doctor.

This defect is found in the early years in weak children. This is caused by over work and by putting on heavy shoes. This weakens the bony bonds which keep, the foot muscles and foot bridge in order. Consequently, the foot becomes flat. Continuously standing or walking also tires out the muscles as the result of which these muscles find themselves unable to function properly and the foot turns flat.

The foot should be rested as soon as symptoms of this defect appear. They should be saved from fatigue. This defect is also overcome by walking on toes. It is also useful to apply pressure on the edges of sole while walking.

Correct body posture represents a healthy and strong body. Faulty posture, on the other hand, mean a weak and sick body. There are two causes of faulty potsures : (1) Relating to home and (2) Relating to school. Many deformities in the body appear due to faulty postures adopted while standing, sitting, reading or writing e. g; spinal curvature, flat foot etc.

The students while reading a book, should sit in an upright position and keep the book at a distance of at least twelve inches from the eye. An angle of 45° should be formed while reading a book in hand.

Special attention should be paid on the manner of holding the paper position, the hand-writing and the way of writing.

The head, shoulders and the hips should form a straight line while sitting. Vertebral column should also be straight.

The body weight should fall equally on both the legs while standing for a short time, but for a longer duration, the body weight should fall alternately on legs, i. e., one leg should remain stretched forward.

Air is as essential for life as food. Life is impossible without air. It is through air that we get oxygen which purifies our blood. The food, too, becomes useful for the body by the action of air which in turn makes the body function efficiently and ensures its proper development.

The air is a gift from nature. The following gases are present in the fresh air:

Oxygen	—	20.96%
Nitrogen	—	79.00%
Carbon dioxide	—	00.04%

Besides the above gases, water vapours, ammonia, organic matter, ozone, oxides of nitrogen etc., are also present.

Their is a difference between the fresh air that we inhale and the foul air which we exhale. The oxygen gas is not present in the air which we throw out of the lungs. The proportion of carbon di-oxide increases by three to four per cent. Besides carbon, mono-oxide and oxide of sulphuric gases are also present in it. The proportion of gases in the discharged air is in the following manner:

Oxygen	—	16.50%
Nitrogen	—	79.00%
Carbon di-oxide	—	04.50%

The foul air adversely affects the body development. It produces physical and mental fatigue, restlessness, worry, headache, sleep and heaviness. The heart beats become slow causing disturbance in the normal respiration. The mind becomes restless with the result that one cannot concentrate on anything. One experiences a lack of appetite. He also feels physical weakness. In these circumstances, there is a likelihood of his getting anaemic.

Science has proved that the condition of physical environment is more important for the healthy development of the body than the chemical proportion of the air. The physical environments affect our health. These are as under:

(a) High temperature, (b) excessive dampness in the air, (c) stand-still air, (d) infectious germs in the air.

The normal temperature of our body should remain at 98.4°F, while that of the living rooms should be between 55°F to 60°F. In this condition, our body maintains a higher temperature than that of the room and heat is produced all the time in the body. This heat warms up the air touching our skin and continuously escape from our body after drying up the sweet. Obstructions arise in the smooth functioning when the outside air becomes too hot. In this condition, the body heat does not remain in a position to warm the air touching the skin because the difference between the temperature of skin and outside air is considerably less. Consequently, it happens that the air does not rise up after getting warm and the fresh air cannot replace it.

The body can remain in a healthy state if the air in the room circulates. Artificial devices may be used for keeping the air in motion, cool and dry to a reasonable extent. Keeping down the temperature of the air, reducing its dampness and maintaining its circulation will keep the respiratory process in a good order. Consequently, the foul air discharged from the lungs will not adversely affect the body. By making provision of cross ventilation of air, the risk of infections is reduced. Cross Ventilation arrangement in a room is absolutely necessary for obtaining fresh air and dispelling the foul air. The numbers of doors and windows in the rooms should, therefore, be as many as possible. This will facilitate the throwing out of foul air from the room and the infectious germs will thus be destroyed. The result will be that children will not fall victim to diseases easily and will remain healthy.

The sole aim of artificial devices is to dispel the foul air and let the fresh air enter the room. The devices are of two categories : (i) Natural and (ii) Artificial. Ventilation of air without the aid of any artificial device is called natural ventilation of air. Natural ventilation is more beneficial that the artificial one. The natural ventilation depends on the ventilation of gases, air action and convection currents.

Passage of Air

When two gases meet each other, they mix up. So the outer air mixes with the room air on opening the doors and windows. In this way the good qualities of the outside air come in the room and the inside air becomes fresh. The room air continuously turns fresh through this action but it is a very slow process, as such it has no importance.

Air Action—The air takes away with itself the foul matter gases from the room and passages. The fresh air enters the room from one end and displaces the foul air which escapes from the other end when all the doors and windows are open. Not only this, but as soon as the foul air rises up and escapes through an outlet, fresh air immediately rushes in and takes its place producing a kind of wave. In this way, the air invisibly plays the role of a mechanical device.

Convection Currents—The movement of hot air upwards and the cold air downwards is called the action of convection currents. This action or movement is possible because the hot waves are lighter and rise upwards while the cooler air that replaces it is comparatively heavier. Sufficient doors and windows are necessary for smooth action so that foul air is displaced by the fresh air, and the hotter air by cooler air.

There are four natural ventilation devices : (1) Chimney or ventilators, (2) Doors and windows, (3) Openings at or near the floor level with vertical shafts. (4) Exits or outlets in the roofs or walls.

Chimney—This is a suitable device of dispelling the foul air. The hot air rushes out tlirough it speedily. Fresh air enters from other inlets to take the place of the dispelled air.

Doors and Windows—In colder countries, the number of doors and windows in houses are comparatively fewer than the houses in hotter countries. In colder countries, it is harmful as well as troublesome to have a large number of doors and windows, but in hotter countries the larger the number of doors and windows the more comfortable and useful the houses are.

Tobin's Tubes—The air under this system enters the room through a six feet high tube in the wall from the air inlet nearest to the floor.

If a valve is fixed at the higher end, the inflow of the air in the room may be controlled.

Wall or Ceiling Air Passage—Many kinds of air passages may be built in the roofs of singlestoried buildings through which fresh air may enter and the foul air may go out. Wall air passages are very useful in this respect. In this system, there are two passages. Through the inner passage, the air goes out and fresh air enters through the outer passage.

Light of the Sun

Life is án impossibility without sun-light. The sun-light is equally essential for animals, birds and plants. The sun-light besides life-giving properties also possess the qualities of destroying harmful germs. It also adds strength to the human skin's power of killing germs. The white corpuscles of blood derive power from sun-light as the result of which it saves the body from falling ill. If increases the health-giving products like iron, calcium, phosphorous, iodine etc., in the blood. The sun-light is also helpful to the digestive and blood circulatory systems. Vitamin 'D' which is so necessary for bones and teeth is produced in the body by sun-light. It also cures rickets. It helps in curing the serious diseases like reumatism and tuberculosis. It will thus be seen that sun-light is very necessary for life.

Children suffer from anaemia due to lack of sun-light. The school buildings should therefore, be so constructed that sufficient light may be available to the students. The sun-light proves very effective in the treatment of diseases like inflammation of tuberculosis glands (neck glands), leprosy, tuberculosis, etc. The deficiencies caused by unbalanced diet is also made good to some extent by sun-light. It helps in the early recovery of health after illness. The sun-light should, therefore, be put to maximum use. The children should play and take exercise in places, where fresh air and sun-light are in abundance.

The quantity of oxygen is less in the air that is exhaled by lungs. Foul air adversely affects the health. It is harmful for body. The physical environments are of more importance than the chemical properties or proportion of air.

Our body is harmed by high temperature of the air, its standstilliness or its lack of circulation and greater number of germs in it.

There are natural and artificial method of propelling the air inside the room, or dispelling it out. The natural process is based on cross ventilation, air-action and convection currents. It needs four special equipments :

(1) Chimney, (2) Doors and windows, (3) Tobin's tubes and (4) The air passages in roofs or walls.

Under the artifical process the system of vacuum and propulsion methods are included. These systems are defective and costly.

The sun-light is absolutely essential for life. It kills the germs. Lack of sun-light causes a number of diseases.

QUESTIONS

1. What are the causes of wrong body postures ? Give a detailed account.
2. Describe with the help of a sketch, the correct posture while writing.
3. What deformities are caused by wrong postures ? How can they be removed.
4. What is the difference between the air that we inhale and that which we exhale ? Which of the two adversely affects the body and why ?
5. Write a short note on the various devices used for keeping the air fresh in the room.
6. What do you understand by phyiscal exercise ? Write an essay giving full details.
7. What is fatigue ? What are its categories ? Describe its symptoms and show how can it be overcome.
8. What do you understnad by rest ? Write an essay on sound sleep.

21

Adult Life

Problem of Fat

Obesity may pose a problem to an adult from his early forties. It develops many difficulties for an individual. This may lead one to have blood pressure, diabetes and liver troubles. There might be two principal causes for obesity. One is eating too much and the other is malfunctioning of endocrine glands. Many fat people are heard saying that they are getting fatter and fatter day by day, although, they do not eat much. In fact, such persons eat four or five times a day and the whole intake totals more than what one should normally eat. So an adult after forty years of age should try to control his diet by gradually reducing the intake per day. Adequate physical exercise, i.e., movements of all the parts of body both in the morning and evening will keep an adult fit. We mention below some points which must be observed by an adult and others for their good health—

1. A doctor should be immediately consulted, if some ailment is felt.
2. Adequate exercise and rest are very necessary for good health.
3. One must never sit idle. One should always be engaged in some fruitful occupation either at home or outside.

4. One should always have adequate fresh air and balanced diet.
5. After any illness, one must never undertake any heavy work. It is very necessary to take complete rest for some days after one recovers fully from some illness.

Increasing Age

The joint family system has been almost broken principally in the urban or rural areas where agriculture is not the main means of livelihood. Even in rural areas in our country the joint-family system which prevailed during the pre-independence days has been disintegrated. Formerly, when agriculture was the principal occupation the eldest man of the family used to be the head and all other members used to obey him. With the growth of industrialization in our country the joint-family system has been broken. Once a person is employed somewhere, he establishes his own independent family leaving the old parents behind to their fate. As a result, old persons have lost the protection of the younger ones. This situation has created certain difficult problems for old people. If for some reason the old parents have to live with their sons at the place of their service, the new set up and mode of living as organized by the latter is not congenial to the old people because they have lived under different cultural biases. It is true that the problem of old people in our country India has not yet assumed that dimension which is seen in some advanced western countries. Nevertheless, the problem is there. This problem is not limited to only bread, clothing and housing. In fact, it is affecting the health of our old people. In Western countries the old people are being rehabilited. The Government has started spending on maintaining houses for old people and looking after their food and other vital needs related to their physical, mental and cultural up-keep. It is difficult to imagine upto what extent the Government in a vast country like India will be able to adopt an identical policy for its old people. There are some apparent difficulties. Naturally, the old people are generally very week and they may be having some ailments. It will be extremely difficult for the Government to shoulder all the responsibilities of old people in our big country. Moreover, so far the old people have been living with their children as one unit. So they will never be happy in living alone. Evidently, we have to strive very hard to find out a reasonable solution for our old people. The best arrangement will be, if the grown-up children keep them with themselves at the place of their work or service and put up with some if their idiosyncrasies.

The Dress

Clothing helps in maintaining a balance in our bodily temperature in addition to presenting ourselves before others in a socially acceptable manner. That is why fashion designers all over the world are making a roaring business over it. During winter we use woollen clothes particularly when we have to go out, but they are not very comfortable inside our houses. So it is only on an unusually cold day that we feel compelled to clothes ourselves heavily inside doors. However, we have to be quite careful when going outside in a shivering weather. Any carelessness in this respect may be harmful to health developing cold and fever.

Rubber, nylon or leather clothes do not have pores in them. Hence they do not permit the touch of air with our body. As a result, perspiration silently remains stuck with the body giving out bad smell or creating itching trouble. Nylon socks are particularly harmful to feet because of lack of pores in them due to which air does not touch the skin over the feet. But some persons for the sake of their easy convenience continue on using them and thus impairing the health of their feet. Undergarments made of nylon must also never be used for the same reasons.

During summer our clothes should be of lighter shade of a colour. But white clothes during summer are more comfortable. Deep colours have a more powerful tendency to absorb the sun-heat. Hence clothes of light colours should be regarded as healthier for summer.

The undergarments generally remain in close touch with our skin. So they should be washed well every day.

Heavy quilt or too many blankets should not be used for protecting oneself during winter, as these will not permit sufficient oxygen to the body. due to this, either one's sleep is disturbed or he does not feel fresh when he gets up in the morning.

As far as possible, the daily sitting in front of fire during winter for protecting oneself from cold should be avoided, as this is likely to impair one's resistance-capacity for obvious reasons.

The Bathing

Some persons are found very lazy and they do not take bath daily even during summer and rainy seasons, then what to speak about them during winter ? Such persons do not realise the importance of bath for health. So they choose to take bath only on Sundays or Fridays or only on some ceremonial occasions. While in U. S. A. during his student days about 46 years ago, the author felt surprised when other contemporary white American students astonishingly exclaimed that "I (author) was a person who persists in taking bath daily." One must take bath daily as far as practicable. Bath cleans the skin. It helps in a balanced circulation of blood and consequent balanced temperature of the body. In bath all those parts of the body which are prone to profuse perspiration should be particularly washed carefully daily. If medically permissible even during winter water of normal bodily temperature should be used for bath. But for the sake of momentary comforts certain persons do not like to use normal water for bath. They prefer warm water for bath. The use of warm water in bath generally creates imbalance in blood circulation and it does not permit the incoming of required energy after bath. That is why, one feels cold after taking warm-water bath. Persons with breathing complications, particularly during winter, may take warm-water bath according to medical advice received. But normal persons should use ordinary water for bath. When especially tired, warm-water bath may be more useful and energy reviving. For some, it may be helpful to take bath before going to sleep at night. But at least 3 to 4 hours must elapse in between meals and bath.

Bath in Sun

In taking sun-bath blood circulation is increased and the necessary 'D' vitamin inherent in the sun-rays is also absorbed in the body. However, sun-bath is possible only during winter season, particularly in tropical countries, as scorching sun-rays of summer is so piercing as to affect the body adversely developing headache, insomnia, fever and vomitting. So the same should be carefully avoided. Sun-bath should be taken for a few minutes in the beginning. Its duration may be increased gradually. Ultra-violet rays ensures better physical health. Ultra-violet rays produce 'D' vitamin from the cholesterol in the food. 'D' vitamin protects young children from the ricket disease. Moderate sun-bath increases haemoglobin in blood and accelerates hunger also to some extent. It also helps the speedier healing of wounds. Sun-bath for a long duration may produce wrinkles and dryness on skin. So too much of it should be avoided.

Care for Body

The face should be softly washed with soap and cold water in order to maintain its lusture and beauty. This process is likely to increase blood circulation adequately over the face area.

Our hands may come in contact with injurious germs and worms at times more easily because they are the principal organs to come in direct touch with certain aspects of the environment. So hands should be well-cleaned before taking meals or eating other things. Nails should be regularly trimmed, otherwise their out-growth may give room to disease worms to settle down into their cavities.

Head hairs easily collect dirt and dust. So the same should be washed with soap and cool water. Warm water must never be poured on head. Regular oil-massage keeps the head-area healthy.

Most of us are not very careful about our feet hygiene. As a result, toes and the entire feet with their muscles get deshaped due to wrong choice of footwears. Pointed narrow and tight footwears should be avoided in order to permit flow of fresh air to the various portions of the feet while one is at his duty during working hours.

Cotton socks (as already mentioned above) are healthier because they have pours which permit the spread of air all over the feet when they are covered with some type of wears. When returned home after the duty hours, the feet should be washed as soon as possible. Washing of the feet will give some relief and comfort. As far as possible, one should not go outside home bare-footed, as the direct contact of the feet with the ground may invite various types of disease germs to penetrate stealthily into the body through them (our feet). Oil massage of feet, particularly during winter, will ensure them better health.

Presonal Habits

One may have good or bad habits. Good habits keep one healthy in a various ways and bad ones impairs his health and longevity. Early rise, early to bed, regular morning walk atleast for an hour, taking of balanced diet ordinarily at some fixed hour, walking straight, sitting and standing in correct healthy postures, sneezing and spitting properly and keeping oneself free of any type of addiction are good habits ensuring good health throughout life. We are hinting onwards at some important points to be kept in view regarding these habits.

Bad Habits

It is not a good habit. In a way it is only a kind of addiction. There are persons who are all the time chewing PAN in their mouth. Such persons are generally in the habits of spitting their 'PAN-refuse' here and there making the nearby surroundings dirty. Such persons are prone to make the tips of their fingers dirty through their pan-juice. PAN-eaters are generally found too-much talkative. This feature with them is most annoying and disgusting for the other non-pan eaters near him. The teeth of pan-eaters become very dirty and sensitiveness of the taste-buds in their mouths are badly impaired.

Some persons are in the bad habit of doing so. Thus they make certain places dirty where disease germs are bred. One's sputum may have various types of disease germs which may spread disease residing in the surrounding areas.

These features in a person are likely to spread disease germs to persons nearby. So one should keep his nose and mouth covered with a piece of hand-kerchief at the time of sneezing and coughing.

We have already explained some of the very important aspects of bodily postures for students. The suggestions given there in are quite pertinant for adults as well. The issue of physical exercise, fatigue and rest. The various aspects as explained there are quite relevant for adults as well in their essential spirit.

The Drugs

Regular use of alcohol impairs the basic phenomena of the entire health of an individual. If one is caught under its grip through some bad company or due to one's own ways of life causing frustrations of various types, it becomes extremely difficult to get rid of the same. A little alcohol in the beginning induces some relief to the higher nerve-centre leading the victim to feel solace and comforts from his self-imposed worries and problems of life. Under its impact, one is not aware of rights and wrongs of his behaviour and he may choose to behave or react as his fancies motivate. The behaviour of an intoxicated person is really very pitiable when he or she just completes his or her over-doze. Excessive drinking may lead to development of various types of diseases, such as, cancer of some vital organ (like heart, lungs, liver-and kidneys etc.) and it may also affect adversely one's various sense organs, eyes, ears, nose, throat, skin and the entire nervous system and some of the very important bones of the body. The very life of a family is terribly disturbed and shaken if some of its members have developed this harmful habit. So one should to give up this habit entirely in the interest of his family and other associates who happen to come in his close contact.

There are certain drugs which physicians use for giving immediate relief to some of their patients. These drugs give relaxation to senses and the patients feel some relief. Such drugs should be taken very sparingly and under strict advice of physicians. Getting habituated to the same will have bad impact on one's health. In fact, no drug can ever cure any disease. So it should be used only as a temporary phase, when some immediate relief is necessary.

Drinking Habits

These items stimulate the heart and nervous system and remove fatigue temporarily. Their ordinary use once or twice a day may be regarded as innocent, but one must not take more than one or two cups during 24 hours. Otherwise it may be harmful. Certain persons get too much addicted to these soft beverages. This feature may develop many problems with them.

Other Habits

The habit of smoking is generally a public nuisance, particularly when one gets addicted to chain-smoking. Smoking makes the lips and teeth dirty. It creates hoarse voice. It may result into dry coughing. The wind-pipe and lungs are injuriously affected by smoking. It may develop heart-troubles as well as cancer of the lungs. It badly affects the reproductory organs. A smoker is generally unmindful of the other person present near him and goes on continuously smoking. Thus he becomes a public nuisance. A smoker is a nuisance to his family members also. It is suggested that for giving-up this habit the following measures should be adhered to:

1. Purchase only one BIRI or CIGARETTE at a time. Do not store it in advance. Do not keep lighter or match box with yourself.
2. In case of chain-smoking reduce the number gradually and come to one or two a day.
3. Do not offer BIRIS, CIGARS or CIGARETTE to any one at your residence.
4. The best way to give up smoking is to make a firm resolve to give it up immediately. Gradual giving up method may not be helpful in getting rid of this nuisance.

This feature is as harmful as smoking is, though it may be regarded as a lesser public nuisance, beacause it does not vitiate the atmospheric air too much as smoking does. However, use of tobacco may develop the same health problems and fatal diseases as smoking does. So it should be given up as soon as possible. Measures sugges-ted above for giving up smoking may be helpful for getting rid of this harmful habit as well.

All these three intoxicants are prepared from leaves and flowers of hemp plants. These intoxicants impair the lungs, brain and eyes. Their frequent use may impair the thinking power of an individual and his very life may be spoiled. Use of Ganja and Charas is more harmful in comparison to Cigarettes and Biris. Infact, these are more vicious and harmful to health. Bhang and Opium spend of the very vitality of an addicted person who makes himself a load over his family and the entire society. N. Â.—The various items in this chapter are explained very briefly. So no summary of the same is given here.

QUESTIONS

1. What should one do for getting rid of his obesity ?
2. Discuss the problems of old age.
3. Explain the role of clothing in personal hygiene.
4. What is the importance of bath for our health ?
5. How should we care about our hands, feet, face and head-hairs ?
6. What are some of the general personal habits of some careless people who are prone to make their surroundings dirty ?
7. What are general intoxicants used by some persons ? How can we help them to get rid of the addiction of the same ?

22

Problem of Population

Today the population of India is more than 100 crore. In fact, our population is increasing every year. Developing population is a world problem.

Increasing Population

Due to illiteracy, ignorance, superstitions and old traditions the birth rate in our country has been generally very high. Similarly, because of inadequate medical facilities and ignorance, the death rate, too, has been quite high. The standard of living has improved a little due to some economic development medical facilities have also been extended to many Parts of the country. This feature has resulted into the reduction of death rate, but the birth rate remains as high as ever. Consequently, the population in our country has been continuously rising. This is an alarming situation for our country and our Central and State governments feel rightly agitated to do something positive for controlling the rise of population.

The standard of living improves with economic development. Consequently, education spreads widely. This leads to reduction of birth rate. Good nutrition and adequate medical facilities reduce the death rate. This situation controls the rise in population. But this has not happened in India. Here population has exploded to an enormous extent. It has been estimated that in every 1.5 seconds a baby is born in India. Every year about 23 crore babies are born. Out of this number about 14 crore die. About 45 percentage of the population in India is below 14 years of age. It has been calculated that one sixth of the world population resides in India, i.e, every sixth person is an Indian. Only 2.5 per cent of the world land is under the control of India, but on this land more than 16 per cent of the world population resides.

The Government of India has estimated that every year the population in the country increases by one crore and 32 lakh. With this rate of increase in population every year 1 lakh 25 thousand schools, 4 lakh teachers, 26 lakh houses, 2 crore metres of cloth, one crore 50 lakh quintals of food materials and 45 lakh employment opportunities will have to be made available. This situation is alarmingly deplorable. For controlling this situation the need of family planning and population education has been very rightly emphasized.

Basic Issues

About 45 per cent of the population of the developing countries is within 14 years of age. This age group is generally at the threshold of adolescence. It is these persons who will in near future begin to play the role of parents. It is this group which will decide the size of the family. So the person within this age group should be educated about the implications of big or small size of their family and its direct hearing on their prosperity and also the prosperity of the nation. So this age group should be well informed on the implied points of family planning. They should be plainly told that the size of the family may be well controlled if there is a definite, healthy and intelligent planning for the same with the help of the medical facilities and other requirements available for the purpose. Thus in the population education we have to inform the youth about the trend of the population in the country and its impact on the growth and economic prosperity of the individual and the nation.

The Objectives

The following may be regarded as some of the more important aims of population education:

1. To tell the young people that the size of the family may be well controlled with the medical aids and relevant advices available for the purpose.
2. To impress upon the youth that a small family is very base to one's happiness and prosperity.
3. To acquaint the young students about the trend of population rise in the country and in the world and the implications of the same on human happiness.
4. To explain to the youth how a small family is necessary for family welfare.
5. To impress on the students the alarming implication of dirty and densely populated localities, food problem, malnutrition and poor individual income.
6. To acquaint the youth how economic social, cultural and political life of a country is closely related with the rise and size of population.

The Requirements

We are mentioning below some of the major points dregarding the need for population education:

1. About 45 per cent of the Indian population is below 15 years of age. For controlling the alarming rise of population it is necessary to influence this age-group regarding the bad consequences of a big population. So in schools and colleges students should be given population education.
2. In most of the developing countries, there is a definitely planned policy of educating people regarding implications of rise of population. For this, newspapers, magazines, radio, television, advertisements and posturers are used. The readers and on lookers cannot be kept away from impacts

of these phenomena. So our young students will definitely come to know about family planning and its implications directly or indirectly. If there is no definite programme for educating them in a healthy manner about population education; they are likely to be misinformed by many undesirable sources. So it will be in individual as well as national interest to run a well chalked out programme of population education for youths.

3. The state is responsible for the welfare and health of its citizens. This responsibility may be well executed only when the people are told about the bad impacts of the population rise.
4. The need of population education in schools were not there, had there not been alarming explosion of population. But the reality is this that there is an urgent need for explaining the points involved in family planning and population education.
5. It is necessary to explain to the students the evil influence on the cultural, social and economic development due to explosion of population.
6. Problem of population is perennial. Hence young people of each generation must be informed about the implication of the same.
7. Through population education the younger generation may be well prepared in advance to fight out successfully realities and complexities of contemporary life which is beset with the evil influences of population explosion. As a result, they can well co-operate with the nation building programme. Hence the need of population education is necessary.
8. In any scheme of population education the youth of the rural area must never be ignored, simply because our population is mostly rural. Hence there is a greater need of spread of population education in the school situated in rural areas.

Various Phases

According to the theory of demographic transition there are the following three stages of population :

High Birth and Death Rates—Population in India is ever on increase. So far its growth has not yet been arrested. The problem of unemployment and food are closely associated with the population rise which has led our country into abject poverty. Ignorance, religious beliefs, superstitions and old traditions have been responsible for high birth rate and lack of medical facilities and food has resulted into high death rate. This situation has persisted till 1947.

High Birth Rate but Lower Death Rate—After achievement of independence in 1947, our standard of living has improved. Now we eat and dress in better ways than what we used to do about 40 years ago. We have now better medical facilities. So death rate has been reduced. But to our great dismay, the birth rate has continued its rise and now it has assumed an enormous size. This situation is very dreadful and it is a great threat to our security, happiness and prosperity.

Low Birth and Death Rates—When the standard of living improves, it results into a wide spread of education. Consequently, people become more conscious about their comforts and they become averse to raising a big family, because a big family consisting of alarge number of children will mean less privileges and comforts to them. That is why it is generally seen that it is the poor man who breeds more children and the rich one does not. No doubt, exceptions are there. So in an affluent society, the birth rate generally decreases and the availability of adequate medical facilities and better nutrition decreases the death rate also. Under this situation the great rise of population is controlled.

Population Explosion—India is undergoing the aforesaid second stage of demographic transition, i.e., we are having high birth rate and lower death rate. This situation is known as the stage of population explosion. We are facing this situation particularly since 1951 and this phenomenon is continuing even today to such an extent that we have now a population over 100 crores, whereas the undivided India of early thirties had only about 32 crore people. It is estimated that by the end of the 21st century our population may touch the limit of about 150 crore or more, because it has been observed that 22 crore children are born every year in India and out of this number 14 crore remain living. Our population is increasing at the rate of 1 crore and 50 lakh per year. We possess only 24% of the land of the earth and this land is inhabited by more than 16.8% of the world population. This alarming condition has struck a death knell to our happiness and prosperity. Hence our Central Government has decided to take certain positive steps to meet this situation. These steps consist of the following measures:

1. To educate women by formal and informal means about family planning.
2. To provide free medical aid under the family welfare programmes.
3. To give more attention to population education.
4. To utilize very widely the state and the Central government services pertaining to family welfare programmes.
5. 21 and 18 years of age have been fixed as the minimum marriage age for boys and girls respectively.

The above measures have been thought of and executed for successfully meeting the problems arising out of population explosion. Needless to mention that this explosion has led to lowering of living standard and aggravating of unemployment problem.

Family Welfare

Necessity has led our Central Government to start a very wide official family planning programme. Perhaps, India is the first country in the world which has started a national programme in this area. Since 1952 the Government of India has taken the Family Planning Programme under its direct control. At the time of finalising the First Five Year Plan it was decided to reduce the birth rate to such an extent that it was suitable for the national economic system. During the Second Five Year Plan it was concluded that the rise in birth rate would adversely influence the living standard. Hence the Family Planning programme was greatly emphasized. At the time of the finalisation of the Third Five Year Plan it was found that the birth rate was much higher than what it was estimated to be at the time of Second Five Year Plan. Hence Family Planning services were greatly advertised and the measures for the same were made available free to all poor or rich. This programme has been further encouraged in each and every Five Year Plan.

People have misconceived that the purpose of family planning is mainly to reduce the birth of children. In fact, to reduce the birth rate is only a process helpful in achieving the purpose. The purpose of family planning is also to make the parents conscious about their great responsibility towards the bringing up of their young ones in future. This planning further provides the necessary information about married life, care of the expectant and nursing mothers and sex education. Thus through family planning we want to make each family a happy unit of the society from the economic, social and cultural view points. Evidently, through family planning we do not mean only to have a control over human life, but we want prosperity of the same. So the family planning programme may be useful from the individual and national view point.

Individual Point of View—Too may conceptions adversely affect the health of a married couple. It is difficult to manage a large family consisting of many children. Too many children become a load to parents instead, of becoming a source of happiness. This attitude on the part of parents may directly affect the growth of children and many of them become a load on society as well in the form of inadequately developed personalities.

Family Point of View—If the family is big, the children are sure to be neglected. They will have poor health and inadequate education. Economic difficulties created by a big family will adversely affect the growth of each one in the family.

National Point of View—Family is a unit of the nation. If families of a nation are not happy, the nation, too, will not be prosperous.

That is why poor and unhappy families in our country have made our nation poor and weak in many respects.

Positive Aspects

On the basis of the above discussion we may now summarise the advantages of family planning in the following manner:

1. It is helpful for ensuring the happiness and prosperity of the family.
2. It provides security to all women and protects their health.
3. It gives an opportunity to the married couple to plan birth of their would-be children in terms of their economic position and other relevant aspects.
4. It ensures security to those married couples who due to some inherited diseases do not want to produce children.
5. It is helpful in making children happy and ensuring their good future.
6. It lays down the foundation of a happy family life.
7. Through good and healthy advice it may help childless ladies to produce babies.
8. It provides useful informations to the expectant and nursing mothers.

Co-operation of the People—It should be particularly noted that no family planning programme may succeed in the absence of people's willing co-operation. Government organisations will be able to do very little, if people are not willing on their own initiative. The success of this programme depends upon people's habits, behaviour and prevailing notions. Hence efforts have to be made to make the attitude of the people favourable to this programme. Towards the achievement of this goal the co-operation of popular leaders, social workers and volunteers are necessary.

Devices of Family Planning—There are many devices of family planning. One should be able to choose the suitable one according to his particular physical and mental disposition. Only one device cannot be recommended for all. Only that device should be considered as suitable which does not mar the happiness of the married life. Below we are hinting at some of the methods of family planning:

Perfect Control—This method is excellent if the couple are able to exercise the necessary control over themselves. But this is not very practicable. Hence it cannot be easily recommended.

Withdrawal Method—This implies that the semen is made to fall outside the female passage. This is risky and seldom sure, as even a single drop, if flown out inside, is sufficient for conception.

Safe Cycle Period—This period is about seven days before the commencement of the monthly course. It is believed that during this period, conception does not take place at the time of intercourse. This method is not reliable because of the unreliability of the physiological phenomenon and possible lack of control on the part of the couple.

Chemical Methods—Certain tablets and jelly are used for preventing conception. This method should be used under medical advice.

Mechanical Methods—Condom is a very popular device under this kind. The Government of India is selling crores of condom every year on nominal prices. They are available even at general stores and grocery shops. This is very easy to use and very reliable also.

Surgical Method : Sterilization—Vasectomy, tubectomy and loop are the devices under this group. In vasectomy, some concerned nerve of the man is tied; This prevents conception. Under tubectomy the fellopian tube of the women is tied in such a manner that conception is prevented. Loop is for women. This is tied by some trained doctors.

Of all the above methods vasectomy is regarded as the best method for the purpose.

Role of Education

The Government of India has made a systematic plan to approach about ten crore iliiterate and literate couples for giving the necessary information and services regarding family planning.

Besides newspapers, magazines, radio, television, films and dramas are some other devices to educate the public about the importance and advantages of family planning. Population education is being added to the courses in schools and colleges. In the adult education programme also the family planning devices are explained. Labour Unions, Pahchayats, Co-operative societies and other local organisations are being mobilized for explaining to the people the advantages of family planning.

The Government of India has also established certain centres of research and evaluation in this field.

It may be noted that even after vasectomy, tubectomy and loop, if some couple want babies due to certain valid reasons, the applied device may be cut out or melted away and the couple may have their normal reproduction cycle into operation.

QUESTIONS

1. Discuss the meaning, aims and need of population education.
2. What is population explosion ? How and why should it be controlled ?
3. What is population explosion ? Explain its underlying causes and its impact on the individual, family, society and the nation.
4. Explain the measures that should be adopted for meeting the problems arising out of population explosion in our country.
5. What is family planning ? Explain its purposes and advantages.
6. Explain the various aspects of the family planning programme in our country. What should be done for making this programme a success ? Suggest some concrete measures for the same.

23

Pollution Factor

Climate plays a very vital role on our health. Bad climate has adverse effect on us. That is why, physicians at times advise their patients to shift from an unfavourable climate to a better one. In this connection they may advise them to go to some hill station or near some sea coast area. An individual becomes used to a certain type of climate during the period of his growth and when circumstances compell him to move to some other climatic region, his health may be adversely affected. However, it may also be admitted that one may get used to even unfavourable climatic condition, if he remains there for a number of months or years.

There is a close relationship between atmospheric pressure and one's health. Within this pressure we may include three principal factors. These are—1. hot climate, 2. cold climate, and 3. damp climate.

Bad Effects

Due to intense heat one may get struck with heat wave causing bleeding from nose, fainting, lowering of capacity for work, unduly decreased heart palpitation, insomnia and nervous instability.

If one has to change his residence suddenly from a hot climatic region to a cold one, he may feel indigestion or have dystentery or some urinary discomfort. Besides, one may fall ill due to severe cold and his heart palpitation may shoot up beyond a normal range.

Dampness, intense or moderate, is always present in climate. Dry climate is a result of less dampness in the air over us. Normal dampness in climate induces more energy in us but its over presence creates uneasiness in us. In this situation there is enough perspiration, the drying power of air is reduced, our clothes become wet due to profuse perspiration. As a result, foul and disgusting smell comes out from our bodies and clothes. Damp climate may lead to breeding of disease producing germs. This may cause spread of some epidemics. This situation will make the entire atmosphere annoying and one may desire to move to some other places for respite.

Sunlight is very vital for our health. Sun-rays convert the ergestiol existing in our skin into 'D' vitamin which is very necessary for good healh now used in medical treatment of various types of diseases.

Rains produce dampness in the atmosphere. This dampness is generally harmful for human beings, this may lead to breeding of various types .of insects and germs.

Pleasant Effects

Trees and ponds create dampness and remove dryness from the nearby atmosphere. Trees and plants attract clouds resulting into good rains. That is why, various types of trees are planted in desert areas for attracting clouds leading to rains which make the soil more fertile. Scientific instruments like thermometer and barometer have been devised for measuring temperature and air pressure respectively. Hygrometer is another scientific instrument for measuring dampness in the air. Through these instruments one may make temporary adjustments in his living conditions for making himself more comfortable.

There is a continual presence of the air on our body. It is estimated that this presence is about 7 kilogram per inch over our body area. We do not experience this pressure in normal circumstances, but the mountaineers experience this pressure as they climb up further and further. This is so because the air on a mountain is thinner than what it is on the ground. As a result, a mountaineer feels difficulty in breathing. This proves that the atmospheric pressure plays an important role on the nature of climate.

24

Construction of School Premises

The place and situation of the school plays an important role on the health of children. Attention should, therefore, be paid to the following factors while establishing and building the school:

(1) Neighbourhood, (2) Water and air, (3) Soil and (4) Direction and surface.

The building of the school should be so situated that as far as possible, the distance is almost equal for all the attending students and they do not experience much fatigue in coming to the school. An ideal school is that which is situated near the locality of prospective students in an open space. Provision for play-gorund should exist so that the students may get open space for games and sports as well as fresh air. A school should not be situated near a slum area, near a railway station or in the centre of a market-place. At such places, the atmosphere is not peaceful and there is always a risk of accidents. Besides dust, smoke and lack of fresh air will prove detrimental to the health of children. Trees, too, near the school building are harmful. These obstruct the flow of fresh air and also stop the light. Dustbins, leather factories and animals should not remain near the school because foul odour coming out of them would affect the health of children.

Pollution Free

The school building should be built at a place where sub-soil water level is at a depth of more than ten feet. Clean and good water is found only after the depth of ten feet because all the foul matter is left in the upper layers of earth. This water is filtered through previous earth and becomes clean and harmless.

Similar to the relation of water and earth is the relation between the earth and air. Air exists in previous earth. The quantity of air in earth depends on the quality of earth. Proportion of air differs in various kinds of earth. Air exists in larger quantity in sand, gravel and chalk soils as compared to clay soil.

There is a difference between sub-soil air and that which exists above the soil. Carbon di-oxide is present in larger quantity in sub-soil air, while the quantity of oxygen is proportionately less. The sub-soil air abounds in impure and harmful gases. The number of germs, too, is larger in it. If this sub-soil air somehow enters the school building it will adversely affect the health of students. They will fall victims to a number of diseases. The position of sub-soil earth depends on sub-soil water. As the sub-soil level of water comes upwards, the air also rises upwards. During rains when the level of sub-soil water rises upwards, the air comes out of the soil and enters the school building, thus polluting the fresh air. It is, therefore, necessary, that the depth of sub-soil water should be examined at the site of proposed school building.

Ordinarily, the Soil may be divided into two parts :

(i) Porous and pervious and (ii) impervious.

The water easily penetrates the porous soil and flows through it. The proportion of air in this kind of soil is greater. Gravel and chalk soils come under this category. Solid and smooth soil absorbs water and does not allow it to flow out. It is because of this that the soil remains damp and wet for a longer time. Such places are cooler and damper. In these places the transformation of sub-soil water into the steam is a continuous process which is harmful for the inhabitants. In places of damp climate diseases like catarrh, gastric pains, measles, cough, malaria and lung diseases abound. The school building should, therefore, not be constructed at such places. Only dry surface with porous soil is suitable for school buildings because the rainy water easily flows through it and the soil dries.

It is, therefore, advisable to examine the soil before constructing a school building, because the climate of that place is affected by the soil and sub-soil water.

The Situation

The face of building should be in such a position that sunlight and fresh air may all the time be present throughout the working hours. South is the correct direction and most suitable one. The plinth level of the school building should be high. Low plinth level will allow the rain water to enter the room making it wet and damp. This dampness may produce many diseases.

Building Plan

The above stated facts should be kept in view before designing and constructing the school building. The foundation should be laid deep with a layer of at least one and half feet of concrete. The walls should then be raised. This will stop dampness and sub-soil air to enter the building.

Walls—The outer walls should be made of bricks and stones. Die walls should be at least of a brick and half thick, that is, about 14 inches or about 36 cm. The stone walls should not be less than about 50 cm in thickness. The plaster of the walls from ground level upto a reasonable height should be of a material that may check dampness appearing on walls. A mixture of cement, moorang (known as Kalpi sand) and damp proofing powder plastered to a height of four feet or 124 cm will prevent dampness. If the walls of the school building are made of clay, that should be painted on die upto four or five feet or 120 to 140 cm in height from the floor. This coating of tar prevents dampness and protects the walls from the reactions of alkaline objects.

The inner walls of the school building should be plastered and painted. Dampness appears on the walls, if these are not painted. Lime or ordinary paints alone are not enough for removing this defect. Germicidal products should be mixed while painting the walls.

Floors—The floor should be strong, smooth and clean. It should neither be slippery nor rough. It should be so constructed that it may easily be cleaned.

Roofs—The roofs should be strong and thick enough so that they may neither become so cold in winter that the room may be affected nor in summer should these become hot and affect the temperature in the rooms. Rain-water pipes should be so placed that the rain-water easily flows out without seeping into the walls. It is advisable, therefore, that the rain water pipes should run down leaving a little gap between the walls and pipes. The walls near the places where rain-water falls through pipes should also be plastered so that water may not find its way in the foundation.

Storeys—The school building, as far as possible, should be single-storied. Although, due to paucity of space in cities, double or treble-storied school buildings are constructed, but these prove unsuitable for school purposes. The children get tired while ascending or descending the stairs and sometimes they fall down from the stairs and receive grate injuries.

Doors and Windows—Sufficient number of doors and windows should exist in the building so that fresh air and light may reach in every corner of the building. The presence of many doors and windows enables the fresh air-to rush inside displacing the foul air within a short time of opening of doors. The school building should have at least two main doors.

Stairs—If due to paucity of space, multi-storied buildings have to be made then careful attention should be given to the design of stairs. There should be a solid wall on both the sides of the staircase and each step should be from 120 cm to 180 cm long, one 30 cm wide and 18 cm high.

Rooms of the School Building—The rooms of the building should be spacy and each student should have 225 cubic feet of space. There should exist a space five feet high and three feet wide for each student. The height of the room should be 15 feet. In this way, a class-room meant for 40 students should be 30 feet long, 20 feet wide and 15 feet high. If it is not possible to construct such big rooms, their area could be reduced but each student should' at least get a minimum of 192 cubic feet of space. The rooms of primary schools may be smaller.

Teachers' Room—In every ideal institution there should be a separate room for teachers, where they can relax during vacant periods. A bath-room should also be attached to it. A separate room should also be provided to the headmaster or the principal as the case may be. Adjoining this room should be the school office.

Doctor's Examination Theatre—An examination theatre is also necessary for the medical check up of students. This room should be equipped with instruments for examining ear, nose, throat, eye and other organs. Such an equipped room is an asset for a school. Medical examination does not in any way disturb the working of the institution. Students of different classes may come and get themselves examined in turns.

Lavatory and Urinals—Lavatories and urinals are necessary for schools. Separate arrangements should exist for boys and girl-students. These places should be at a reasonable distance from the main building and special attention should be paid towards their cleanliness. The lavatories and urinals should be so designed that sufficient air and light may reach there. The floors should be made of cement so that it may be easily washed with water. Attention should be particularly paid towards the level of the floor so that after washing it no water remains on it and easily dries up. The walls should be made of smooth bricks. Tiles may serve this purpose well. The walls should be plastered. In case it is difficult to make this arrangement, provision may be made of 'earth closet' or automatic earth closet. The urine and excreta of the day should be get removed daily and thrown in an open space far away from the school.

Arrangement of Light and Air—Existence of a number of windows in the room will ensure a good supply of air. Windows should exist on both sides so that there is a cross ventilation and the air may enter from one side and pass out from the other. Arrangements should be made of exhausts, air circulation of fans during summer and rainy seasons because it is hot in these months and fresh air is needed most.

Size of the School Building—For maintaining control and keeping eye over the activities of the students the building should be so designed that all the things may be visible from one place. With this end in view an ordinary school building is constructed in three ways : (1) building which has a central hall, (2) those which are oval in shape and (3) which have field inside.

Central Hall Plan Schools—In such schools there is a central hall around which there are class-rooms. Such institutions do not need more space. This design is, therefore, suitable for schools in cities. Such buildings may be made double-storied and each story may have a central hall.

In this kind of building natural air cannot reach in sufficient quantity. As such, this shortage of air has to be made good through mechanical devices. This needs plenty of money. Even then this arrangement is not very suitable. The number of windows on walls is less because except the corner rooms other rooms do not possess their independent walls. Consequently, there is no arrangement of cross ventilation. The rooms of such buildings get insufficient light because with the hall in centre is only an inlet for air.

During cultural or physical shows in the hall, teaching in class-rooms is disturbed, because the sound attracts the attention of children sitting in other rooms.

Pavillion or Staffordshire Schools—This type of building was for the first time built on a plan made by Dr. Reed in which an attempt was made to remove the shortcomings of the Central Hall Plan type buildings. According to this plan, the proposed building is divided into two wings. In one wing are held teaching classes and in the other are situated teachers' rest room, hall and other rooms. The two wings join like straight lines forming and angle. Classes are pavillion like with a verandah in the front. There are windows on both the sides of the rooms through whom fresh air and sufficient light enter the room. From the health point of view this type of building is better than the former type, but it is unsatisfactory as far as educational utility is concerned. This type of building may be multi-storied. Generally, this type of building remains single-storied, because ascending or descending the steps creates difficulties.

Courtyard Plan School—In this kind of school buildings there is a rectangular field in the centre around which rooms are consturcted. In this type of building more air and light is available in the rooms as compared to the Central Hall Plan type of building. In the centre field of this building there may be constructed a hall bisecting the main building into two parts.

1. Hall, 2. Playground, 3. Open path, 4. Cloak-room, 5. Laboratory, 6. Teachers' Room, 7. Principal's Room, 8. Entrance, 9. Classrooms.

This type of building is most suitable from control or discipline point of view. Its utility from educational point of view is greater. This type of building is superior to those mentioned earlier.

Furniture and other Equipments

The school furniture has an important bearing on the health of students. The size and shape of the desk is particularly important but unfortunately much attention is not paid towards this in our country.

The absence of suitable desks affects the vertebral column. If the desk is high, the student with a short stature will have to bend his backbone on one side and the distance between the book and eyes decreases. Consequently, defects appear in eyes. The student cannot write smoothly as a result of which his hand-writing becomes ugly and bad. Similarly, unsuitable chairs, too, have a bad affect on the body.

Desks—The desk should be slopy. It should not have a slope more than 15°. Both the eyes experience equal strain if the book is read at an angle of 45° and in so doing, less body energy is lost. Ordinarily, desks are of three kinds :

(1) Zero, (2) Plus and (3) Minus.

The front edge of the zero desk is in line with the front edge of the chair. This type of desk is most suitable for writing purposes.

There exists some distance between the plus desk and the chair. This type of desk produces many defects in the body because the student has to bend his body forward.

The front portion of the minus desk facing the child and the front side of the chair cross each other vertically. The chair cuts inside the desk. This type of desk is more useful than the other two mentioned earlier. But this type of desk should also be made according to the height of the students. The upper plank of the desk should be above the stomach of the boy. In the case of minus desk, the children experience difficulty in standing up and they cannot move their body freely.

Faringdon desks are the best amongst the joint type of desks. Chairs are attached to them which may be changed to desired positions according to the needs of the students. These may easily be fixed in zero, plus or minus positions.

Blackboard, Almirah and Stage—Blackboards made of slate are more suitable as compared to those made of wood or cement. These may be easily cleaned. The colour of the slate should be black. The wooden blackboards should be placed in such a position that they may not dazzle and the students may see without straining their eyes. The blackboard should be at least four feet wide and two to four feet above the floor level. The blackboards made on the walls are more useful.

Besides the blackboard, an almirah, a platform, a table and a chair are also required by the teacher. Almirah should be made in the wall itself. It is used for safely keeping the books, pen, inkpots, chalk, duster and the students' exercise books. The platform is of great use for short-statured teachers. Many schools have big wooden rectangular desks (chaukis) that serve the purpose of platform but these make the cleaning of room difficult. The brick platform is the most suitable one. The platform should be six to twelve inches in height. On this platform the table and chair of the teacher should be placed.

The Checkup

The need of a separate room in the school building for medical examination has been emphasised earlier. Provision of medical check-up of students is absolutely necessary. A number of students in every school suffer from one or the other diseases. Provision of medical facilities in a school considerably helps in the treatment or early diagnosis of diseases.

Every student should be medically examined at least four times during his early education period. First, at the age of five or six years when the child is admitted in the school, next when he is ten years of age and completes the primary education. The third time, he should be examined when he leaves the junior high school. He should also be examined, for the fourth time when he enters the high school.

The first medical check-up should take place in the presence of parents. Special attention at this time should be paid to the physical deformities and uncleanliness. The second medical check-up should be conducted in the presence of a teacher. During this check-up eyes, ears, throat, lungs etc., should specially be checked. The third check-up should concentrate on the physical development of the body and attempts should be made to find out if there are special changes. In the fourth check-up, it should be ascertained whether the school life had any special effect on the physique of the student and whether the student is fit to undertake heavy work.

Generally, during medical examination, the weight of the student is taken. Besides, his height and the breath of the chest are also measured. This gives an idea about his physical development. The clothes of the child and his head, eyes, ears, nose, teeth, nails etc., should particularly be examined. The successful result of the medical check-up depends upon the way in which the guardians, teachers and other persons concerned feel their duty and responsibility towards the child. These persons should ever remain vigilant and perform their duty towards the child with devotion.

The school physician should regularly examine the health of the student. On his advice, special diet should be given to the students and they should be admitted in schools, accroding to his advice. It is the duty of the school doctor to find out children suffering from infectious diseases and make arrangements for their isolation so that other students may not catch any infection. He should supervise the work of the school nurse and maintain a record of child's health. He should also inspect the arrangements of light, air, sanitation and physical exercise in the school.

Provision of a nurse is also necessary besides a physician, because with her co-operation, it becomes easier to gain knowledge of children's health. The school nurse should daily keep an eye over the cleanliness of children. She should inform the students of the date and time of medical examination so that they may appear at the appointed hour. It is also her duty to maintain a card recording the facts about the student's health. It is necessary to have the .previous history of the student in preparing his card. She should visit every house and acquaint herself with the family and home environment of the student.

The medical examination work in the school will remain incomplete in the absence of teacher's co-opearation with the doctor. It is, therefore, necessary that their co-operation is available to the doctor. Besides, the teacher should have a reasonable knowledge of infectious diseases, their diagnosis and treatment.

Proper treatment should be started of the diseases diagnosed during medical examination. If careful and proper treatment is not undertaken, all the labour of the school doctor will be lost. A school dispensary for proper treatment is necessary for treating cases of ear, nose, throat, teeth, eyes, vertebral column diseases. In India, such dispensaries are very few in number. There are hardly some school dispensaries in rural areas. Attention should, therefore be paid to this aspect.

The neighbourhood, water, air, earth direction and surface should be carefully examined before constructing a school builidng.

The school building should not be built in thickly populated and dirty localities and slums. It should also be not near a railway station, workshop or market-place. The foundation of the school building should be laid deep. Its walls, roofs and floors should be strong. The school building, as far as possible, should be a singlestoried one.

The rooms of the school should be spacious and provision of 325 cubic feet space should exist for each student. It is necessary that a teachers' rest room, medical examination room, lavatory and urinals should be provided in the school building.

The school buildings are made in three ways : (i) Central Hall Plan building, (ii) Pavillion building, (iii) Courtyard Plan building. The third type of school building is the most suitable one.

Amongst the school furniture, desk, chairs, blackboard and almirahs are important. Desks are of four varieties: (i) Zero, (ii) Plus, (iii) Minus and (iv) Faringdon desks. Separate desks are more suitable than the combined ones.

Desks and chairs should be made according to the physical stature of students. The blackboard made in the wall is better than a separate wooden blackboard.

Arrangement for medical check-up of the student should exist in schools.

Clean Environment

According to the World Health Organization environmental sanitation implies controlling of all those surroundings of man which in any way is likely to affect his development adversely, i.e; his health and longevity. A committee of experts appointed by the World Health Organization has presented a plan for controlling the following important items which may have bad effects on man's life:

1. To look after milk and other food articles.

2. To control the water resources in order to ensure pure and adequate water supply.
3. To control such insects, rats and other small animals which generally spread diseases.
4. To ensure cleanliness of drainage and refuse.
5. To see that the residential areas and surroundings of industries are clean and congenial to human health.
6. To see that in future only such houses are built which are health ensuring in all respects and do not permit any possibility of spread of diseases.
7. To see that big and small industries are situated in helathy surroundings and the dwelling places of their workers and roads, lanes and approaches to their residential places are clean and free from any danger due to pollution of air, noise and water.
8. To see that only such houses are constructed in future which are conducive to healthy life.

The Difficulty

Man wants to live in a group or community. Various types of communities may be found in a certain locality. Hence the problems of environmental sanitation are likely to differ according to the living ways and conditions of the communities concerned. We may think the following four such types of communities whose problem of environmental sanitation may be varying:

(1) Such people who have to work as labourers and are compelled to remain in temporary sheds or on road sides or beneath trees near the places of their work. Amongst such people may be mentioned labourers engaged in construction of roads, bridges and big building complexes. Such labourers may be seen on the skirts of any big city around which some sorts of construction are usually in process.

(2) People residing in big cities like Bombay, Madras, and Kanpur.

(3) Scattered hilly or rural communities which have to reside here and there separately in their own houses which they happen to construct near their fields or places of fruitful occupation.

(4) People in rural areas whose major occupation is agriculture. Such people happen to group themselves in small or big villages. A small village may have only eight or ten houses and a big one may consist of about fifty or even more.

The above four types of people have to face their particular problems of environmental sanitation.

Bad Effect on Health

Bad environmental sanitation may lead to many diseases. We are mentioning some of the major ones below:

Disease Spreading Insects—Lice and ticks are responsible for spreading of certain skin diseases. Sand fly may cause some type of serious fever, pests may spread plague and mosquitoes may cause malaria. Occurrence of such diseases may be checked if the insects responsible for them are destroyed before they breed into millions. It is also true that the general public does not know how various types of insects and pests cause fatal diseases.

Surface Contamination Development Infection—Tetanus, Septic Ulcer. Ulcers beneath the lower and upper bids of the eyes may be grouped under disease caused due to infection.

Alimentary Infection—This type of infection in the ailmentary canal is caused due to unhealthy environmental sanitation. Under this category of infection we may group typhoid, fever, dysentery, non-pulmonary tuberculosis, cholera, diarrhoea.

Generally all these diseases are caused due to unhealthy environment consisting of refuse and pits having urine and stool etc.

QUESTIONS

1. What factors should be kept in view while constructing a school building and why ?
2. Describe the various types of school buildings ?
3. What kind of furniture should be used in schools ?
4. What do you understand by school medical examination ? Discuss its ideal nature for a school.
5. What do you understand by environmental sanitation ? How has the W. H. O. defined it ?
6. Discuss the problems of environmental sanitation.
7. What are the ill effects on man's health due to bad environmental sanitation ?

25

Clean Village

India is a land of villages. About 80 per cent of its population, *i.e.*, about 80 crores of its people live in villages. In a way, our villages have always been away from the main currents of the upheavals of our land, although they have always remained the backbone of the nation. That is why, Gandhiji—the Father of the Nation, used to say that the soul of India resides in villages and unless their condition is unproved, the country cannot prosper. Therefore, it was in fitness of thing that in 1947 after achievement of Indpendence, our government diverted its attention to the upliftment and regeneration of the village people. Towards this end, a number of programmes in the areas of agriculture, health, sanitation, education and building of houses and many others have been started in rural areas through out the whole country. The starting of the Panchayat system infused a new life in the village people and they began to think that they had a say in making their own destiny. Because of the efforts so far made, now there are found schools, health centres, wells for drinking water, family planning centres within the easy reach of some of the villages.

Below we shall understand the items that may be included with in the village sanitation programme.

Mass Education—Most of the villagers are illiterate. They are almost ignorant of health laws and principles. They are badly in need of the requisite knowledge about the same. They must be told about dirty habit pertaining to food, clothing, bath, use of dirty and good water, unhealthy surroundings, dense localities and dirty lanes and unhealthy effects of ponds and tanks full of dirty water. Hence the villages are in great need of education regarding these things. Slides, lectures, posters and films etc. may be profitably used for their education. With the help of these things they will begin to understand the importance of healthy living and will save themselves from many diseases they often fall victims to.

Food Sanitation—One falls ill if he consumes dirty and unhealthy articles. Many of our villagers do not understand how to maintain sanitation of food materials. They should be told about the role that flies and dirt play in spreading many diseases. They should also be told so to how to protect food articles from flies and dirt. They should be educated as to what measures should be adopted for protecting oneself from epidemics and other diseases. They should also be informed as to how to purify the unhealthy water of wells, ponds and tanks. In certain ponds washermen should be restrained from washing clothes. They must also know how to protect food materials and water from cats, dogs, flies and other insects.

Water Supply—The importance of suitable water for human consumption cannot be over-emphasised. People in the villages must know how to obtain healthy water for drinking and for preparing food. Generally, it is seen that in most of the villages wells and tanks are not very deep. Hence their water easily becomes contaminated and spreads diseases: very easily. The drainage system in villages should be imporved. There are many villages which are either surrounded by unhealthy water or have dirty-inside drainages. Health of our villagers will always be in danger as long as this situation exists. As far as possible a few tube wells may be constructed for providing healthy water to villagers and at some places good wells and tanks should be dug with adequate enclosures with a view to protect them from flies, insects and domestic and other animals. Some adequate arrangements should be made for pumping out dirty water of wells and tanks periodically. Disinfectants should also be used for purifying water from time to time.

Disposal of Dead Bodies—It is generally seen that there is no arrangement, good or bad, for the disposal of dead bodies in villages. Dead bodies dogs, cats and other animals are generally thrown out in the near vicinity. Consequently, the whole atmosphere becomes dirty and unhealthy. For sanitation of villages suitable arrangement should be made for disposal of dead bodies of animals.

Disposal of Excretory Substances and House Refuse—There are no private lavatories in villages. So the villagers use banks of ponds and rivers, open fields, standing cropfields and other open places for excretions. This feature makes the vicinity of a village very foul. Sewer system is not possible in villages so trench lavatoreis and septic tanks may be more economical for villages. Through mass education the villagers must be told that the open air latrine system is very unhealthy as it may spread many diseases of intestines.

The house Refuse and the cow and buffalo-dung etc. are generally thrown at the skirts of the village or near some houses. This situation makes the whole atmosphere very dirty. Here various typs of flies and insect breed. They make the whole vicinity unhealthy. Consequently, water and food materials are also affected and they become prone to spread various types of diseases. Our villagers must be saved from this unhealthy atmsophere. They should be advised to dig pits for house refuse and those pits should be covered with earth whenever some refuse is thrown into them.

Rural Town Planning—The above account indicates that our villages are situated in a very unsystematic manner. There is no arrangement worth the name for water supply, light and fresh air there. Consequently, our villagers live in unhealthy surrounding. So there is a need of rural town planning with all the facilities of a healthy living.

Primary Health Centres and Dispensaries—A number of health centres and dispensaries should be established in villages for rendering services in case of simple and seasonal diseases, if not for chronic and serious ones.

Precautions—For rural sanitation the following points must be taken into consideration, otherwise any programme for the same may not yield the desired results:

1. Generally it is extremely difficult to execute any programme for the welfare of villages because of their peculiar situation, such as lack of suitable means of communications, minimum amenities of life and lack of co-operation from the villagers themselves due to party politics and rivalries. Hence competent persons with missionary zeal should be selected for executing any programme for villages. Moreover, they must be given the minimum possible amenities of life for working in unfavourably situated villages.
2. For the success of any programme, it is necessary that a programme should be very humble and simple in the beginning and should be framed after the necessary survey.
3. In making a programme, other suitable persons of some relevant department or area should also be consulted for avoiding any mistake.
4. It is better if a number of allied departments co-operate in making and executing any plan for villages.
5. The village people should be continually and consistently educated about health laws and principles, i.e., their health education must never be neglected.
6. It must always be kept in mind that our main purpose is to guide the villagers and to seek their willing co-operation for their own welfare. In other words, we must let them understand that they should be able to help themselves.

In this part of the book, onwards we shall deal with some such burning problems of public health in some greater details.

The Refuse

Refuse may be grouped into the following four types:

(1) Refuse coming from the cleaning of markets, stables, slaughter-houses and factories.

(2) Dry refuse, such as panicles of broken glass, bottles, broken rusted iron pieces, ashes and pieces of bricks and wood.

(3) Refuse consisting of dirty things collected through sweeping of lanes and roads. This refuse consists of both dry and wet types. This may also have cattle dung and dry leaves of trees and plants.

(4) Wet refuse collected from the useless matter of vegetables, meat and fish.

Near all dwelling places or residential areas arrangements of scavenging are supposed to exist. If scavenging is not done, there will be a great danger to public health. So authorities are particularly careful for engaging persons for scavenging of sweeping and when scavenging is stopped flies and insects will breed and will spread various types of infectious diseases.

It is very necessary that all types of refuse are collected at a place for their disposal at some suitable place every day both in the morning and evening. It is generally seen that some people throw out refuse here and there. This habit on their part pollute the environment. Dustbins should be provided at various street and lane corners in order that people place their refuse into them. Dustbins should be placed at convenient places. The people should utilise them properly. It is generally seen that some people instead of throwing their refuse into the dust bins, they place it near it or throw it into the dustbin in such a manner that the whole of it does not go into the dustbin. For collecting refuse wheel burrows should be provided. Wheel-burrows are to be used for those places where buffalo-cart cannot enter into narrow lanes. Wheel-burrows bring the refuse from certain corners and place it into the dust-bins. Arrangement should be made for removal of refuse at least twice every day. The refuse cart or the wheel burrow should have a lid over it in order that the refuse does not drop or come out of it in the process of removal. In big cities like Kanpur, Lucknow, Bombay, Calcutta and Delhi lorries are used for removal of refuse. These lorries, too, should be covered while moving loaded with refuse, otherwise the refuse put into them will pollute the air and some portions of refuse will fall down in movement from one place to another.

Disposal Arrangements

There are various methods of disposal of refuse. One method is that of dumping it into some tank, pit or low lying area far away from any inhabitance. If dumping is not done carefully, flies, rats and snakes may hover around the same jeopardising the health and life of the people neraly. The ground which is thus prepared by dumping refuse into low lying area or ponds is called made soil. It will be dangerous to construct houses on made-soil unless the same is left to subside at least for a decade or so.

If some sea is very near, the refuse may be disposed into it. Composting is another method of removal of refuse. Through composting good quality of fertilizer is prepared. Pits are dug for composting or the refuse may be collected at some suitable place just on the ground surface. In both the cases the refuse should be turned over up and down in order to obtain good fertilizer.

Suitable arrangement of urinal is necessary at places where a number of persons happen to passby or work. This means that on road sides, lanes and in markets, mohallas, hostels and all types of big offices urinals should be provided. The provision of urinal may be of three types, such as trough urinal, bore-hole urinal or funnel urinal. If necessary, some other type of urinal may also be provided.

There are various ways of disposal off dead human bodies in different parts of the world. In some country dead human bodies are thrown for consumption before dogs which are purposely kept for this purpose. In some they are thrown out in dense forests where birds and wild animals may devour them. Besides, there are two principal ways of disposal off dead human bodies. One is that of cremation and the other is that of burial. We shall understand these two principle ways below.

Last Spots

Cremation is a very old practice with Hindus for disposing off dead human bodies. If there is a river, tank or lake nearby, then the dead body is carried on its bank and it is burnt with dry pieces of wood. If there is no river, tank or lake in the surrounding areas, the dead body is burnt away from human abode in open plains. In some western countries also this method is now followed. There is no doubt that this is best method of disposing off dead human bodies. Electric cremation ground or platform has also been now raised for burning dead human bodies in big cities all over the world.

Fire is a great natural cleaner. We generally get rid of useless things by buring them off. Harmful effects of most of the edibles are removed through proper cooking.

Some poor families in India burn only the lace of the dead body and throw it in a river, because they do not have money to purchase pieces of wood for burning the whole body. This is an unhealthy method of disposal off a dead body, because it poses a great danger to public health, as the river water is polluted thereby. Therefore some big cities have enacted municipal laws for proper disposal off dead human bodies.

This method is usally followed in Muslims and Christians in India. In other parts of the world also this method prevails. In this method a pit about five or six feet deep is prepared for placing into it the dead body. Dead bodies of young children of Hindus within the age of one or two years are also buried, instead of being burnt. When the dead body is placed in the prepared pit then it is covered well with earth in such a way that wild animals are not able to take it out. Within a period of four to ten months the various parts of the dead body are merged with soil and they become a part of the ground. Certain precautions should be observed in burying dead bodies. The place of burial should be soft and not rocky. It should be on a higher level than the general ground and it should be much away from any river or tank, or human abode. The place of burial should be quite spacious in order to permit burial of other dead bodies also in future.

This may be done by dumping it into some pit, or it may be spread in agricultural fields as a fertilizer. It is also a practice with some people to prepare cakes from cattle dung for using it as fuel. If dung is not properly disposed off, it will spread foul smell and flies will also surround them and breed themselves into millions. Methane gas is also prepared from cow-dung for cooking purposes. The residual portion after preparing methane gas is called humus which may be used as fertilizer.

Sometimes the refuse is burnt in a furnace especially prepared for this purpose. The residual portion after the incineration or burning down the refuse may be used in construction of roads.

Cattle Care

Cattle House. The following points should be kept in view while erecting a cattle shed or a stable:

1. The cattle shed should be made at such a place that excreta are easily cleaned out.
2. The shed or stable should be at least twenty feet away from a human dwelling place and fifty feet away from a tank or river.
3. The space to be provided for each cattle should be about five or six feet wide and the space in front of the cattle should be at least four feet long. In this manner it will be easy to feed them and milk cows and buffaloes.
4. Each animal should be provided a window at least three to four feet wide and long.
5. The manger for each cattle should be separately provided at such a distance from each other that another cattle does not mouth in the fodder of another cattle.
6. There should be adequate provision of pure water for each animal.
7. The shed should be so constructed that it may easily be cleaned before milking the animals concerned.
8. The animal which is allowed to graze in field should have at least 700 cubic feet space and for that which is not taken out for grazing in open field should be allowed at least 900 cubic feet space.
9. The floor of a shed should be well bricked roughly but strongly cemented in order to permit cleansing.

10. Goats and sheep should not be kept with cows, buffaloes and horses for obvious reasons. Separate sheds should be erected for them. Their shed, too, should be spacious enough and should be at such a distance from a residential place that their foul odour does not pollute the atmosphere. These animals, too, have to be protected from extreme heat and cold. So in the erection of a shed for them also all the aforesaid precautions should be reasonably observed.

Slaughter House

Before an animal is taken to a slaughter house, it should be thoroughly examined. It should look healthy in appearance from all points of views. Its body should be smooth in touch. There should be no secretion from its nostrils, eyes and mouth. It should have no wound. It should have no foul smell from its nose. In fact, it should be got thoroughly examined by some veterinary doctor.

Now we shall understand the points to be observed in erecting and maintaining a slaughter house.

It will be better if no particular individual is permitted to run a slaughter house, as he is liable to be careless in the matter. Hence the municipal board or the township authority should erect and maintain a slaughter house. In such an arrangement it will be easy to ensure all hygienic conditions. Generally, bad and unhealthy meat is sold from a slaughter house run by private persons. The vicinity of such a slaughter house is generally very dirty. When the slaughter house is maintained by a municipal body, there will be proper arrangement for medical examination of the cattle and rules of cleanliness and general hygiene of the slaughter place are likely to be better observed. Only licensed butcher should be permitted to slaughter and he should not be suffering from either asthma or any infectious disease. There should be a fixed hour for slaughtering. The morning hour is generally regarded, as the best time for it. The pieces of meat taken out for sale should be sealed and have a particular mark identifying its purity and genuineness. The butcher should see that blood does not flow hither and thither in the process of slaughtering. Some iron utensil should be used for collecting and throwing out such a type of blood. The blood must never be permitted to throw into a drain or gutter. The hide and other useless portions of the slaughtered animal should be placed at a particular place especially provided for the same. The meat should be taken out in a covered can or vehicle and the inner portion of the same should have a lining of zincsheets.

The following precautions should be observed in erecting and maintaining a slaughter house:

1. A slaughter house should have adequate light and fresh air. The particular place of slaughter should be well iron-screened in order to ward off flies and other insects.
2. A number of water taps should be provided for occasional necessary washing of hands, tools and equipments.
3. The ceiling should be at least fourteen or sixteen feet high.
4. A separate well ventilated room should be maintained within the slaughter house for storing blood, bones, and other waste materials.
5. Necessary scaffolding with hooks should be provided for taking off the hides of the slaughtered animal.
6. There should be enough slope in the drain in order that the blood and waste water may go out easily.
7. The floor should be pucca and quite smooth and it should not look cruel to the eyes.
8. The waiting place for customers should be at least 25 or 30 feet away irom the slaughter house.
9. The slaughter house should be at least 80 or 120 feet away from human habitations.
10. The animals brought for butchering should be kept in a waiting shed at least 20 feet away from the slaughter house in order that the animal does not get afraid while looking at another animal being slaughtered.

Construction of the House

A house should be constructed in such a manner as to permit adequate fresh air, sunlight and other minimum comforts. Proper arrangement of cross-ventilation should also be there. In a way the problem of housing particularly for women is more difficult in rural areas in our country than in the urban one, because the menfolk generally sleep outisde in the open and the women have to be inside their house for most of the time except when they are also working in open fields. Most of the houses in villages in India are generally constructed without windows. This situation does not permit fresh air to come in. Moreover, no proper outlet is made for flowing out rain-water. Such houses remain generally damp. Such a housing provision is not congenial to health. So the inmates neither feel comfortable during summer nor during winter.

The condition of housing in urban area is different, because there is a municipal or town-area board to regulate construction of houses according to certain plans which have to be governed by certain by-laws and other regulations prescribed for the purpose. The rules made for constructing houses for urban area should also be followed in rural areas upto some extent for obvious reasons. In fact, in daring so there will be no difficulty, because there is generally enough ground in villages for constructing houses.

The Objectives

1. A house provides protection from rains, winter and hot sun.
2. A house ensures personal and family privacy.
3. Within a house it will be easy to control the passage of air and light.
4. House protects the inmates from infectious and other diseases.
5. Within a house one may feel protected from possible accidents.
6. One feels great satisfaction in owing one's own house.

Bright Side

The Selection of a Suitable Place—While deciding about a place for constructing a house the soil of the ground should be particularly noted. Its level from the surface ground is also quite important. This level should be about 30 to 35 cm higher than the common ground surface. The house should be constructed at such a place as to permit enough light and fresh air. The provision for pure water should also be kept in view. Either a deep well should already be near at hand or enough space should be left for consturcting a suitable well near the new house in view. The site for the house should be far away from a factory, brick-field or trenching ground. The soil of the place should soak rainy water easily. The chosen place should be such that the house to be constructed on it should be open from the Eastern and Southern side. This position will permit sufficient fresh air and sunlight for the house.

Construction—After selection of the place the style of construction should receive serious consideration which may pertain to foundation, ceiling height, roof, windows, doors, size of rooms, verandahs and toilets etc.

Foundation—The foundation of the outer and inner walls should be so deep as to sustain onslaughts of both rains, extreme'heat or any possible storm which may occur at least once or twice a year. So the foundation should be about a metre deep.

Walls—Walls should be at least 30 to 35 cm thick. The outer and inner walls should be well plastered if they are made of bricks. In villages where bricks are not used for constructing houses due to paucity of funds, such a quality of soil should be used for raising the walls as to make them strong durable and reasoning smooth after clay-plastering.

Ground Floor—The ground floor of the various rooms should be at least twelve to fifteen cm higher than that of the verandahs and courtyard. This position will permit out-flow of water when the rooms are washed.

Roofs—The roof may be either having slope or of an even level. The even level makes the roof useable in winter and summer. So it is always better if the roofs are laid in one regular level and not slopary. It is a pity that many persons build roofs of their bricked houses in cities slopary. In such a situation, they are deprived of the use of an even roof during summer and winter.

Kitchen—The kitchen should be so designed away from the toilet as to have enough fresh air and light. The windows and ventilation for it should be sufficiently big in order that smoke may blow out easily. For a family of about six persons, the size of the kitchen should be about 4 metres by 6 metres. This size may be further enlarged if considered necessary.

Latrine—Latrines should be constructed away from the kitchen and well. Normally, in many village latrines are not constructed and all have to go in the open air to respond to their natural calls. This situation in our country will remain as it is so long as the standard of general living in our rural area is so raised as to enable every one to have a brick wall of his house and have deep tube well constructed through boring.

Building Materials—Under building materials we have to be careful about the quality of bricks, timber, iron bars, mortar, lime, cement and sand. Regarding qualities of all these, expert engineers should be consulted. Engineers have made experiments in this connection. So their expert advice must not be overlooked.

QUESTIONS

1. What are the factors that we should attend to and how in rural sanitation ?
2. What are the precautions that we should observe in rural town planning and why ?
3. Describe the various types of refuse.
4. How should the refuse be collected?
5. What arrangement should be made for disposal off refuse?

26

Role of Education

Teaching is an essential part of education. Its special function is to impart knowledge, develop understanding and skills. It generally excludes inculcation of values like truth. It is usually associated with the in parting of knowledge of 3 R's—Reading, Writing and Arithmetic—representing various school subjects. Education, on the other hand, has a wider connotation. It implies 7 R's - Reading, Writing, Arithmetic, (All three denoting school subjects), Rights, Responsibilities, Relationships and Recreation (Requirements and ideals of a modern democratic state). In teaching we limit our outlook omitting those more important means of education which are involved in the school as a systematically organised social community, including its tone or general moral environment, its government and discipline, and that potent influence—the personality of the teacher. James Welton observes, "We treat teaching by itself, because it is an aspect of school life which can be singled out in thought, though it cannot be separated in reality, from the whole of which it forms a part and because it covers a fairly consistent body of doctrine. It is true that the value and success of all school teaching depends on those wider and deeper elements of school life-tone, discipline, etc. - which are omitting. But it is true that whilst the latter may be excellent the former may be of poor quality.

Albert Einstein (A Swiss Physicist 1879-1950): The supreme art of teaching is to awaken joy in creative expression and knowledge.

American Educational Research Association Commission in 'Handbook of Research on Teaching' (1962): Teaching is a form of interpersonal influence aimed at changing the behaviour potential of another person.

Amidon and Hunter (1967): Teaching is an interactive process, primarily involving classroom, which takes place between teacher and pupils and occurs during certain definable activities.

Anatole France (French novelist 1844-1924): The whole art of teaching is only the art of awakening the natural curiosity of young minds for the purpose of satisfying it afterwards.

B.O. Smith (1963): Teaching is a system of actions involving an agent, an end in view, and a situation including two sets of factors those over which the agent has no control (class size, size of classroom, physical characteristics of pupils etc.) and those that he can modify (ways of asking questions almost instructions and way of structuring information or ideas gleaned.)

Burton (1963): Teaching is the stimulation, guidance, direction and encouragement of learning.

Clark (1970): Teaching refers to activities that are designed and performed to produce change in student (pupil) behaviour.

Floyed Well (1958): Children are notoriously 'curious about everything except the things people want them to know. It then remains for us to refrain from forcing any kind of knowledge upon them and they will be curious about everything.

CaWeo Calieleo (Italian astronomer 1564-1652): You cannot teach a man anything, you can only help him to find it himself.

HE. Morrison (1934): Teaching is an intimate contact between a more mature personality and less mature one which is designed to further the education of the latter.

Israel Sheffler (1966): Teaching may be characterised as an activity aimed at the achievement of learning and practised in such a manner as to respect the student's intellectual integrity and capacity.

John Dewey (1859-1952): One might as well say he has sold when no one has bought, as to say he has taught when no one has learned.

John Bmbacher (1939): Teaching is an arrangement and manipulation of a situation in which there are gaps and obstructions which an individual will seek to overcome and from which he will learn in the course of doing so.

John Chapman (1960): The gift of teaching is a peculiar talent, and it implies a need and craving in the teacher himself.

Joyce and Well (1972): Teaching is a process by which teacher and students create a shared environment including set of values and beliefs (agreement about what is improvement) which in turn colour their view of reality.

J. Wilton: To know where the pupils are and where they should try to be are the first two essentials of good teaching.

Michael Oakeshort (1966): Teaching is two-fold activity of communicating information and communicating judgement.

N.L. Gage (1962): Teaching is a form of interpersonal influence aimed at changing the behaviour potential of another person.

Ned. A. Flanders (1970): Teaching is an interaction, process. Interaction means participation of both teacher and students and both are benefited by this. The interaction takes place for achieving desired objectives.

Paul Goodman (1980): A good teacher feels his way, looking for response.

Thomas P. Green (1971): Teaching is the task of a teacher which is performed for the development of a child.

W.R. Ryburnt (1946): Teaching includes the training of emotions of the child. It is one of the means of giving right feeling to the children.

William Lyon (1970): In my mind teaching is not merely a life work, a profession, an occupation, a struggle, it is a passion. I love to teach, as a painter loves to paint, as a musician loves to play, as a singer loves to sing, as a strongman rejoices to run a race.

Yoakm and Simpson: Teaching is a means whereby society trains the young in a selected environment as quickly as possible to adjust themselves to the world in which they live.

Analytical Approach

In the type of teaching as mentioned by Morrison, teaching is reduced to what the teacher does. There is interaction but the flow of instruction is from the teacher. In this type of teaching, the learners may become passive listeners

Brubacher's definition of teaching assigns more place to the learner. This approach tends to be child or learner-centered.

B.O. Smith seems to be more pragmatic in his approach to teaching. He accepts certain limitations of the learner in the teaching learning process.

Smith's definition contains the following three elements:

(a) Teaching is a system of action.
(b) Teaching is a goal-directed action.
(c) Teaching takes place in a situation comprising the controlable and uncontrolable set of factors.

A review of the definitions given above reveals that to play his role competently in teaching, a teacher is expected to understand the significance of the following:

Who is to teach. The teacher is to teach and he must understand himself thoroughly his strengths and weaknesses and strive to present a reasonably good model before his students.

Whom to teach. The child is to be taught. Therefore, a teacher should understand him thoroughly his abilities, aptitudes, attitudes, manners and temperaments and accordingly cater to the individual differences of students.

Why to teach. The teacher should always keep in view that the aim of education is to develop harmonious personalities, who are culturally refined, emotionally stable, ethically sound, mentally alert, morally upright, physically strong, socially efficient and spiritually enlightened. He should not forget even for a moment that the traditional 3 R's have been replaced by 7 R's, that is, reading, writing, arithmetic (representing various disciplines), rights, responsibilities, relationships and recreation.

Where to teach. The teacher ought not to visualise the school to be merely a place of imparting information but a place where men of tomorrow are trained to take their place as enlightened citizens in the society and contribute to national development.

What to teach. The teacher must have mastery over the subject he teaches.

How to teach. The teacher must use new teaming-learning technology to make his teaching. Effective and inspirational.

When to teach. Appropriate steps need to be taken by the teacher to develop motivation of the student in the entire work.

Instructions in Practice

Instruction is primarily concerned with the development of knowledge and understanding in the pupil about a thing, system or process. Imparting of knowledge and understanding merely represents one of the several objectives which we want to achieve through teaching. Teaching is concerned with all the domains of pupil's behaviour, i. e., cognitive, conative and affective. Instruction is a part of teaching.

The distinction between teaching and instruction may be seen from another angle. The face to face interaction of the teacher and taught found in teaching is not so much essential in the process of instruction . In instruction, a teacher may be replaced by the programmed material, computer, teaching machine, radio and television etc. A teacher cannot be replaced by these aids. Of course, in teaching a teacher makes use of them. Thus, instruction is one of the several modes of teaching.

Salient Features

Teaching is giving Information. There are many things that the students cannot find out for themselves. There are many things that they can never know unless they are told. There are many things the use of which they do not know. These things they have to be told. So one essential part of teaching is communicating knowledge. Knowledge must be given in a systematised manner. Teaching should be-made interesting. It must, however, be stressed that knowledge aspect should not be unduly emphasized.

Teaching is Causing to Learn. It is wrong to think, that knowledge can be passed on from one person to another like money. Knowledge will be received only when the students are prepared to receive it. Real teaching consists in persuading the child, by one method or the other to learn for himself. The teacher is an instrument in helping a child to learn how to do things for himself.

Teaching is a Matter of Helping the Child to Respond to his Environment in an Effective Manner. F.N. Freeman observes, "It is not what is presented to the child which educates him, but rather the reaction that he makes to what is presented. Certain children may fail entirely to respond to a lesson, or may respond in a wrong manner. If a child's response to his geography is to memorize the words, without any understanding of the facts they represent, the lesson is ' educative for him (he has not been taught), although it may be educative for the child next to him who reacts properly."

Teaching is Helping a Child to Adjust himself to his Environment. A child is reacting in some way or the other to his physical and social environment, from his very birth. His reactions are both fruitful and harmful. Teaching should help the child to make successful adjustment. This may be done in two ways. Sometimes we modify the environment and at other times strengthen the child. Teaching should make the child socially efficient, that is, a worthy member of society, making his contribution to the common good. Yoakam and Simpson: write, "Teaching is a means whereby society trains the young in a selected environment as quickly as possible to adjust themselves to the world in which they live. In primitive societies this adjustment means conformity with things as they are. In more advanced civilizations, such as ours, effort is made not only to adjust to things as they are but also to make an advance in the improvement of conditions of life by training the young in modes of thinking and acting which will help to improve the conditions of living that surround them."

Teaching is Stimulation and Encouragement. Teaching should fire the enthusiasm of the child. It is to encourage the child in the development of his natural desires to work, and to be active.

Teaching is Guidance. Teaching is to guide the pupils to learn the right things in the right manner and at the right time. Teaching is to guide the students to do things in such a way that time, material and energy are not wasted.

Teaching is Training the Emotions of the Child. Ryburn observes, "It is also the encouraging and training of the emotion all life. This is an aspect of teaching which is very commonly neglected', at least in practice. But our teaching will be only one-sided and distorted unless we take into account the 'necessity for helping the child to develop a stable emotional life." Teaching is to develop the emotional life of the child by providing an atmosphere of love, affection and freedom. Teaching is to provide such activities as will sublimate their instinctive urges to action.

Teaching is Both a Conscious and an Unconscious Process. Teaching is both a conscious and an unconsciously process and the most effective part of it is generally the part of which we are unconscious. The personal relationships between the teacher and the taught have a great bearing on the growth of the child.

Teaching is a Means of Preparation. Though preparation for future is not the only aspect of teaching, yet it is an important aspect: Teaching is to help the immature child to develop physically, intellectually, emotionally and spiritually to participate effectively in the life of the community.

Teaching is Formal as well as Informal. Formal teaching is deliberately planned, systematically organised and is always purposive. Teachers are just formal agents of teaching. School is not the only agency of teaching. Informal teaching is carried on by the parents, brothers and sisters at home, playmates, student community outside the classroom, etc. The few hours of the school are insufficient for the full development of the child. Formal and informal teaching must coperate, if good results are to be achieved. School should 'supplement' not 'supplant', the training imparted by the home and *vice-versa.*

Teaching as a Skilled Occupation. Every successful teacher is expected to know the general methods of teaching and instruction in creating suitable learning situations. He is also expected to be familiar with the general objectives of education.

Teaching is an Art. Art implies the intelligent action of a human being through which it is possible to modify an ordinary course of events. Teaching is an art which can be improved through research.

Teaching is a Form of Social Service. The teaching profession is regarded to be a sort of social.servjce and the teachers as servants of society in whose hands has been entrusted the task of shaping and developing the behaviour and conduct of the young children for maintaining and improving the social patterns.

Teaching as a Relationship. Teaching is a, relationship which is established between three focal points in education, the teacher, the child and the subject. Teaching is the process by which the teacher brings the child and the subject together. The teacher and the taught are active, the former in teaching and the latter in learning.

Teaching as a Skilled occupation. Every successful teacher is expected to know the general methods of teaching and instruction in creating suitable learning situations. He is also expected to be familiar with the general objectives of education.

Teaching is Both an Art and Science. Silverman (1966) has expressed the nature of teaching in these words, "To be sure teaching-like the practice of medicine-is very much an art which is to say, it calls for exercise of talent and creativity. But like medicine, it is also a science, for it involves a repertoire of techniques, procedures and skills that can be systematically studied, described and improved. A good teacher, like a good doctor, is one who adds creativity and inspiration to the basic repertoire."

Teaching in Practice

1. Creating learning situations.
2. Motivating the child to learn.
3. Arranging for conditions which assist in the growth of the child's mind and body.
4. Utilizing the initiative and play urges of the children to facilitate learning.
5. Turning the children into creative beings.
6. Inspiring children with the nobility of thoughts, feelings and action.
7. Giving information and explaining it.
8. Diagnosing learning problems.
9. Making curricular material.
10. Evaluating, recording and reporting.

Qualitative Aspects

Sri Aurobindo describes the marks of good teaching in these words, "The first principle is that nothing can be taught. The teacher is not an instructor or task master, he is a helper and guide. His business is to suggest and not to impose. He does not actually train the pupils's mind, he only shows him to perfect his instruments of knowledge and helps and encourages him in the process. He does not impart knowledge to him, he shows him how to acquire knowledge for himself. He does not call forth the knowledge that is within, he only shows him where it lies and it can be habituated to rise to surface. The distinction that reserves this principle for the teaching of adolescent and adult minds and denies its application to the child, is a conservative and unintelligent doctrine. Child or man, girl or boy, there is only one sound principle of good teaching. Difference of age only serves to diminish or increase the amount of help and guidance necessary, it does not change its nature."

John Dewey (1859-1952) states, "The more a teacher is aware of the past experiences of students, of their hopes, desires, chief interests, the better will he understand the forces at work that need to be directed and utilized for the formation of reflective habits." Further he writes, "The teacher is a guide and director, he steers the boat but the energy that propels it must come from those who are learning."

Albert Einstein (1879-1955) has observed, "It is the supreme art of the teacher to awaken joy in creative expression and knowledge.

Montaigne, a French philosopher (1533-1592) advises, "A tutor should not be continually thundering instruction into the ears of his pupil, as if he were pouring it through a funnel, but, after having, put the lid, like a young horse, on a trot before him, to observe his paces, and see what he is able to perform, should according to the extent of his capacity, induce him to taste, to distinguish, and to find out things for himself, sometimes opening the way, at other times leaving it for him to open."

Joseph Payne (English educator, 1808-1876) writes, "The teachers part in the process of instruction is that of guide, director or superintendent of the operation by which the pupil teachers himself."

Swami Vivekananda (1863-1902) describes the role of the teacher in teaching as, "The true teacher is he who can immediately come down to the level of the student."

Good teaching recognises individual differences—Good teaching treats each child as unique. Good teaching recognises that catering to individual differences brings strength. It must be remembered that standardized procedures do not fit every pupil.

Good teaching is causing to learn—Good teaching enables the child to learn for himself. It is not stuffing the mind of the child with information. Good teaching is what we can make the child do for himself.

Good teaching provides opportunities for activity—The child is inherently active. Passiveness on the part of the child implies that he is not in good physical and mental health. A good teacher keeps the students active. He is aware of the fact that to keep the students disciplined, he must fill the time with work and he does so accordingly.

Good teaching involves skill in guiding—A good teacher motivates his teaching. He stimulates " through his personality and his activities the personalities and activities of the pupils." He creates such situations as lead to desired types of learners.

Good teaching is kindly and sympathetic—Good teaching must create an environment of acceptance, sympathy and understanding.

Good teaching decreases the distance i.e. to either teacher and the taught—Teachers should come out of their ivory tower and come as close with the students as possible.

Good teaching is not tied to any method—Methods, techniques and devices should be adopted to local situations and considered as servants and not masters.

Good teaching is cooperative—Good teaching is an active and living process. A good teacher seeks the cooperation of the learners.

Good teaching is kindly and sympathetic—A good teacher always creates. A cordial atmosphere in the classroom. He always ensures his pupils's emotional stability and security. He is loving, kind, affectionate and sympathetic to his pupils. He bears in mind this fact "love the child and he will love you, hate him and he will hate you." He avoids scolding and sarcasm.

Good teaching involves careful planning—Good teaching keeps in view that everything cannot be taught to children at every time. A good teacher carefully studies the mental make-up of the pupil he teaches, studies the individual differences of pupils and then prepares his subject-matter. An unplanned lesson often results in a failure and involves a waste of time, energy and money also.

Good teaching is democratic—A good teacher always respects the individuality of his pupils. He keeps democratic ideals, contents, methods and objectives in view.

Good teaching provides desirable and selective information—The good teacher does not try to teach all the available information that he gathers form books and experience. On the other hand he makes a judicious selection and teaches all that is useful to live a good life as responsible member of the society.

Good teaching helps the child to adjust himself to his environment—Man has been struggling against natural forces since ages. He is expected either to adjust himself to these natural forces or to adjust the forces to himself. A good teacher helps the child in both directions.

Good teaching is progressive—A good teacher aims at improving his modes and techniques steadily. He also helps the child to make suitable progress in life.

Good teaching leads to emotional stability—There are very powerful inherited urges which always cry for expansion. A good teacher knows that unguided expression leads to wilderness, and therefore, helps in providing his pupils suitable opportunities which assist in training and sublimating their urges and emotions.

Good teaching is both diagnostic and remedial—A good teacher makes use of the various measuring instruments which have been provided by psychology and discovers the intelligence, aptitudes and interests of children and accordingly plans his work.

Challenge of Education-A Policy Perspective (1985). A publication of the Ministry of Education, and a forerunner of The National Policy on Education-NPE 1986, has something worth quoting, on quality of education. It states, "It is difficult to define quality, particularly with reference to educational processes. However, it could be stated that a quality conscious system would produce people who have the attributes of functional and social relevance, mental ability and physical dexterity, efficacy and readability and above all, the confidence and the capability to communicate effectively and exercise initiative, innovative and experiment with new situations. To these personal attributes one could add the dimensions of a value system conducive to harmony, integration and the welfare of the weak and disadvantaged."

Quality teaching also known as effective teaching is the chief instrument of quality education. It is essentially concerned with translating the objectives of education into action and practice. It is concerned with how best to bring about pupil learning by various activities. Quality teaching may be defined as the teacher's ability to stimulate students intellectually and move them emotionally to instill in them love for learning and develop suitable skills and attitudes.

Quality teaching is based on the premise 'All teachers should teach well and all students should learn well'.

An understanding of the following facts would go a long way in quality teaching:

1. Effective teaching is a comprehensive concept. Several variables are involved in teaching.
2. All types of variables play their part in teacher-learning situation.
3. 'What' and 'how' of effective teaching should be carefully comprehended.
4. There are several models of teaching and each should be considered in the overall context of teaching.
5. All models are complimentary to each other.
6. A teacher should adopt an electric approach in the selection of a model.

7. Developing a personal model of teaching in consonance with the requirements of quality teaching should become the cherished goal of every teacher.
8. Skill in creating intellectual excitement has two components: The clarity of an instructor's communications and their positive emotional impact on students.
9. Quality teaching results from a teacher's skill attracting both intellectual excitement and positive rapport with students.
10. The development of good rapport is based on three qualities in the teachers interaction with students: the teacher cares for student progress, the teacher has consideration for students as learners and the teacher respects students as individuals.
11. The three elements involved in teaching competence while contribute to teacher's authority and prestige are: Mastery over the subject, interest in the subject and effective learning situations and experiences.
12. Quality teaching presupposes an understanding mind; a feeling heart and a lofty personality.
13. In quality teaching the environment is of mutual cooperation and of purposefulness. A play-way spirit is the chief characteristic of the work.

Impressive Styles

A *'A'* is for alertness on the part of the teacher to the multifarious needs of the learners. Alertness is very helpful in taking appropriate decisions and timely corrective measures.

'A' is also for adaptability in handling several situations.

B 'B' is for businesslike attitude. It is to be ensured that every learner in the class, remains busy in realizing the goals set.

'B' is for balanced behaviour.

C 'C' stands for cooperative teaching-learning. The learners must be made active partners.

'C' is for clarity of purpose. The teacher and the learners must be clear about the goals for the achievement of which they are working.

'C' is for clarity of the subject-matter taught. A teacher must make all possible efforts to make his lesson clear. Difficulties of the learners must be appreciated and clarified.

D 'D' stands for democratic classroom environment.

'D' is for discovery. Children should be guided to find out new facts, ideas and principles. It helps children in becoming independent and resourceful learners.

'D' stands for democratic discipline.

E 'E' stands for expectancies. Each learner should be expected to learn. No learner should be considered without any potential.

'E' stands for enthusiasm. The teacher himself must demonstrate enthusiasm for his work.

'E' stands for appropriate etiquettes.

F 'F' is for feedback. Feedback helps the teacher and the learners to take timely corrective measures for the completion of the task.

'F' stands for faith of the teacher in himself.

G 'G' is for goal-setting. Appropriate goals should be set for the learners. They should also be made clear about the suitability of goals. Efforts may be made to associate the learners with the setting of goals.

H 'H' is for hard work on the part of the students as well as teachers. .

'H'is for humour. Humour on the part of the teacher releases fatigue and tension.

'H' stands for human touch.

I 'I' stands for involvement of all the learners in classroom activities and experiences.

'I' stands for impartial attitude.

'I' stands for inspirational teaching-learning.

J 'J' stands for just attitude.

'J' stands for judicious rewards and punishments.

K 'K' stands for knowing children's abilities, aptitudes and interests.

'K' stands for the knowledge of the sub-matter.

L 'L' stands for linking present, past and future knowledge.

'L' stands for leadership qualities.

M 'M' stands for motivation.

'M' stands for management of the class.

N 'N' stands for needs of the learners and their satisfaction.

O 'O' stands for open-mindedness.

'O' stands for out of class activities.

'O' stands for objectivity in approach.

P 'P' stands for praise. Verbal and non-verbal praise of children can motivate them to hardwork.

'P' stands for personal contact with every learner.

Q 'Q' is for quiz. From time to time, quiz competitions may be arranged in the class.

'Q' stands for quality teaching.

'Q' stands for question-answers.

R 'R' stands for review of the lesson.

'R' stands for relationships.

'R' stands for resourcefulness.

S 'S' stands for success experience. Success motivates the learner to achieve more.

'S' stands for scientific temper.

'S' stands for self-analysis and self-control

T 'T' stands for technology of teaching.

'T' stands for tutoring which involves removing difficulties, individually or in small groups.

U 'U' stands for undivided attention to teaching.

'U' stands for unbiased attitude to the treatment of controversial issues.

V 'V' stands for visual aids.

'V' stands for variety of experiences.

'V' stands for voice-modulated.

'V' stands for variation in the presentation.

W 'W' stands for welcoming attitude.

'W' stands for warmth towards students.

X 'X' stands for X-ray of the teaching process. It implies finding out of the difficulties and potentials of the students.

Y 'Y' stands for yardstick i.e. same standard basis of making a judgement on the performance of the students.

'Y' stands for you, implying that you (student) are the most important element in the teaching-learning process.

'Y' stands for zenith or excellence.

Either J. Swenson in the Teacher's Letter (1952) states that each of the following seven wonders brings a new challenge to the classroom teacher:

First wonder. How much children are ready know before they come to school. They bring with them rich resources of knowledge, skill and understandings-mostly self-learned.

First challenge. How much do I know of these rich resources? How far do I go in searching them out? How do I use what I find?

Second wonder. Children's eagerness to learn. It is natural for children to inquire, to discover. It is unnatural for them to be passive, disinterested.

Second challenge. How do I use this eagerness to learn? In what direction should it be channelled? Am I feeding it or killing it?

Third wonder. The never-ending process of learning. Every hour of the day, no matter where he is with whomever or whatever he works, the child learns.

Third challenge. Is he learning what is best for him, now and later? Am I setting the stage for constructive learnings?

Fourth wonder. The infinite variety of abilities, personalities, needs, and interests of pupils. He who says, "I know children" has not taken time to study the marvels of their growth.

Fourth challenge. Do I know as much as I should about each child's abilities, personalities, needs, interests? How can I learn more? Do I accept differences or rebel against them?

Fifth wonder. The concomity of learning. Simultaneously, children learn subject matters, traits of personality, habits of working, attitudes and appreciations-many of them permanently.

Fifth challenge. Do I push so hard toward a single goal that I push the children away from another of equal importance? Do I leave these "marginal learnings" to chance?

Sixth wonder. The faith, respect, loyalty and tolerance to children. When a teacher treats them well—sometimes even when' he does not—they will respond with respect and understanding.

Sixth challenge. Do I have an equal faith in them and in their motives? Am I as loyal to them and their welfare? Do I treat them with respect and understanding?

Seventh wonder. The ability of children to teach. Each child learns form the other, and even the teacher can learn much from children.

Seventh challenge. Do I use my opportunities to learn from children? Do I listen, literally and figuratively, to the lessons they can teach?

Several attempts have been made to analyse activities involved in teaching with a view to understand it scientifically, design teaching materials and methods for realising the specific objectives efficiently, and to evaluate and modify it in the light of the feedback.

Plenlders, Ned. S. (1959) of the University of Minnesota was the first educator to categories all the sets of verbal behaviours (teaching activities) of a teacher in the classroom while interacting with students. He classified these activities into three categories:

1. Teacher Talk. 2. Pupil Talk and 3. Silence/confusion.

Teacher talk was further categorised as under:

(1) Indirect influence which includes (a) Accepts feelings, (b) Praises or encourages, (c) Accepts or uses pupil ideas, (d) Asks questions.

(2) Direct influence which includes (a) Lecturing, (b) Giving directions, (c) Criticising or justifying.

2. Pupil talk which induced (a) Pupil talk response, (b) Pupil talk initiation.

3. Silence or confusion.

Komesnr, N.P. (1966) tried to analyse teaching into various specific activities like introducing, demonstrating, contrasting, explaining, proving, justifying, explaining, defining, appraising, amplifying, rating, interpreting, questioning, elaborating, identifying, conjecturing, confirming etc.

Gagel N.L. (1968) attempted .to analyse teaching in terms of technical skills. According to him, "Teaching skills are specific instructional techniques and procedures that a teacher may use in the class room. They represent an analysis of the teaching process into relatively discrete components that can be used in different combinations in the continuous flow of the teacher's performance."

Clarles, S.C. (1970) analysed teaching in terms of some specific activities that are designed and performed to produce change in student's behaviour. Those activities may be of cognitive, affective or conative nature and belonged to different levels.

Brown, B.B. (1968) analyses teaching by considering it as a manysided activity which includes several activities like questioning, giving information and listening etc.

Passi, B.K. (1976) states that teaching constitutes a number of verbal and non-verbal teaching acts like questioning, accepting pupil response, rewarding, smiling, nodding to pupil response, movements, gestures, etc. These acts, particularly in combination, facilitate the achievement of objectives in terms of pupil growth.

Dhingra, N.K. and Singh Ajit (1982) present the analysis of teaching as, "Teaching can be analysed in terms of teacher behaviour at least at three levels viz, component teaching skills, competent teaching behaviours and atomistics teaching behaviours."

Old and New Techniques

Teaching Technology : Concept and Meaning

Teaching technology involves the mechanism of instructional process in the classroom situations, levels of teaching, theories of teaching, principal teaching operations and establishing relations between theories and teaching operations.

Teaching technology as a concept can be classified into four well-defined components. These components are: (i) Manpower, (ii) Methods, (iii) Materials, and (iv) Media.

As a method, it implies making use of a few devices such as programmed learning, team teaching, micro-teaching, personalized system of instruction, etc.

As materials, it comprises instructional materials, comprising programmed text-books, manuals, guides, text and other written/ print materials, which expose to the learner the contents of these sources of materials.

As media, it implies audio or visual or both audio-visual media such as radio, tape recorders, films, educational television as teaching aids to supplement effective teaching and to promote better learning.

Whatever be the method, material or media, it requires manpower to operate/ utilise in the teaching learning environment.

Thus, the four M's constitute a whole sequence of chains of; inputs/facilities in teaching technology.

Structure of Teaching

Structure of teaching consists of three variables which operate in the process of teaching and create learning conditions or situations. These are classified as under:

1. Teacher as an independent variable.
2. Students as dependent variables.
3. Content and the strategy of presentation as 'intervening variables.

Teacher as Independent Variable. The teacher plans the role of an independent variable. Students are dependent on him in the teaching process. The teacher does the planning, organizing, leadling and controlling of teaching for bringing about behavioural changes in the students. He is free to perform various activities for providing learning experiences to students.

Student as the Dependent Variable. The student is required to act according to the planning and organization of the teacher. Teaching activities of the teacher influence the learning of the students.

Content and the Strategy of Presentation as Intervening Variables. The intervening variables lead to interaction between the teachers and the students. The content determines the mode of presentational using, showing and doing etc.

The independent and dependent variables perform three functions: (i) Diagnostic function (ii) Prescriptive function and (iii) Evaluative function.

Diagnostic function. The initial task in bringing about desirable changes in the behaviour of the students is to have a proper diagnosis of the existing situation. Accordingly a teacher has to perform the following diagnostic functions:

1. Diagnosing the entering behaviour of the students in terms of cognitive, conative and affective abilities.
2. Formulating specific educational objective, the type and quality of behavioural changes to be introduced in the students in the light of the entering behaviour and environmental conditions.
3. Analysing the content, instructional material and environmental facilities available for carrying out the task.
4. Diagnosing his own capabilities and potentialities and bringing about desirable changes in his own behaviour for achieving success in his mission of moulding the behaviour of the students under his charge.

Like the teacher, a student has also to perform certain diagnostic functions as listed below :

1. Diagnosing strength and weakness of his entering behaviour.
2. Assessing himself in terms of the tools of learning like power of expression, ability to think and analyse, psychomotor skills, and emotional behaviour. etc.
3. Making efforts to understand the behaviour of the teacher, the type of teaching methods and strategies, the nature of the content and instructional material for the purpose of initiation on his part. In the process of initiation, both the teacher and the student diagnose for initiation and response.

Prescriptive Function. Prescriptive function is based on the diagnosis for achieving the stipulated objectives. In the prescriptive function, teacher is more active. He has to, work for the meaningful interaction. Cooperation of the student is also very essential in carrying out the prescriptive function by the teacher. The prescriptive function involves.

1. Selecting appropriate contents and organising them into proper sequence.

2. Selecting proper teaching methods, media and strategies and feed-back devices in view of the individual differences of the students.
3. Seeking desired cooperation from the students for a purposeful interaction.

Evaluative Function. Evaluative function is concerned with the task of finding out the progress and outcome of the teaching process. It is done in order to test the diagnostic and prescriptive functions of teaching. Evaluation is very important from the teacher as well as the point of view of the student. Evaluation is conducted with the aid of several measures like tests, inventories, observations, interviewing, rating scales etc. If the results are favourable, it is taken for granted that the prescriptions were correct. In case the results are contrary, necessary changes are made in the teaching learning process to get the desired results. Evaluation serves as a feedback. Teaching strategies are planned in the light of the feedback obtained from evaluation.

Different Stages

Teaching is a complex task. For performing this task, a systematic planning is needed. Teaching is to be considered in terms of various steps and the different steps constituting the process are called the phases of teaching. Jackson thinks that if we are to obtain a complete description of the teaching activity, we must consider what the teacher does before and after his regular teaching in the class. Jackson divides the teaching act into three phases of teaching.

Pre-active Stage. Before actual classroom teaching or what Jackson calls "calm" part of teaching, a teacher has to perform many tasks. These tasks include such as preparing lesson plans, arranging furniture and equipment within the classroom, manning papers, studying test reports, reading sections of a textbook and thinking about the aberrant behaviour of a particular student. These activities are very crucial to teacher's performance during regular, teaching session. Pre-active behaviour is, more or less, deliberative.

The teacher at this stage hypothesises about the possible outcome of his action. As the teacher decides what textbooks to use or how to group the children for reading or whether to notify students's parents of their poor performance, his behaviour is at least analyzable.

Following operations or substages are involved:

(1) Forming or fixing up goals.

(2) Taking decisions about the content.

(3) Managing or sequencing appropriate means and ways of presentation.

(4) Deciding about appropriate strategies and tactics of teaching.

(5) Developing teaching strategies for the specific subject matter.

Inter-active Stage. This is actual classroom teaching. At this stage, the teacher uses a number of strategies for achieving the goals already set. In the inter-active setting, the behaviour of the teacher is more or less spontaneous. Research suggests that things happen quickly during the teaching session. For example, the elementary teacher may change the focus of his concern as many as 1000 times daily. Amist all this hustle and bustle the teacher often has little time to think. Many teachers try to devote sometime alone with individual students but the teacher-student dialogue is usually public; rather than private. When a teacher is alone with a student, he is not face to face with the problem of control and management that frequently take up a major portion of his energies in a group setting. There is a greater sense of physical and psychological intimacy between the teacher and the student during individual sessions than when the teacher is responding to the class as a group. The task of keeping pupils involved may entail explanation, demonstration, definition, and other logical operations that have come to be thought of as the heart of teaching.

Operations at the Inter-active Stage. The inter-active stage of teaching involves the following:

(i) Perceiving the size of the class by the teacher to identify students.

(ii) Diagnosing the achievements of the learners.

(iii) Action or Achievement (Initiation or Response). This involves the following operations:

In the above paradigm :

(a) Selection of stimuli

(b) Presentation of the stimuli

(c) Feedback of reinforcement

(d) Development of strategies of teaching.

Post-Active Stage. The post-active stage concerning evaluation provides necessary feedback to the teacher and the students in bringing desirable improvement in their performance. It is related with both teaching and learning. The teacher analyses as to what extent the students have grasped the material presented to them. It is in fact the assessment of the Interactive process. It helps the teacher to teach things better in future. It also helps the students to learn things better. It enables the teacher to decide whether he should proceed with the new contents or reteach what has already been taught.

In short, following operations are involved at the post-active stage of teaching:

1. Assessing the suitability of the objectives determined.
2. Deciding regarding re-teaching the content or further taking up the contents.
3. Assessing the suitability of the instructional material and aids.
4. Assessing the impact of the classroom environment and effecting desired changes.

It may be stressed that all the above mentioned three phases of teaching are closely interelated. All those stages may be depicted by the following paradigm.

1. *Pt* stands for the teacher's perception of the pupil's behaviour.

2. *Dt* is the teacher's diagnosis of the pupil's state of interest, readiness, knowledge etc., made by inference from the behaviour of the pupil.
3. *Rt* is the action taken by the teacher in the light of his diagnosis.
4. *Pp* is the pupil's perception of the teacher's behaviour.
5. *Dp* is the pupil's diagnosis of teacher's state of interest what he is saying and is inferred from the teacher's behaviour.
6. *Rp* is the reaction of the pupil to the action of the teacher. Each unit marked off by the double vertical line is an example of a teaching unit.

Each unit consists of a teacher-pupil interaction. There are two sub-units within the teaching cycle which are divided by single vertical line.

The sub-unit *(Pt* -t *Dt* -t *Rt)* is referred to as an act of teaching. The sub-unit (P -t D -t *R*) is what we call the act of learning or taking Instruction.

The act of teaching and the act of taking instruction are reciprocating acts and when performed under appropriate conditions they result in behavioural changes or achievement.

Teaching according to this paradigm implies that someone gives instructions and someone takes it.

QUESTIONS

1. "To know where the pupils are and whom they should try to be are the first two essentials of teaching." Explain this statement.
2. What are the most essential things that a teacher should know to make his teaching effective?
3. "Teaching is a tripolar process or relationship." Elucidate this. "Good teaching is giving information." Do you agree with this view? Give arguments in support of your answer.

4. Explain the marks of good teaching.
5. What is quality teaching? On what factors does it depend?
6. State the factors which determine effective teaching.
7. List any ten activities involved in classroom teaching.
8. Explain the 4 M's of teaching technology. How does modern teaching technology differ from the traditional one?
9. Describe briefly the structure of teaching.
10. Distinguish diagnostic functions of teaching from its prescriptive function.

27

Process of Learning

The Concept

Teaching-learning process is as old as human beings are on earth. It has been carried out not only by human beings but also by animals to teach their young ones to adjust themselves successfully with their environment. With the passage of time, it has undergone revolutionary changes.

If the teaching-learning process is effective, then the child is able to make the best use of the things in the world around him. If a child has not learnt the art of living harmoniously with others, he will find himself beset with more difficulties than the person who has learnt how to establish social relations with his fellows. So the acquisition of knowledge, skills and attitudes which enable us to adjust ourselves in an effective manner to the environment may be said to be the aim of teaching-learning.

Teaching-learning process is a means whereby society trains its young ones in a selected environment (usually the school) as quickly as possible to adjust themselves to the world in which they live. In primitive societies this adjustment meant conformity with the things as they were. In advanced civilisation of the modern times, effort is made not only to adjust to things as they are but also to make an advance in the improvement of conditions of life by training the young in the modes of thinking and acting which will help to improve the conditions of living that surround them.

Teaching-learning has four aspects: teacher, student, learning process and learning situation. The teacher creates the learning situation for the student. The process is the interaction between the student and the teacher.

Teaching-learning process is a means through which the teacher, the learner, the curriculum and other variables are organised in a systematic manner to attain pre-determined goals and objectives.

Teaching-learning process simplifies the various elements of the teaching-learning situation have to be brought into an intelligible whole. The teaching-learner activities which are varied and complex have to be harmonised. These elements and activities induce learners and their individual differences, the methods of teaching, the material to be taught, class-room conditions, teaching devices. and aids, questioning and answering, assignments, thinking, enjoying, creating, practicals skills, discussions and many others.

Teaching-learning process is influenced by the totality of the situation. Teaching learning is fruitful and permanent if the total situation is related to the life situations. Teachers can play an important role in, facilitating learning when they take into account the needs of the learners.

Communication in three Dimensional Form

Interaction between the teacher and the learners is the core of the teaching learning process. This interaction through a sort of three way communication, results in behaviour changes in the learners.

A learner needs the help of a teacher when he wants to learn any subject and to solve any problem. The process of guiding the learner involves eight steps—communication from the teacher to the learner (steps 1 and 2), from learner to teacher (steps 3 to 5), and again from teacher to learner (steps 6 to 8). Through this 3-way communication, teacher could direct his course of teaching concretely. On the other hand, learner can know how well his learning is progressing and how sure he can make his way of learning. So teacher should establish firmly this 3-way communication between many learners and himself.

The formative evaluation in step 7 and KR in step 8 are important to conduct the effective teaching learning processes. KR is a kind of feedback information which has many types. For example, in responding to his behaviour, teacher, says: "good," "wrong," "no," "well," "hum," "wonderful," "interesting" and some times repeats and summarizes learner's opinions. Sometimes teacher gives many non-verbal KR, nodding, smiling, winking, and making gestures.

Important Angles

Teaching and learning are interlinked. We cannot think of teaching without learning. The teacher teaches and the students learn. Teaching is not in a vacuum. It is therefore obvious that for making teaching learning sound and effective in our educational institute the teachers must look into its various aspects very carefully and critically so that they contribute in making teaching-learning inspirational and relevant. Following are the chief aspects:

Command, planning and organisation of the subject matter or content and activities. There are no two opinions about the important factors that the success of the teaching-learning process greatly depends upon the thoroughness of knowledge of the subject matter to be taught by the teacher. The soul of effective teaching learning is good command of the subject matter. The next aspect is to present the subject matter to the class. Here we enter into the field of organisation of the subject-matter and the use of methods of teaching and teaching technology. The teacher's endeavour will be to use different dynamic and progressive methods of teaching and learning. He should encourage the students to develop proper habits of learning. He should stress self-learning on the part of the students.

Class control and discipline. Appropriate class control and discipline is one of the most important characteristics of a successful teacher. A good teacher is one who can control his class not through fear or high-handedness but by virtue of his interest in the learner, good command on the subject-matter and the ability to present it interestingly and effectively. The learners also appreciate good teaching and cooperate with the teacher in the teaching-learning process.

Psychology of Learners. It must be realized by a teacher that all his knowledge of the subject-matter, his ability to present it methodically and effectively and his ability to control the class situation ably, while teaching will be effective only if he takes into consideration the interests, abilities, aptitudes and limitations of the learners. A teacher must learn to understand his learners and encourage them. He has to be sincere and honest towards his learners. An ideal teacher is always humble. He has to practise tolerance and patience in dealing with the learners. The participation of the learners is very important and necessary if the teaching learner has to have a broader and meaningful process.

Evaluation. Evaluation has an important place in the teaching learner process. A teacher should carefully evaluate his students to find out how they can make more progress. He may use a variety of methods for this purpose. Self-evaluation by both the teacher and the student is very important.

Assessment in Practice

Teaching remains central to both learning and evaluation. There is an interrelatedness between teaching objectives (ends), learning experiences (means) and evaluation (evidence of what is taught and learnt). Evaluation is the process of determining : (1) The extent to which an objective is achieved (2) The effectiveness of the learning experiences provided in the classroom and (3) How well the goals , of teaching have been accomplished.

In evaluation one has to know where students were at the beginning if we are to determine what changes are occurring.

In evaluation one has to obtain a record of the changes in pupil by using appropriate methods of appraisal.

In evaluation one has to judge, how good the changes are in the light of the evidence obtained.

Evaluation may lead to changes in teaching technology and also in learning technology.

Thus, evaluation comes in at the planning stage when teaching objectives are identified. At every point of learning, evaluation is an attempt to discover the effectiveness of the learning situation in evoking the desired changes in students.

Evaluation is integrated with the whole task of teaching and learning and its purpose is to improve learning and not merely to measure its achievement. In its highest sense, evaluation brings out the factors that are inherent in student growth such as proper attitudes and habits, manipulative skills, appreciations and understanding in addition to the conventional acquisition of knowledge.

It has been rightly observed, "The definition of evaluation places it in the stream of activities that expire the educational process; these activities can be reduced to four essential steps: identification of educational objectives, determination of the experiences students must have to attain these objectives, knowing the pupils well enough to design appropriate experiences and evaluating the degree to which pupils attain these objectives."

Objectives provide the starting point on which are based all the learning experiences which in their turn are the material of evaluation.

Teaching Objectives. Our teaching objectives are the changes we wish to produce in the child. The changes that must take place through education are represented in:

1. The knowledge children acquire
2. The skills and abilities children attain

3. The interest children develop
4. The attitudes children manifest

If education imparted is effective, then the child will behave differently, from the way he did before he came to school. The pupil knows something of which he was ignorant before. He understands something which he did not understand before. He can solve problems he could not solve before. He can do something which he could not do before. He revises his attitudes desirably towards things.

Specific Classroom Objectives. These objectives must involve points of in formation,the skills and attitudes to be developed and interests that could be created through the particular topic or subject taken up for work in the classroom:

A statement of classroom objectives:

(1) serves as a basis for the chores of classroom procedures that should provide for suitable experiences to the children.

(2) serves as a guide in seeking evidence to determine the extent to which the classroom work has accomplished what it set out to do.

Learning Experiences. A learning experience is not synonymous with the content of instruction or what the teacher does. Learning results from the active reaction of the pupil to the stimulus situation which the teacher creates in the class. A pupil learns what he does. He is an active participant in what goes on in the class. Changes in a pupil's way of thinking and developing concepts, attitudes and interests have to be brought about gradually. No simple experience will result in the change. Many experiences, one reinforcing another, will have to be provided. They may have to be repeated in increasing complexity or levels in meaningful sequence extended over a period of time. A cumulative effect of such experiences will evoke the desired change of behaviour with reference to a specific objective.

The following considerations will be useful in the selection of such experiences:

1. Are they directly related to goals?
2. Are they meaningful and satisfying to the learners?
3. Are they appropriate to the maturity of the learners?

It is worth bearing in mind that learning is what students do, teaching is what the academic staff does and that improvement in teaching can only be demostrated if there is consequential improvement in learning. On the other hand, improvement in learning may occur for reasons that have nothing to do with teaching, for example, students are able to spend more time, gain better access to libraries and become more strongly motivated.

As observed by prof. R.S. Adams and others, "Students may learn what the teacher intended them to; they may not. Furthermore, teachers, like others, are fallible, they may not always teach correctly. It follows then that in any learning situation, students may learn correctly what the teacher taught incorrectly or may learn incorrectly what the teacher taught correctly-or fortunately, the opposites."

Finally, although students certainly do learn because of the instructions they receive, they also learn in spite of the instructions they receive. In the process of accommodating to what is being taught students attempt to 'fit' the new experience—into their past experience in to the knowledge, insights and understandings that they have accumulated previously. It is this capability of human beings to transcend their immediate circumstances, to, add into their 'learning' their past experiences, that complicates the instructional process and makes it difficult for teachers to tailor the learning experience appropriately for their (unusually diverse) students. As a consequence, the instructional strategies are often based on different assumptions. Some deliberately set out to exercise control over the learner by : (i) either trying to exclude outside influences; or (ii) by trying to build beyond them; or (iii) by trying to overpower them. For example some earlier attempts at programme learning tried to confine student attention precisely and exclusively to the material to be mastered. Other more sophisticated mastery learning programmes attempt to both discover and start from what the learner's basic knowledge is and to provide 'branch' programmes catering for individual differences. Operant conditioning, of course, has always represented an attempt to 'override' other influences, however powerful they might be. Outside these more mechanistic strategies, other instructional strategies have been based on other assumptions. For example, where students are expected to learn by emulating their instructors (e.g. as in medical and veterinary training) reliance is placed on observational 'learning'.

Practical Aspects

Teaching operations and learning operations are interlinked. Nevertheless teaching operations to be successful must take into account the learning operations needed to accomplish the teaching objectives which themselves are based on learning objectives. It is therefore, desirable to consider the learning operations first. Learning operation are as under:

1. Discrimination of stimulus situation.
2. Response or cognition.
3. Assimilation of relationship between specific elements of the situation and the response.
4. Developing application and control over the environment.
5. Definite behavioural changes.

Teaching operations may be enumerated as under:

1. Presentation of stimulus in a specific control.
2. Bringing suitable responses by organising appropriate learning experiences.
3. Elucidation and elaboration.
4. Setting up drill and review exercises for fixing up the behaviour in the repertoire of learning.
5. Evaluating learning outcomes.

Variables and Components in the Learning Process

1. Task to be learned.

2. Characteristics of the task to be learned.
3. Characteristics of the learner.
4. Conditions under which effective learning takes place.

Components of the Teaching Process

1. Instructional goals
2. Entering behaviour
3. Instructional procedures
4. Performance assessment

A close review of the components of learning and teaching processes reveals that there is a close correspondence between the two. Performance assessment becomes a part of the teaching process so as to confirm whether or not the instructional objectives are realised and it provides a feedback to other components and also supplies data for developing teaching technology.

Two Way Procedure

Modern teaching-learning process assigns an important place to student-activity. It calls for a child-centred approach. The most distinctive feature of modern society is its science-based technology which has been making a profound impact not only on the economic and political life of a country but also on its educational system. The changes that occur as a result of the impact are broadly described as 'Modernisation'. This modernisation has affected the teaching-learning process in many ways. The recent changes in the concept of teaching-learning process have led to the development of newer areas of educational endeavour. In a traditional society the aim of teaching-learning was the assimilation of the accumulated-stock of knowledge. But in the modern society, the main aim of teaching learning is not acquisition of knowledge alone. It is the awakening of curiosity, the stimulation of creativity, the development of proper interests, attitudes and values and the building of essential skills such as independent study. Teaching-learning process has to serve as a powerful instrument of social, economic and cultural transformation .of the society. Teaching-learning process is conditioned by the nature and demands of society to which the learner should get adapted and attuned. One of the main aims of teaching-learning in the modern society is to keep pace with the advancement of knowledge and skills.

For a pretty long period, the teaching-learning process has been by and large, a process dominated by the institution of professional teachers. Now, the process is to be replaced to a great extent by a process in which the individual learner is expected to take up challenges through an inevitable intellectual revolution. The intellectual revolution has been enabled futher by forces of hardware technologies at low cost, socialization process due to interdependence. Besides, projects, farms, factories, markets, excursions and playgrounds will become classrooms in the new teaching-learning process.

QUESTIONS

1. "Teaching-learning is interaction between the teacher and the pupil." Explain.
2. Describe the teaching learning process.
3. "Teaching-learning is a three-way communication." Elucidate this statement.
4. Explain the principal aspects of the teaching-learning process.
5. "Child is a unique being." Elaborate this statement and point out the role of the child in teaching-learning.

28

Programmed Learning

Technological Changes

Programmed learning is one of the important invocations of the 20th century in the teaching-learning process. It is a self-instructional technique for providing individualized instruction or learning experience to the learner. In programmed learning, the subject matter or learning experience is logically sequenced into small segments. The learning experience is self-corrective.

The English writers prefer to use the term programmed learning and the American authors prefer the use of programmed instruction.

It is held by some educators that 'Gita' is the first example of programmed learning. They hold that the text of the 'Gita' has several ingredients of programming: initial behaviour, small steps, active participation of the learner, terminal behaviour, immediate feed-back and self-evaluation by the learner.

Several educators regard Socrates as the earliest programmer. Socrates used to guide his followers to gain knowledge by conducting them conversationally along a path from fact to fact and insight to insight.

Programmed learning emerged in the beginning of the 20th century from the efforts of American psychologists. E. L. Thorndike (1874-1949) was the first psychologist whose findings bear direct relevance to programming. Other important psychologists who have made significant contribution in the field are Sidney L. Pressy, Robert M. Gagne, Robert Mager and B. F. Skinner.

Programmed learning is related with the 'Law of Effect' as explained by Thorndike. Sidney L. Pressey, a psychologist of Ohio State University, is credited for developing in the middle 1920's practical machines which could teach as well as test. The teaching machines as developed by Pressey present a series of questions to a student and inform him immediately whether his response is right or wrong.

In 1943, Skinner and his two other colleagues started programming by teaching a pigeon to roll a small bowling ball by operant conditioning. By 1954, Skinner and James G. Holland devised the auto-instructional methods which have served the present generation as the basis for present work in programmed instruction. In Skinnerian programmed instruction, whether mechanised or otherwise, the learner is initially asked a question which he can easily answer correctly without any previous study of the particular lesson. The learner is taught by the sequence of questions. He is asked more and more as the lesson proceeds in very small steps.

In 1955, Norman A. Crowder developed what he calls "automatic tutoring by intrinsic programming" as against "extrinsic programming" developed by Skinner.

Robert Mager (1958) gave a new concept known as "Learner Controlled Instruction" which is a kind of Socratic dialogue in reverse, in which the learner led the instructor. The instructor remained silent until the learner himself stimulated the instructor with questions that suggested the needed illustrations, demonstrations, practice or some other help.

Stoluron, at Illionis, aimed at developing a process which should provide for greater individualization by measuring needs and developing programmes that require a computer to assist instruction.

In 1962, T. F. Gilbert gave formalized expression of his technology of education called Mathetics. Pennington and Slack expressed in 1962 further detailed methods of preparing lessons from mathetic principles.

Programmed learning is a process of arranging material to be learned in a series of small steps designed to lead a learner through self-instruction from what he knows to the unknown of new and more complex knowledge and principles. A programme takes the place of a tutor and leads the learner through a set of frames of specified behaviour designed and sequenced to make it more probable that he will behave in a given derived way.

In programmed learning, it is said that the most efficient, pleasant and permanent learning takes place when the student proceeds through a course by a large number of small, easy-to-take steps. Wilbur L. Schramm (1962) lists the essential elements of programmed instruction as: (*a*) an ordered sequence of stimulus items, (*b*) to each of which a student responds in some specific way, (*c*) his responses being reinforced by immediate knowledge of results, (*d*) so that he moves by small steps, (*e*) therefore, making few errors and practicing mostly correct responses, (*f*) from what he knows by a process of successively closer approximation, toward what he is supposed to learn from the programme.

Following definitions provide a comprehensive view of programmed instruction.

Dale, Edgar (1962). Programmed learning is a systematic, step by step, self-instructional programme aimed to ensure the learning of stated behaviour.

Das, R. C (1993). Programmed instruction is a method of individualised instruction where each individual learns by himself at his own rate. Programmed learning consists of elements of new knowledge called 'steps' which are arranged in a sequence in such a way that a student can easily learn by himself.

Espich, James E. and William B (1965). Programmed instruction is a planned sequences of experiences, leading to proficiency in terms of stimulus response relationship.

Gulati and Gulati (1990). Programmed learning as popularly understood is a method of giving individual instruction in which the student is active and proceeds at his own pace and is provided with immediate knowledge of results. The teacher is not physically present. The programmer, while developing programmed material has to follow the laws of behaviour and validate his strategy in terms of student learning.

Jacobs and Others (1966). Self-instructional programmes are educational materials from which the students learn. These programmes can be used with many types of students and subject-matter either by themselves, hence the name "self-instruction" or its combination with instructional strategies.

Kampfer (1970). Programmed learning is a device which presents an exercise or a problem to a student, inducing him to respond; and revealing to him whether or not his response is correct.

Leith, G. O. M (1966). Programme is a sequence of small steps of instructional material (called frames), most of which require a response to be made by completing a blank space in a sentence. To ensure that expected responses are given, a system of cueing is applied, and each response is verified by the provision of immediate knowledge of results. Such a sequence is intended to be worked at the learner's own pace as individual self-instruction.

Luonsdaine Arthur, A (1964). An instructional programme is a vehicle which generates an essentially reproducible sequence of instructional events and accepts responsibility for efficiently accomplishing a specified change from a given range of initial competencies or behavioural tendencies to a specified or terminal range of competencies or behavioural tendencies.

Marke, Susan (1969). Programmed learning is a method of designing a reproducible sequence of instructional events to produce a measurable and consistent effect on the behaviours of each and every acceptable student.

Navi, N. S. **(1984).** Programmed instruction is a technique of converting the live instructional process into self-learning or auto-instructional readable material in the form of micro-sequence (the segments of subject-matter) which the learners are required to read, make some right or wrong response, correct wrong responses or confirm right responses and attain the complete mastery of the concept explained in the micro-sequences.

May, K. O. **(1965).** Educational programming is the scheduling and control of student behaviour in the learning process.

Smith and Moore **(1962).** Programmed instruction is the process of arranging the material to be learned into a series of sequential steps. Usually it moves the student from a familiar background into a complex and new set of concepts, principles and understandings.

Stolurow **(1966).** Programmed learning can be described as a process in which a teacher presents (*i.e.*, communicates), a subject matter to a learner so that he responds to it (i.e. communicates to the teacher) the next item of information to be presented.

Main Features

From the above mentioned definitions of programmed learning, following characteristics may be derived:

1. It is a method of individualized instruction.
2. In this technique, instructional material is logically sequenced and broken into suitable small steps or segments of the subject matter called 'frames'.
3. For sequencing a particular unit of the instructional material, the programmer has to pay due consideration to the initial or entering behaviour of the learner.
4. In actual operation, the beginning is made by presenting a 'frame'. The learner is required to read or listen and then respond actively.
5. Programmed instruction system has an adequate provision for feed-back.

6. The interaction between the learner and the learning material or programme is very important.
7. Programmed learning provides self-pacing to the learner.
8. Programmed learning provides for continuous evaluation.

Material in Use

There are three basic types of programmed instructional material—The teaching machines, the programmed textbook and scrambled textbook.

The teaching machine. A teaching machine is intended to function as a private tutor. It is simply a mechanical devise or piece of apparatus designed to present to the student a sequential programme of learning activities comprising instructional items which requires the student to make an overt response and which provides the student with immediate knowledge of the accuracy of his response. It represents the practical application of laboratory technique of education.

Programmed textbook. Each page of the programmed textbook consists of usually four or five panels. The student begins with the top panel on page one, responds to it, turns to page two to get his answers confirmed on the top panel, goes to the top panel on page three, responds to it, confirms the answer by turning the page, and so on.

The scrambled textbook. In a scrambled textbook, branching or intrinsic technique is used.

Important Rules

Principle of Small Steps. It is shown by experiments that even the dullest students can learn as effectively as the brightest students if the subject matter is presented to them in suitable small steps. When we divide the task to be learnt into very small steps, and ask the students to learn only one step at a time, then probably all the students will be able to learn one small step at a time and sequentially learn all the steps. It is a difficult task to climb a mountain but once steps are built even a child can climb the mountain very easily. This is known as the 'Principle of small steps'.

Principle of Active Responding. The second psychological principle is that the students learn better and faster when they are actively participating in the teaching-learning process. In our classroom teaching the teachers to ask a few questions and the students respond. But is not possible for the teachers to ask all the students to respond at each small step. A teaching machine text or a programmed text contains a large number of questions—one question at each small step and the students respond actively. The principle of active responding is used for the programmes. The teaching machines and programmes have proved to be superior because they provide opportunity to every learner to respond at every small step.

Principle of Reinforcement. Every response even approximately correct must be reinforced immediately. Delayed reinforcement fails to work. This is possible only when a teacher has to teach only one student at a time. The most ideal situation is when the teacher can cater to the needs of his students individually. But in classroom teaching this is hardly possible. No teacher, however efficient and sincere he may be, can reinforce each correct response of each of his students as soon as it is made in a classroom situation where he has to teach abut 40/50 students. The teaching machines and the programmes do the job more efficiently.

Principle of Self-Pacing. The programmed instruction is based on the basic assumption that learning takes place effectively if the learner is allowed to learn at his own pace. Therefore, a good programme of the material always takes care of the principle of self-pacing. A learner moves from one frame to another according to his own speed of learning.

Principle of Student-Evaluation or Student Testing. Continuous evaluation of the student and the learning process leads to better teaching-learning. In the programmed instruction, the learner has to leave the record of his responses because he is required to write a response for each frame on response sheet. This detailed record helps in revising the programme.

Important stages in the Development of the Programmed Instruction

Preparation. This is the first stage in the development of the programme. It includes:

(*i*) Selection of the topic.

(*ii*) Writing assumptions about learners.

(*iii*) Defining objective in behavioural terms.

(*iv*) Writing the entry behaviour (present status) of the learner.

(*v*) Developing specific outline of the content.

(*vi*) Preparing a criterion test.

Construction or writing of the programme. The programme is written under these heads (*i*) Writing draft frames in a sequence i.e. from simple to complex. (*ii*) Editing the draft frames by a team of experts usually comprising a subject-matter expert, a skilled writer and the programmer.

Try Out Revision. It includes (*i*) Trying out the programme on a few individual learners and finding out their reactions and making necessary changes in the light of reactions, (*ii*) Trying out the programme on a group of learners and making necessary changes on the basis of their reactions; and (*iii*) Trying out the programme in the field.

Evaluation. This implies finding the success or the failure after implementing a programme.

Assessment in Practice

Merits of programmed instruction. 1. A well-programmed instruction is a great thrust in the direction of individualised instruction, as it is tailored to the needs of the individual learner in the class. 2. It permits individual learner to progress at his own speed. An intelligent learner needs no longer to be bored or allowed to lose interest on account of his slow progress of other learners of the class. He can make progress as he is capable of. 3. Since a programme requires continuous response from the learner, it overcomes the inertia and passivity on the part of the learner. 4. The teacher can give explanation in the classroom if the error is common or he may arrange individual conferences on specific points. 5. Learning material in a programmed instruction is presented in such a way that learning becomes an interesting game and the learner is motivated to meet the challenges set by his own capabilities. 6. Programmes are developed by experts. They are empirically tested and modified till they are standarised. A number of learners can use a single good programme and thus evade textbooks. 7. In programmed instruction the learner is immediately reinforced to correct his response and this reinforcement sustains the motivation of the learner. 8. The self-instructional technique presents material in which its complexity is simplified through the analysis of the subject-matter into small and more easily assimilated segments of information. 9. The introduction of programmed instruction is of great significance for developing countries which are set on the path of educating millions of learners and are short of teachers. 10. Good teachers are freed from the boredom of routine classroom teaching and they are in a position to devote more time to more creative activities. 11. The programmed instruction has been used more successfully in teaching the discernment of the logic of various disciplines and inspiring students to creative thinking and judgement. 12. Certain motor skills and intellectual abilities normally taught by frequent drills and rote memorisation can be very efficiently taught by self-instructional devices. 13. Self-instructional materials have been found to be very useful in the West in revolutionisng the social setting of the classroom. Problems of discipline have been solved and a new hope for eliminating emotional and social problems has been generated. 14. Programmed instruction enables the teacher to diagnose the problems of the individual learner. 15. The introduction of programmed instruction is very helpful in certain situations where human instructors are not easily available in the required number, for instance small schools in the isolated or hill areas.

Programmed materials have been severely criticised as a threat to replacing the teacher.

It is also argued that there is too much emphasis in learning facts and very little emphasis on the mastery of principles and concepts.

Some critics of programmed instruction maintain that the user of a programme does not now where he is headed to.

They also point out that the learners are not aware of the organisation and programmed instruction is unrelated to other aspects of instruction.

It is also argued that the programmed instruction material is very costly and only rich nations can afford it.

It is also stated that the development and use of programmed instructional material require expert knowledge and training. An average teacher finds it very difficult to make use of this device.

Various Categories

As a result of experimental studies and research, following types of programmed instruction have emerged.

1. Linear or Extrinsic Programming
2. Branching or Intrinsic Programming
3. Mathetics Programming
4. Rules System of Programming
5. Computer Assisted Instruction (CAS)
6. Learner Controlled Instruction. (LCS)

The first three styles—linear, branching and mathetics are the basic formats. The rules system represents the deductive and inductive approach to teaching. The other two types, Computer Assisted Instruction (CAI) and Learner Controlled Instruction (LCI) are not the basic format of Programming. They are, infact, the ways and means of providing instruction. Here we have taken up only the basic type of programming.

B. F. Skinner is the originator of linear programming. It is also called a single tract programme. According to Skinner, a creature, a bird or a human being can be led to a desired behaviour by means of a carefully constructed programme consisting of small steps leading logically through the subject-matter from topic to topic, provided each step is reinforced by some kind of favourable experience or reward. The increments in information which the learner is expected to absorb are small. The favourable experience or response increases the probability of the same response to occur again in the future. The process of rewarding the correct response to a stimulus increases the general tendency to give a response.

The sequence of frames and path of learning in programmed learning is systematic and linear. That is why, this type of programming is referred to as linear programming. Hence all the learners have to proceed through the same frames and in the same order.

In a linear programme, learner's responses are controlled externally by the programmer sitting at a distant place. Hence linear programming is also termed as extrinsic programming. In branching programming, learner's response is controlled by the learner himself internally. It is, therefore, also called intrinsic programming.

Merits. 1. Immediate knowledge of results acts as a great motivator and releases anxiety and tension. 2. The smallness of the frames brings the sub-goals within the reach of the learner and thereby facilitates secondary reinforcement. 3. Repetition strengthens the responses and ensures learning. 4. Easy nature of the programme provides 'success experience' to the learner.

Limitations. 1. In linear programming, the learning process becomes quite dull on account of the following reasons (*a*) Subject matter is broken into very small pieces, (*b*) Responding is quite mechanical and restrictive, and (*c*) The learning process is quite slow. 2. The use of linear programming is limited to some subjects and topics. 3. Linear programming cramps the imagination of the learner and initiative for creative, integrative and judgement learning. 4. Linear programming encourages guessing. 5. Linear programming does not develop the discriminating power of the students.

Branching or intrinsic programming was developed by Norman A. Crowder (1954) an American technician. According to Crowder, branching or intrinsic programme is one which adopts to the needs of the learners without the medium of any extrinsic device such as a computer. It is not controlled extrinsically by the programmer.

Norman A. Crowder was a technician who was working in the United States Air Force. He was faced with the problem of efficiency of vocational training. His programme is based on intuition. His approach at the most is practical. This type of programme employs multiple choice response patterns. The learner is required to select one right answer out of several responses presented to him.

Merits. 1. Big size of a frame as well as the branching minimises unnecessary repetitions and responding, thus reducing the amount of learning time and fatigue. 2. The pitfalls and consequences of erroneous logic are usually explained in the remedial frames so that the learner not only gets the correct responses but also understands why some other response is not correct. 3. Instead of simple response it provides alternatives in the form of multiple choice. 4. Through its broad frames, branching programme provides for more freedom to respond and scope of choosing one's path of learning according to one's need. Thus, it helps in maintaining the interest and initiative of the teacher. 5. Branching programme is helpful in the development of the power of discrimination of the learner. 6. Branching programme helps in the development of creativity and problem-solving ability. 7. Branching is most useful in the areas beyond facts, definitions and basic skills. 8. The frames being of a large size contain a good deal of information and this may enable the programmer to enrich the style and expand his ideas.

Programmed Instruction	*Traditional Method*
1. It is an individualised technique of instruction.	1. It is a group technique.
2. It is based on the teaching principles that have been known for years.	2. It becomes difficult to apply teaching principles in crowded classrooms.
3. It presents the instructional matter step by step in logical order.	3. It presents the instructional matter as a whole.
4. The size of the unit of information presented to the pupils is a small bit of information.	4. The unit is a lengthy one. There is very little provision for response from the students in the form of answers to questions.
5. Immediate feedback is given to the learner.	5. The learner does not get immediate feedback.
6. Objectives are defined very clearly in operational terms.	6. Objectives are not well-defined and are usually vague.
7. The programmer prepares his programme with care and precision.	7. Very little preparation is made.
8. Programme is prepared in such a way that the student automatically participates actively by making responses continually.	8. The student usually remains a passive listener and the teacher himself does the summarising and reviewing.
9. A programme is developed empirically through a series of tryouts and refined gradually. Effective sequences students reaction of frames are retained and ineffective ones discarded.	9. It is usually found to be very difficult to modify traditional instruction.

Limitations. 1. The multiple choice questions provided in this programming may lead to guess work on the part of the learner and he may not understand the subject matter of the frame. 2. The setting of appropriate multiple choice questions suiting to the entire material of the frames proves a difficult task. 3. No branching method can provide infinite branching to take care of all possible needs of every individual student. 4. The cost of branching programme is very high when compared with traditional teaching approaches. 5. The branching programme is not suitable for small children as they are unable to express symbolisation. 6. The programme needs revision after every five years. 7. It is difficult to cover the entire subject matter of the curriculum in the stipulated time. 8. The diagnostic questions framed by the programmer may or may not suit the needs of the individual learner. 9. The programme cannot shape the behaviour of the learner.

Teaching Instruction and Programmed Instruction. According to Edger Dale, "Teaching' is a broad, vague, ill-defined term and instruction' is a purposeful, orderly, controlled sequencing of experience to reach a specified goal. 'Programmed instruction' is a sub-head under instruction and represents a more rigorous attempt to develop a mastery, over specified goals to secure 'insured' learning."

Role of the Teacher

Programme learning cannot replace the teacher. Any innovation in the school programmes and practices must remain in the hands of the teachers. The radio and T V did not displace the teacher. Similar is the case with programmed instruction. It is upto the enlightened teachers to take up the challenging task of preparing programmes. We have got a wide market. The programmes can be sold all over the country. A student who is convinced that he can learn better, achieve more with the help of this programme, will definitely prefer instead of buying this programme to buying a text book. By taking up this challenging task we will not only help the cause of education, help our fellow teachers by setting them free from the routine task of information, giving help to the students to achieve more, but we will be helping ourselves also.

It may also be remembered that these gadgets can be used mainly in the cognitive field and possibly in the psycho-motor field to develop certain abilities and skills of the students as an individual. A teacher is something more than all these gadgets put together. He has to bring about socialization of the individual; he has to promote socially desirable attitudes and interests and mould the personality of the students. The effective domain is almost reserved for his care. At present the teacher is not able to devote his energy and time to this important task as most of his time and energy is consumed by his routine job as an information giver. We always talk of education for three 'H's'—the head, the hand and the heart. But it has almost remained a mere slogan. Programmed learning, teaching machines and other gadgets will set teacher free from routine work. These are labour-saving devices for the teacher so that he may function more effectively in a field of his own choice.

Technique involved in programmed instruction can be used in teaching different subjects. Teaching of mathematics, science, social studies and elements of Indian languages can be done effectively with the help of this new technique. The teacher has to formulate objectives of teaching a particular subject, undertake content analysis of the subject matter in the light of objectives, frame a chain of questions which will lead the pupils in the direction of the objective and present the questions to his pupils who are expected to try their hand at answering the questions independently. The teacher will have to play the role of a friend, guide and philosopher in the class when the pupils are engaged in solving the riddle and at the same time acquiring knowledge or skill. The question of class discipline may not arise as the pupils will be found busy doing the task assigned to them by the teacher. The teacher will have to do remedial or corrective teaching as the weakness of his pupils will be located in the very act of learning. The pupil will also undergo a process of self-evaluation as he completes his work.

Role of the teacher in the changed context of Programmed Learning may be stated as under :

1. Teacher as an advisor in helping students in the selection of programme learning material.

2. Teacher as a discussion leader for focussing the attention of the learners on important points.
3. Teacher as a guide to clarify doubts and elaborate on various points asked by the learner.
4. Teacher as an evaluator of the learning outcomes.
5. Teacher as a consultant to the various agencies engaged in production of programmed material.

Inside Classroom

The programmed learning approach can be adopted in normal classroom teaching in the following ways:

1. A teacher can make use of the principles of programmed learning such as active responding, minimal errors and confirmation while teaching various subjects in the conventional manner.
2. A teacher can define behavioural objectives in advance of teaching.
3. A teacher can validate the instructional systems of a class in terms of the performance of learners immediately after teaching is over.
4. A teacher can regulate questions and answers. The answer of a learner can be immediately reinforced by informing or telling whether it is correct or incorrect.
5. A teacher can plan the entire instructional programme of a classroom and can treat the terminal behaviour, the pre-requisite skills and content analysis in advance.

Komoski (1960) an expert has observed "Two thousand years ago the world's first public administrator, a gentleman by the name Quintilian wrote what might be called a handbook for teachers." In it he has one bit of advice which will serve as an excellent starting point for a discussion of programmed learning and its potential uses. His advice is: "Do not neglect the individual student. He should be questioned and praised."

Programmed Teaching

Programmed instruction is still in its infancy in India. Programmed instruction as an optional or elective paper has been included at the B. Ed./M.Ed. level in a few universities in India. It also forms a part of the paper of Educational Technology/Educational Innovation. However, as regards its classroom use, it may be observed that it is almost nil. As far back in 1966, the Kothari Commission suggested to develop programmed material in different subjects to test the suitability of the technique in Indian conditions. An Association of Programmed Instruction has been formed to coordinate the research being done at different centres in the country. The association also disseminates the information on new studies through its journal issued from time to time. The National Council of Educational Research and Technology has also done some work in the field. In spite of all these efforts, it may be stated that the application of programmed instruction has not yet made an appreciable impact on our classroom teaching. Our methods of teaching still remain traditional, by and large.

Following are the important factors which stand in the way of introducing programmed instruction in Indian schools:

1. Resistance to change.
2. Lack of good programmes.
3. Lack of facilities.

QUESTIONS

1. Explain programmed learning. How does it differ from traditional teaching?
2. State the meaning, characteristics, merits and limitations of programmed learning.
3. Name the major styles of programming. Discuss their features and limitations.

4. What is programmed learning? Does it replace the teacher? Outline the role of the teacher in programmed learning.

5. "Programmed instruction, in spite of its important place in teaching-learning, is still in its infancy in 'India'? Explain. Suggest measures for its popularisation.

6. What are the various steps in programming? Prepare a programme on any topic.

29

The Showcases

Fairs in our country are generally held at or near sacred places of pilgrimages. Such fairs are very popular in our religious country. Old men, women and children are greatly interested in going to fairs. The fairs serve as a stimulant for sale and purchase of various items such as, kitchen-kits, ready made dresses, articles of daily use, pets, horses, cows, goats, sheeps, bullocks, camels, elephants and other useful animals. Dramas, circus shows and religious discourse are also organized in fairs. In fairs like KUMBHA at Prayag (Allahabad), Hardwar and Ujjain and solar eclipse at Kurukshetra (Haryana) the gathering has a religous colour. Still at such places as well various articles of daily use are sold. Some of the fairs of social nature are principally organized for sale of useful animals and other items of utility. Some of these fairs are of such a great dimension that lacs of people attend them and they continue even for days or weeks. Considering their great importance the Government has to depute a section of its administrative officers with magistrial powers and some police force for the necessary arrangements and safety of the people in the fair. Some staff and a mobile medical unit are also sent to the fair ground for its cleanliness and for giving first aid in emergency cases. Onwards we shall hint at some main items that must be done on the occasion of a fair for physical safety and health of the people attending it.

The Organisation

A committee should be formed for thinking about the needful, that should be attended to for good arrangement of the fair. This committee should be a representative body of some experienced persons from the various departments of administration of the district. This committee should prepare an outline of arrangement for the fair. The co-operation of the district health-officer and district engineer is very necessary for making suitable arrangements. The engineer should plan how and where stalls will be organized and how the various temporary roads and pathways on the fair ground should be designed and constructed. The health officer will look after arrangement for drinking water and will give suggestions regarding pluses of lavatories and urinals. Many people have to stay in the fair for days and weeks in connection with their sale or purchase. For such persons arrangements for stay should be made at safe places. The fair ground should be cleaned before the fair is held. A number of portions should be demarcated in the fair-ground for such items as roads, pathways, bazars, various functions and dwelling places. If animals have to be brought for sale, different areas should be allotted for various types of such animals as pets, goats, cows, camels and others.

Refuse and Conservancy—Bore-hole type of latrines should be constructed in a fair. They should be one foot deeper below the first water level beneath the ground surface. If trench-latrine is constructed, then it should be about twenty feet long. It should be divided by pieces of mat in such a manner that five persons may use it at a time. The pit for the trench latrine should be about 9 to 12 inches wide and 20 to 40 inches deep. This type of deep latrine may be adequate for about 1000 persons. A sweeper should be appointed for every 1000 persons for covering store and supervising cleanliness. It will be better if septic tank latrines are constructed at places where fairs are held every year for some weeks. They should be thoroughly cleaned before the fair is held. Some lime and bleeching powder should provided near the latrine in an earthen pit. Separate latrines should be provided for men and women.

Control of Epidemics—Adequate arrangement for some isolation hospitals should be made in order that the affected persons may be nursed separately. A number of stretchers should be provided for carrying patients to the isolation hospitals. Besides, at some place first-aid centres and temporary dispensaries should also be run.

Water Provision—Pure water should be adequately provided for a fair. This provision is likely to reduce the chances of spread of infectious diseases. Deep wells should be dug if filtered water supply cannot be arranged. Before the fair is started, all the wells in the surrounding 20 to 30 kms area should be besilted and disinfected.

Slaughter House—At some distance from the fair a slaughter house should also be provided. Its floor should be well-bricked or plastered giving a smooth face.

Disposal of Dead Bodies—It is just possible that some persons die in the fair which continues for weeks. For such a fair suitable place should be provided for disposal of dead bodies.

Provision of Light—Suitable provision of light should also be made in a fair. In big fairs like that of Magh Mela of Allahabad and Kumbha Fair at Allahabad, Hardwar and Ujjain temporary electric posts are erected for running electric wires for giving light to various roads, pathways and bazars in the fair.

Arrangements for Cleanliness—A duty list should be prepared for various types of officers and workers deputed for a fair. Under the officer group we may mention sanitary inspector, health inspector, and medical officer. Each one should be acquainted in writing about his specific duties in the fair. It is necessary to have a number of sweepers for cleaning the whole area of the fair every day. The work of each sweeper should be supervised in order to keep him alert about his duties. It is necessary that a sweeper is appointed for each 4000 persons. The number of person engaged for disposal of refuse should be at the ratio of one person for each group of 2500 persons.

Food Arrangement in the Fair—It should be seen that the food that is made available for the people in the fair is free from any such undesirable matter which may make them ill or spread infectious diseases. From the shops opened in the fair food article samples should be obtained for chemical analysis. The Government administrative officers should see that the shop-keepers sell only good quality food articles.

QUESTIONS

1. Discuss the nature of preliminary arrangements for a fair.
2. Describe the details of arrangement for a fair.